THE ENGLISH POETS

GENERAL EDITOR: CHRISTOPHER RICKS

Also available in this series

Samuel Johnson
The Complete English Poems

EDITED BY J. D. FLEEMAN

NEW HAVEN AND LONDON
YALE UNIVERSITY PRESS

First published in 1971 in the United Kingdom in a paperback edition by Penguin Books Limited in the series Penguin English Poets. First published in 1982 in the United States of America by Yale University Press.

Introduction and notes copyright © 1971 by J. D. Fleeman.

Printed in the United States of America

Library of Congress Cataloging in Publication Data

Johnson, Samuel, 1709–1784.
    The complete English poems.

    (The English poets; 11)
    Reprint. Originally published: Harmondsworth, Middlesex:
Penguin Books, 1971.
    Bibliography: p.
    Includes index.
    I. Fleeman, J. D. (John David) II. Title.
III. Series.
PR3521.F5 1982   821'.6   81–16065
ISBN 0–300–02824–5   AACR2
ISBN 0–300–02826–1 (pbk.)

10 9 8 7 6 5 4 3 2 1

To Isabella

Contents

Introduction

Two important editions of Johnson's poetical works are already available: the first, *The Poems of Samuel Johnson*, edited by David Nichol Smith and Edward L. McAdam, Jr, at the Clarendon Press in 1941, and the second by E. L. McAdam, Jr and George Milne as volume 6 of the Yale Edition of *The Works of Samuel Johnson* in 1964. This present edition is much indebted to the work of those editors, and for full bibliographical and historical details the reader should consult them.

The texts here presented are not, however, simply reprinted from those editions: wherever possible, reproductions of the original manuscripts have been consulted to confirm their readings, and it has been the aim of the present editor to provide a truly critical text in which the characteristics of Johnson's own practices in spelling, punctuation and capitalization are preserved, whilst at the same time his final authoritative revisions, which represent his definitive intentions in the substantive readings of his text, have been admitted. This procedure will explain any divergences from other editions, in which the editors tended in general to print the best contemporary text they could find, and to supply variants from it. One advantage of the construction of a critical text is that the recorded variants will illustrate the progress of composition by which a rough draft develops into a finished work.

The policy of this series would ordinarily have required a modernized text for Johnson, but a number of factors have led to the decision to make an exception in his case. First of all because his spellings often serve as helpful guides to the stresses of his metre. Johnson had a sound metrical ear and to modernize some of his spellings might lead to a shift in the stress, as in, for example, the word *harass*. Johnson's spelling, *harrass*, leaves no doubt that the stress falls on the first syllable. Modern English has a tendency to let any stress slip away from a final syllable, but Johnson's spelling of words ending in *–ful*, as *artfull, banefull, carefull, chearfull, deathfull, direfull, dolefull, dreadfull, fearfull, forcefull, forgetfull, fruitfull, gratefull, joyfull, mournfull, ruefull, scornfull, tastefull, tunefull, vengefull, wrathfull,* or in *–ic*, as *angelick, critick, despotick, domestick, electrick, extatick, fabrick, frantick, frolick, Gallick, logick, mechanick, mimick, musick, mystick, philosophick, politicks, publick, sympathetick, reliques,* and in *–or*, as *horrour, superiour, terrour, warriour,* are useful reminders that though no stress lies heavily on those final syllables, yet they are not to be elided. A secondary stress may be indicated when a consonant is doubled, as in *alass, annuall, cancell, counsells, cruell, dispell, excell, expell, repell, royall, scandall, unequall,* or in *allmighty, forrests, harrass, sollicitude.* When a syllable is designedly unstressed, then again the spelling will indicate the weakening or elision, notably in past participles, as *addrest, blesst, blest, confest, crop'd, deprest, disgracd, dispossesst, distrest, drest, fan'd, grov'ling, kist, mist, prest, purchasd, tost, trickd, unballast, unfetterd,* and may even by an additional doubling show where the stress is to lie, as *infesst.* When the position of the stress is clear in any case then a normally doubled consonant may be written singly, as *cripled, crop'd, dulness, fan'd, griping, grizly, rufled, shriveling, strugle,* but failure to double consonants was one of Johnson's own quirks: he habitually wrote Boswel, Cromwel, Dod, Farewel and Pot ('If Pot says so; Pot lies'), and very occasionally his spelling may be no clear guide to the stress, as in *imerse* or *worshiper.*

In spelling long vowels Johnson is often uneasy. A single vowel is never really clear in its quantity, and so he (and his contemporaries) would often add another vowel (and sometimes a consonant) as a 'lengthener', so that he writes *compleat, controul, choak, cloath'd, doat, skaiter, shoar, smoaking,* and even *rowl.* On the other hand two vowels pronounced short may be written as one, as *herse* or *stedfast.* Similarly the final 'mute *e*' may be omitted if it might appear to be lengthening the preceding syllable, so he will write: *chast, darksom, hast, laureat, tast, vultur*; but after a long vowel it may even be added, as in *heroe* or *troopes.*

The second reason for retaining these old-fashioned features in Johnson's writings was advanced by Johnson himself when he was talking of Lord Hailes's then *modernized* edition of John Hales of Eton:

An author's language, Sir, is a characteristical part of his composition, and it is also characteristical of the age in which he writes. Besides, Sir, when the language is changed we are not sure that the sense is the same. No, Sir, I am sorry Lord Hailes has done this.

Many spellings have no relation to prosody but are simply 'characteristical of the age'. Just as we may still hover uneasily between an *inquiry* or an *enquiry*, so too the eighteenth century was not only uncertain in its choice between *in-* and *en-* (Johnson writes: *encreas'd*, *intrust* and *incumber'd*) but also between a number of similar alternatives. The choice between *ie* and *y* seems to have been uncertain, and he wrote *citys*, *dy'd*, *try'd*, *flie*, *fortifie*, *mossie*, *Pygmie*, *skie*, *vallies*, and even *hyperbolies*.

The long *i* vowel is often written with *y*, as *gyants*, *lye*, *lyon*, *lyoness*, *pye*, *tyde*, and *y* is certainly preferred for the semi-vowel, as in *oyl*, *traytor*. Like many people today he was not infallible in his preference between *ie* and *ei*, so he can write *mein*, *theives* and *viel*. Other uncertainties affect words whose spelling has now become settled, as *croud*, *drousy*, *flour*, *shour*, but *asswage*.

Some spellings reflect his linguistic theories and result from his insistence upon analogous formations, so that from *beauty* he derived *beautious*, though when he compiled his *Dictionary* he was wiser and accepted the more usual form. He seems to insist on the kind of distinction between noun and verb which we still exemplify in *practice/practise*, and wrote *expence*, *extacy* and *suspence*.

Yet other spellings are more than merely characteristic of a past age; they illustrate and illuminate the etymological significances which he wished to give them. Most obvious perhaps are his adjectives ending in *–full*, but others are *burthen*, *murther*, *persue*, *spritely*. Others can emphasize the shift of meaning since the eighteenth century, a shift which might be missed if the spelling were not a signal: *antient*, *awefull*, *griping*, *strait*, *teizing*.

Some few of his spellings may reflect sources and influences, and it may not be entirely fanciful to suggest that in his early usages of *grizly*, *gyant*, *lyon* and so on, there may be discerned echoes of his youthful reading among the old romances in his father's bookshop.

Perhaps the strongest argument for the retention of Johnson's spelling is that it serves as a warning that he is not a modern author, that not only is his language (despite its close resemblances) not modern English, but that his is not a modern mind. All great poets speak to all ages and Johnson is no exception, but it would be misleading to suppose that the modes of thought exemplified in his language are the same as ours.

Johnson's punctuation has little that is peculiar in it. He punctuates lightly, a practice to which we have today returned, and so there should be no obstacles to our understanding in his own practices, which have been retained here. The eighteenth-century emphatic comma which adds an emphasis to the words it immediately follows seems not to be exemplified in his English poetry.

Capital letters were freely used in Johnson's day, and they will perhaps be the most obviously odd feature of the following pages. The problem of their significance remains undecided, though some useful comments will be found in B. H. Bronson's *Personification Reconsidered.** To retain capitals strictly in accordance with modern practice for proper names and personifications only would place interpretations on the words which might well be unwarranted. There is a difference between 'Let Observation with extensive view/Survey mankind from China to Peru' and 'Let Observation with extensive View/Survey Mankind from China to Peru' which, though not a point affecting immediate comprehension, nevertheless raises important questions about the modes of thought which lie behind the words. It has seemed unwarranted for an editor to impose a simplified solution on such a complex issue.

Because of its length, *Irene*, Johnson's verse tragedy, is not here presented in its entirety, but in the selection on pp. 53–60 an attempt has been made to give the reader a fair indication of its poetic quality.

*Cambridge University Press, 1964; paperback edn, University of California Press, 1964.

Because so many of Johnson's very minor pieces are in Latin, the products of casual occasions and slight impulses, and because many others are brief and indeterminate contributions to the works of others, it has been decided to offer only a selection of the more interesting examples of his writing in both these kinds in Appendixes 1 and 2 (pp. 143 and 157).

The survival of the complete manuscript version of *The Vanity of Human Wishes* affords a remarkable opportunity of presenting Johnson's major poem in its earliest known form. Even in this state it is a poem in its own right, and so it has not been dissected and distributed into textual notes, but retained and presented as it stands. To Mrs Mary Hyde I am indebted for permission to publish a complete transcript of this invaluable manuscript in Appendix 3 (p. 165), where the reader will be able to trace the growth and development of Johnson's thought and expression.

Over forty holograph manuscripts of poems by Johnson are known to survive and many others are known in contemporary copies. The Boswell Papers at Yale University contain many transcripts of Johnson's poems which Boswell acquired while writing the *Life of Johnson* and which presumably led him to declare his intention of publishing a complete edition of Johnson's poems 'in which I shall with the utmost care ascertain their authenticity, and illustrate them with notes and various readings'.* It is a pity that Boswell did not carry out his design, but many of the materials have survived and they include transcripts by Edmund Hector, Johnson's Lichfield schoolfellow and lifelong friend who became a surgeon in Birmingham. Hector was able to give Boswell valuable information about the date of composition of several of these pieces. Other early compositions were preserved by Johnson's Stourbridge schoolmaster, John Wentworth, who seems to have been one of the first to appreciate Johnson's ability – not many schoolmasters are willing to preserve the exercises of their pupils. Wentworth's nephew lent twelve such pieces† to Boswell, who had them copied by his servant

* *Life*, I, 16n.
† M. Waingrow (ed.), *The Correspondence &c. of James Boswell relating to the making of the 'Life of Johnson'*, 1968, p. 244.

James Ross. Transcripts by Ross are thus presumed to be of Johnson's Stourbridge compositions. Other transcripts of Johnsonian verses are known in the papers of several others of his contemporaries. Four were transcribed by or for Henry Hervey, the scapegrace son of the Earl of Bristol, brother of Pope's 'Sporus' and soldier turned clergyman, whom Johnson seems to have known from 1728 onwards until Hervey's death in 1748. Others were made by Mrs Thrale, the blue-stocking wife of a Southwark brewer whose kindness 'soothed twenty years of a life radically wretched'. David Garrick kept a copy of Johnson's *Prologue* for Garrick's tragedy *Lethe*; Fanny Burney recorded a couple of light pieces in her diary; and Baretti noted an improvised piece in his Commonplace Book.

Johnson's extensive knowledge of classical literature means that he alluded freely and frequently to its mythology and history. The explanation of these allusions would have laid a severe burden upon the notes, and they have therefore been collected, together with other references to persons and place, into a Dictionary of Proper Names (p. 239) which has eliminated repetition and perhaps made consultation easier.

Acknowledgements

No work of this kind can be performed single handed, without the assistance of others who have endured importunate enquiries with patience and given freely of their time and knowledge. For permission to publish copyright materials and to consult and make use of manuscripts, I am indebted to the following owners and institutions: the Henry W. and Albert A. Berg Collection in the New York Public Library, Astor, Lenox and Tilden Foundation; the Folger Shakespeare Library; the Horace Howard Furness Memorial Library; the Henry E. Huntington Library and Art Gallery; Mrs Mary C. Hyde; the Yale University Library; the Bodleian Library; the British Museum; the City Council of Lichfield; Major C. Congreve; the Earl of Crawford and Balcarres; Messrs William Heinemann Ltd; the Hornby and Picton Libraries, Liverpool; the Central Library, Manchester; and the John Rylands Library, Manchester.

For particular help of various kinds I am grateful to Mrs Mary C. Hyde, Mr A. J. Lockett, Professor Alan T. McKenzie, Mr E. V. C. Plumptre, Professor W. K. Wimsatt, Miss Marjorie G. Wynne and Mr K. K. Yung. Professor J. P. Sullivan prepared the translations of the Latin poems, and also helped with the Latin texts.

Table of Dates

1771   Publishes *Thoughts on the late Transactions respecting Falkland's Islands.*

1773   Tours Scotland with Boswell.

1774   Visits North Wales with the Thrales; publishes *The Patriot.*

1775   Publishes *A Journey to the Western Islands of Scotland,* and *Taxation no Tyranny;* receives D.C.L. from Oxford; visits Paris with the Thrales.

1777   Writes *Prologue* to Kelly's *A Word to the Wise,* and several pieces in defence of the convicted forger, Rev. William Dodd; undertakes to write the *Lives of the Poets.*

1779–81   Publishes ten small volumes of 'Prefaces Biographical and Critical' to the *Works of the English Poets,* later known as the *Lives of the Poets.*

1781   *4 April* Death of Henry Thrale.

1782   Break with Mrs Thrale.

1783   Founds Essex Head Club. *16–17 June* Has a stroke.

1784   *July* Mrs Thrale marries Gabriel Piozzi.
13 December Dies. *20 December* Buried in Westminster Abbey.

1785   *Poetical Works of Samuel Johnson, LL.D.* published by George Kearsley; *Prayers and Meditations composed by Samuel Johnson, LL.D.* edited by George Strahan; *The Journal of a Tour to the Hebrides, with Samuel Johnson, LL.D.* by James Boswell.

1786   *Anecdotes of the late Samuel Johnson, LL.D.* published by Mrs Piozzi, formerly Mrs Thrale (containing many of Johnson's minor verses).

1787   *The Works of Samuel Johnson, LL.D.* in eleven volumes with a Life by Sir John Hawkins (Johnson's poems in volume 11).

1788   *Letters to and from the late Samuel Johnson* edited by Mrs Piozzi, in two volumes (a few poems appended).

1791   *The Life of Samuel Johnson, LL.D.* by James Boswell in two volumes (many of Johnson's juvenile poems appear here for the first time).

Further Reading

The best general introduction to Johnson is still James Boswell's *Life of Samuel Johnson, LL.D.*, which contains intelligent comments and pertinent information on Johnson's writings and his literary career. The standard edition is that of G. B. Hill, revised by L. F. Powell, 6 vols., Clarendon Press, 1934–64; but it is handily comprised in a single volume in the Oxford Standard Authors series.

Johnson's letters are valuable illustrations of his informal moods. The standard edition is by R. W. Chapman, 3 vols., Clarendon Press, 1952, but there is a useful selection by the same editor in the World's Classics series.

Critical studies of Johnson are innumerable, though in general (except for the major poems – *London* and *The Vanity of Human Wishes*) his poetry is relatively neglected. Approximately four thousand studies and books on Johnson are listed in J. L. Clifford and D. J. Greene (eds.), *Samuel Johnson: A Survey and Bibliography of Critical Studies*, University of Minnesota Press, 1970. The following cursory list includes pieces which the present editor has found helpful.

GENERAL

Sir W. A. Raleigh, *Six Essays on Johnson*, Clarendon Press, 1910.

W. J. Bate, *The Achievement of Samuel Johnson*, Oxford University Press, Inc., 1955.

T. S. Eliot, 'Eighteenth-Century Poetry', in *Pelican Guide to English Literature 4: Dryden to Johnson*, Penguin, 1957.

E. L. McAdam Jr, *Johnson and Boswell: A Survey of their Writings*, Houghton Mifflin, 1969.

PARTICULAR STUDIES

J. Sutherland, *A Preface to Eighteenth-Century Poetry*, Oxford University Press, 1948.

I. Jack, *Augustan Satire*, Clarendon Press, 1952.

F. R. Leavis, 'Johnson and Augustanism' and 'Johnson as Poet', in *The Common Pursuit*, Chatto & Windus, 1952.

H. Gifford, 'The Vanity of Human Wishes', in *Review of English Studies*, VI (1955), pp. 157–65.

C. F. Chapin, *Personification in Eighteenth-Century English Poetry*, King's Crown Press, Columbia University, 1955.

T. S. Eliot, 'Johnson as Critic and Poet', in *On Poetry and Poets*, Faber, 1957.

S. I. Tucker and H. Gifford, 'Johnson's Latin Poetry', *Neophilologus*, XLI (1957), pp. 215–21.

J. Butt, 'Johnson's Practice in the Poetical Imitation', in F. W. Hilles (ed.), *New Light on Johnson*, Yale University Press, 1959.

M. M. Lascelles, 'Johnson and Juvenal', in *New Light on Johnson*, 1959.

D. Nichol Smith, 'Johnson's Poems', in *New Light on Johnson*, 1959.

E. A. Bloom, '*The Vanity of Human Wishes*, Reason's Images', in *Essays in Criticism*, XV (1965).

C. B. Ricks, 'Johnson's Poetry', in *New Statesman*, 6 August 1965.

C. B. Ricks, 'Johnson's Battle of the Pygmies and Cranes', in *Essays in Criticism*, XVI (1966).

R. Trickett, *The Honest Muse: A Study in Augustan Verse*, Clarendon Press, 1967.

A. Sachs, *Passionate Intelligence*, Johns Hopkins Press, 1967.

J. P. Hardy, 'Johnson's *London*, The Country versus the City', in R. F. Brissenden (ed.), *Studies in the Eighteenth Century*, Australian National University Press, 1968.

H. D. Weinbrot, *The Formal Strain*, University of Chicago Press, 1969.

H. Gardner, 'Johnson *Improvisatore*', *Transactions of the Johnson Society of Lichfield*, December 1970, pp. 34–47.

The Poems

On a Daffodill

THE FIRST FLOWER THE AUTHOR HAD SEEN
THAT YEAR

Hail lovely flower, first honour of the year!
    Hail beautious earnest of approaching spring!
Whose early buds unusual glories wear,
    And of a fruitfull year fair omens bring.

Be thou the favorite of the indulgent sky,
    Nor feel the inclemencies of wintry air;
May no rude blasts thy sacred bloom destroy;
    May storms howl gently o'er and learn to spare.

May lambent zephyrs gently wave thy head,
10   And balmy spirits thro' thy foliage play,
May the morn's earliest tears on thee be shed,
    And thou impearl'd with dew appear more gay.

May throngs of beautious virgins 'round thee crowd,
    And view thy charms with no malignant eyes:
Then scorn those flowers to which the Ægyptians bow'd,
    Which prostrate Memphis own'd her deities.

If mix'd with these, divine Cleora smile,
    Cleora's smiles a genial warmth dispense;
New verdure ev'ry fading leaf shall fill,
20   And thou shalt flourish by her influence.

But while I sing, the nimble moments fly,
    See! Sol's bright chariot seeks the western main,
And ah! behold the shriveling blossoms die,
    So late admir'd and prais'd, alas! in vain!

With grief this emblem of mankind I see,
    Like one awaken'd from a pleasing dream,
Cleora's self, fair flower, shall fade like thee,
    Alike must fall the poet and his theme.

Translations of Horace Odes *I xxii*
(Integer vitæ)

The man, my friend, whose conscious heart
   With virtue's sacred ardour glows,
Nor taints with death th'envenom'd dart,
   Nor needs the guard of Moorish bows.

Tho' Scythia's icy cliffs he treads
   Or torrid Africk's faithless sands;
Or where the fam'd Hydaspes spreads
   His liquid wealth o'er barb'rous lands.

For while by Chloe's image charm'd,
10   Too far in Sabine woods I stray'd,
Me singing, careless and unarm'd,
   A grizly wolf surpris'd, and fled.

No savage more portentous stain'd
   Apulia's spacious wilds with gore;
None fiercer Juba's thirsty land,
   Dire nurse of raging lions, bore.

Place me where no soft summer gale
   Among the quivering branches sighs;
Where clouds condens'd for ever veil,
20   With horrid gloom the frowning skies.

Place me beneath the burning line,
   A clime deny'd to human race;
I'll sing of Chloe's charms divine,
   Her heavenly voice, and beautious face.

TO ARISTIUS FUSCUS

The Man, my Friend, whose conscious Heart
   With Virtue's sacred Ardour glows,
Nor taints with Death th'envenom'd Dart,
   Nor needs the Guard of *Moorish* Bows.

O'er icy *Caucasus* he treads,
   Or torrid *Afric*'s faithless Sands,
Or where the fam'd *Hydaspes* spreads
   His liquid Wealth thro' barbarous Lands.

For while in *Sabine* Forests, charm'd
10   By *Lalagé*, too far I stray'd,
Me singing, careless and unarm'd,
   A furious Wolf approach'd, and fled.

No Beast more dreadful ever stain'd
   Apulia's spacious Wilds with Gore;
No Beast more fierce *Numidia*'s Land,
   The Lion's thirsty Parent, bore.

Place me where no soft Summer Gale
   Among the quivering Branches sighs,
Where Clouds, condens'd, for ever veil
20   With horrid Gloom the frowning Skies:

Place me beneath the burning Zone,
   A Clime deny'd to human Race;
My Flame for *Lalagé* I'll own;
   Her Voice and Smiles my Song shall grace.

An Ode on Friendship

Friendship, peculiar Gift of Heav'n,
   The noble Mind's delight and pride,
To Men and Angels only giv'n,
   To all the lower World deny'd:

While Love, unknown among the blest,
   Parent of Rage and hot Desires,
The human and the savage Breast
   Inflames alike with equal Fires.

With bright, but oft destructive Gleam,
10   Alike o'er all his Lightnings fly;
Thy lambent Glories only beam
    Around the fav'rites of the Sky.

Thy gentle flows of guiltless joys
    On Fools and Villains ne'er descend;
In vain for thee the Monarch sighs,
    And hugs a Flatt'rer for a Friend.

Directress of the Brave and Just,
    O guide us thro' Life's darksom Way!
And let the Tortures of Mistrust
20   On selfish Bosoms only prey.

When Virtues kindred Virtues meet,
    And Sister-souls together join,
Thy Pleasures, permanent as great,
    Are all transporting, all divine.

O! shall thy Flames then cease to glow
    When Souls to happier Climes remove?
What rais'd our Virtue here below
    Shall aid our Happiness above.

*Translation of part of the Dialogue between
Hector and Andromache; from the Sixth Book
of Homer's* Iliad (*VI 390–502*)

Hector, this heard without a moment's stay,
Back through the city trod his former way.
Soon as the chief approach'd the Scæan Gate
About to rush into the field of fate
He met Andromache his beauteous wife
Far dearer than his own or father's life
Whose sire Eëtion in Cilicia reign'd
Where Hypoplacus' lofty shades extend.
The nurse attending bore a lovely boy

10   Pledge of their love and source of all their joy
     By Hector call'd Scamandrius from the god
     That laves proud Ilion with his rapid flood,
     But call'd Astyanax because his sire
     Alone preserv'd the town from Grecian fire.
     From Hector's breast each gloomy trouble flies
     And secret pleasures sparkled in his eyes.
     Mournfull Andromache the silence broke,
     Her tears in show'rs descending as she spoke.
         'Why gen'rous warriour will you rashly run
20   On dangers which your safety bids you shun,
     Forgetfull of your wife, forgetfull of your son?
     Soon shall you fall by num'rous hosts opprest
     And Grecian spears shall quiver in your breast.
     But, ah! before arise that hapless day
     May I lye cold beneath a load of clay.
     While Hector lives I tast of ev'ry joy
     With Hector's life away my pleasures fly.
     My father fell by fierce Achilles' hand
     Whose direfull rage destroy'd my native land.
30   Pleas'd with the conquest, he forbore the spoil
     And burnt him decent on a funerall pile.
     The nymphs bewail'd his fall with loud lament
     And planted elms around his monument
     By that dire sword my sev'n brave brothers dy'd;
     All stemm'd in one sad day the Stygian tyde.
     Among their flocks the blooming heroes fell
     And stain'd with blood Pelides' vengefull steel.
     My mother who alone escap'd the grave
     The victor hither brought, a royall slave.
40   Soon as with gold appeas'd, he set her free
     To tast again the sweets of liberty.
     Provok'd Diana with a vengefull dart
     Ended her wretched life and pierc'd her heart.
     But dearest Hector while thou liv'st I see
     A father, brother, husband, all in thee.
     Rush not impetuous to the bloody fray
     Nor tempt the dangers of this deathfull day

Think shouldst thou fall how wretched shall we be,
A widow I, an helpless orphan he.
50   Within the town assemble all thy powers
And man the walls and fortifie the tow'rs.
Where the wild fig trees join their darksom shade
The bravest of the Greeks the wall invade.
Th'Atridæ there and Tydeus' mighty son,
Idomeneus, and godlike Telamon·
Thrice to the wall their dreadfull hosts have led
And thrice to mount the battlements assay'd
Whether urg'd on by seers from heav'n inspir'd
Or their own souls with hopes of vict'ry fir'd.'
60   She ceas'd, then godlike Hector answer'd kind,
His various plumage sporting in the wind.
   'That post, and all the rest shall be my care
But shall I then forsake th'unfinish'd war?
How would the Trojans brand great Hector's name!
And one base action sully all my fame
Acquir'd by wounds and battles bravely fought!
Oh! how my soul abhors so mean a thought
Long since I learn'd to slight this fleeting breath
And view with chearfull eyes approaching death.
70   Th'inexorable Sisters have decreed
That Priam's house, and Priam's self shall bleed.
The day will come in which proud Troy shall yield
And spread its smoaking ruins o'er the field.
Yet Hecuba's nor Priam's hoary age
Whose blood shall quench some Grecian's thirsty rage
Nor my brave brothers that have bit the ground,
Their souls dismiss'd through many a ghastly wound,
Can in my bosom half that grief create
As the sad thought of your impending fate
80   When some proud Grecian dame shall tasks impose,
Mimick your tears, and ridicule your woes.
Beneath Hyperia's waters shall you sweat
And fainting scarce support the liquid weight.
Then shall some Argive loud insulting cry,
"Behold the wife of Hector, guard of Troy."

Tears at my name shall drown those beauteous eyes
And that fair bosom heave with rising sighs.
Before that day, by some brave heroe's hand
May I lye slain and spurn the bloody sand.'
90   Hector, this speaking, with extended hands
From the fair nurse Astyanax demands.
The child starts back affrighted at the blaze
Of light reflected from the polish'd brass.
And in his nurse's bosom hides his face.
The parents smil'd, the chief his helm unbound
And placed the beamy terror on the ground
Then kist his son and raising to the skies
In fervent prayer addrest the deities:
    'Immortal Gods! and thou allmighty Jove
100   That reign'st supreme among the pow'rs above,
Propitious hear my prayers, protect the boy,
Grant him like me to guard the walls of Troy.
Let distant regions echo with his name
And his more glorious acts eclipse his father's fame.
May then his mother's heart with joys o'erflow
And may she ne'er returning sorrows know.'
    The chief, this spoke, into the mother's arms
Returns his child; she views his infant charms,
Tumultuous passions strugle in her breast
110   And joy and sorrow stand by turns confest.
This Hector saw; his soul was touch'd with grief.
He grasp'd her hand endeav'ring kind relief.
    'Ah! let not tears down that fair count'nance rowl,
Restrain your sorrows, calm your troubled soul.
Your sighs are spent in vain; if fates withstand
Hector shall perish by no warriour's hand.
But if by their irrevocable doom
My death is now decreed my death will come.
The bravest hero and the fearfull'st slave
120   Shall sink alike into the gloomy grave.
Hence to the palace and your maids repair; ⎫
There let the web and distaff be your care. ⎬
To men belongs the dreadfull work of war.' ⎭

Then on his brow the mighty soldier plac'd
His shining helm with nodding horse hair grac'd.
Swifter than lightning to the fight he flies.
Andromache looks back with weeping eyes,
Then sought the palace where the menial train
Shed floods of tears and sympathiz'd in pain.
130 With dolefull cries their living lord they mourn
Nor from the battle look for his return.

An Epilogue to The Distrest Mother

Ye blooming train who give despair or joy,
Bless with a smile, or with a frown destroy,
In whose fair cheeks destructive Cupids wait,
And with unerring shafts distribute fate,
Whose snowy breasts, whose animated eyes,
Each youth admires, tho' each admirer dies,
Whilst you deride their pangs in barb'rous play,
Unpitying see them weep and hear them pray,
And unrelenting sport ten thousand lives away;
10   For you, ye fair, I quit the gloomy plains,
Where sable night in all her horror reigns;
No fragrant bow'rs, no delightful glades,
Receive th'unhappy ghosts of scornful maids.
For kind, for tender nymphs the myrtle blooms,
And weaves her bending boughs in pleasing glooms,
Perennial roses deck each purple vale,
And scents ambrosial breathe in every gale;
Far hence are banish'd vapours, spleen, and tears,
Tea, scandal, ivory teeth, and languid airs;
20   No pug nor favourite Cupid there enjoys
The balmy kiss for which poor Thyrsis dies;
Form'd to delight, they use no foreign arms,
Nor tort'ring whalebones pinch them into charms;
No conscious blushes there their cheeks inflame,
For those who feel no guilt can know no shame;
Unfaded still their former charms they shew,

Around them pleasures wait, and joys for ever new.
But cruel virgins meet severer fates;
Expell'd and exil'd from the blissful seats,
30 To dismal realms, and regions void of peace,
Where furies ever howl and serpents hiss.
O'er the sad plains perpetual tempests sigh,
And pois'nous vapours, black'ning all the sky,
With livid hue the fairest face o'ercast,
And every beauty withers at the blast;
Where e'er they fly their lovers ghosts persue,
Inflicting all those ills which once they knew;
Vexation, Fury, Jealousy, Despair,
Vex every eye, and every bosom tear;
40 Their foul deformities by all descry'd,
No maid to flatter and no paint to hide.
Then melt, ye fair, while crouds around you sigh,
Nor let disdain sit low'ring in your eye;
With pity soften every awful grace,
And beauty smile auspicious in each face;
To ease their pains exert your milder power,
So shall you guiltless reign, and all mankind adore.

Translation of Horace 'Epode the 2ᵈ' (Beatus ille)

Blest as th'immortal Gods is he
Who lives from toilsome bus'ness free,
Like the first race in Saturns reign
When floods of Nectar stain'd the main,
Manuring with laborious hand
His own hereditary Land,
Whome no contracted debts molest
No griping Creditors infesst.
No trumpets sound, no Soldiers cries,
10 Drive the soft Slumbers from his eyes,
He sees no boist'rous Tempests sweep

The Surface of the boiling Deep,
Him no contentious suits in law
From his belov'd retirement draw,
He ne'er with forc'd Submission waits
Obsequious, at his Patrons gates;
But round the lofty Poplar twines
With artfull hand the teeming vines,
Or prunes the barren boughs away;
20 [Or] sees from far his Bullocks play
Or drains the Labour of the Bees,
Or sheers the Lambkins snowy fleece.
Or when with golden Apples crown'd
Autumn o'erlooks the smiling Ground
When rip'ning fruits perfume the year,
Plucking the blushing Grape and Pear,
Gratefull, rewards the Deities,
That, fav'ring, listen to his cries.
Beneath some spreading Ilex Shade
30 On some green bank supinely Laid,
Where Riv'lets gently purl along
And, murm'ring, balmy Sleep prolong,
Whilst each Musician of the Grove
Lamenting, warbles out his love,
In pleasing Dreams he cheats the Day
Unhurt by Phœbus fi'ry ray.
But when increas'd by Winter shours
Down cliffs the roaring Torrent pours
The grizly foaming Boar surrounds
40 With twisted toils, and op'ning hounds;
[So]me times the greedy Thrush to kill
[He] sets his nets, employs his skill.
With secret springes oft ensnares
The screaming Cranes and fearfull Hares.
Would not these pleasures soon remove
The bitter pangs of slighted love?
If to compleat this heav'nly Life
A frugal, chast, industrious, Wife,
Such as the Sun-burnt Sabines were,

50 Divide the burden of his care,
    And heap the fire, and milk the Kine
    And crown the bowl with new-prest wine
    And waiting for her weary lord
    With unbought dainties load the board;
    I should behold with scornfull eye
    The studied arts of Luxury:
    No fish from the Carpathian coast
    By Eastern Tempests hither tost,
    Nor Lybian fowls, nor Snipes of Greece,
60 So much my Appetite would please
    As herbs of which the forrests nigh
    Wholsome variety supply.
    Then to the Gods, on solemn days,
    The farmer annuall honours pays
    Or feasts on Kids the Wolves had kill'd
    And frighted, left upon the field,
    How pleas'd he sees his Cattle come,
    Their dugs with milk distended, home!
    How pleas'd beholds his Oxen bow
70 And faintly draw th'inverted Plow.
    His chearfull Slaves, a num'rous band,
    Around in beauteous order stand.

    Thus did the Us'rer Alphius praise,
    With transports kindled, rural ease,
    His money he collected strait,
    Resolv'd to purchase a retreat.
    But still desires of sordid gain   ⎫
    Fix'd in his canker'd breast remain: ⎬
    Next Month he sets it out again.   ⎭

Translation of Horace: Epode xi

Pettius no more I verses write;
   My bosom glows with fiercer fire;
No more I sing, no more delight
   To handle the melodious lyre.
Venus, the sacred Sisters dispossest,
Invades my soul, and rages in my breast.

Thrice has December strip'd the tree
   And thrice deform'd the verdant year
Since from Inachia's charms set free
10   I first forsook the scornfull fair.
I then (my cheeks still glow with shame) was grown
The sport of boys, and scandall of the town.

No feasts could e'er my cares dispell;
   Sighs issued from my heaving breast;
The pains I labour'd to conceal
   My silence and my groans confess'd.
Then when repeated bowls unlock'd the heart
To thee I told the causes of my smart,

To thee I then with tears complain'd
20   That all the fair their favours sold;
No wit nor honesty could stand
   Against th'omnipotence of gold
And wish'd my rising anger could remove
Those anxious fears that fan'd the flame of Love.

Then would I free from torments live
   And quit Inachia's venal charms
Nor with too powerfull rivals strive
   But take another to my arms.
Thus I t'effect this mighty change design'd
30 And gainst the pow'r of Venus steel'd my mind.

But being counsell'd to go home
    And see my mistress face no more
Confus'd about the streets I roam
    And stop'd unwilling at her door.
Then to the inclement skies expos'd I sat
And sigh'd and wept at her relentless gate.

Lyciscus whose soft arms excell
    A girls, inflames me with desire;
Nor counsells nor reproach expell
40   The raging of the kindled fire
But the next blooming virgin's beauteous face
Or boy, whose snowy neck the flowing ringlets grace.

Translation of Horace: Odes *II ix*

Clouds do not always viel the skies
    Nor show'rs imerse the verdant plain,
Nor do the billows always rise
    Or storms afflict the ruffled main.

Nor, Valgius, on th'Armenian shores
    Do the chain'd waters always freeze;
Not always furious Boreas roars
    Or bends with violent force the trees.

But you are ever drown'd in tears;
10   For Mystes dead you ever mourn.
No setting Sol can ease your care
    But finds you sad at his return.

The wise experienc'd Grecian sage
    Mourn'd not Antilochus so long,
Nor did King Priam's hoary age
    So much lament his slaughter'd son.

Leave off at length these woman's sighs;
   Augustus num'rous trophies sing.
Repeat that Princes victories
20   To whom all nations tribute bring.

Niphates rolls an humbler wave;
   At length th'undaunted Scythian yields,
Content to live the Romans slave
   And scarce forsakes his native fields.

Translation of Horace Odes II xiv
(Eheu fugaces)

Alass, dear Friend, the fleeting years
In everlasting Circles run,
In vain you spend your vows and prayers,
They roll, and ever will roll on.

Should Hecatombs each rising Morn
On cruel Pluto's Altar dye,
Should costly Loads of incense burn,
Their fumes ascending to the Skie;

You could not gain a Moments breath,
10 Or move the haughty King below,
Nor would inexorable Death
Defer an hour the fatal blow.

In vain we shun the Din of war,
And terrours of the Stormy Main,
In vain with anxious breasts we fear
Unwholesome Sirius' sultry reign;

We all must view the Stygian flood
That silent cuts the dreary plains,
And cruel Danaus' bloody Brood
20 Condemn'd to everduring pains.

Your shady Groves, your pleasing wife,
And fruitfull fields, my dearest Friend,
You'll leave together with your life,
Alone the Cypress shall attend.

After your death, the lavish heir
Will quickly drive away his woe,
The wine you kept with so much care
Along the marble floor shall flow.

Translation of Horace: Odes II xx

Now with no weak unballast wing
A Poet double-form'd I rise,
From th'envious world with scorn I spring,
And cut with joy the wond'ring Skies.

Though from no Princes I descend,
Yet shall I see the blest abodes,
Yet, great Mæcenas, shall your friend
Quaff Nectar with th'immortal Gods.

See! how the mighty Change is wrought!
10   See! how whate'er remain'd of Man
By plumes is viel'd; see! quick as thought
I pierce the Clouds a tunefull Swan.

Swifter than Icarus Ill flie
Where Lybia's swarthy offspring burns,
And where beneath th'inclement Skie
The hardy Scythian ever mourns.

My Works shall propagate my fame,
To distant realms and climes unknown,
Nations shall celebrate my Name
20   That drink the Phasis or the Rhône.

Restrain your tears and cease your cries,
Nor grace with fading flours my Herse,
I without fun'ral elegies
Shall live for ever in my verse.

Translation of Virgil: Pastoral I

MELIBAEUS
How Tit'rus you supine and careless laid
Play on your pipe beneath this beechen shade,
While wretched we about the world must roam
And leave our pleasing fields and native home,
Here at your ease you sing your amorous flame
And the wood rings with Amerillis name.

TITYRUS
Those blessings, friend, a deity bestow'd
For I shall never think him less than God.
Oft on his alter shall my firstlings lye;
10   Their blood the consecrated stones shall dye:
He gave my flocks to graze the flowery meads
And me to tune at ease the unequall reeds.

MELIBAEUS
My admiration only I expres'd
(No spark of envy harbours in my breast)
That when confusion o'er the country reigns
To you alone this happy state remains.
Here I tho' faint myself must drive my goats
Far from their antient fields and humble cots.
This scarce I lead who left on yonder rock
20   Two tender kids the hopes of all the flock.
Had we not been perverse and careless grown
This dire event by omens was foreshown;
Our trees were blasted by the thunder stroke ⎱
And lefthand crows from an old hollow oak ⎬
Foretold the coming evil by their dismal croak. ⎰

Translation of Virgil: Pastoral V

MOPSUS

The nymphs bewail'd poor Daphnis hapless death
Ev'n in the bloom of life depriv'd of breath.
The limpid streams with ruefull murmurs flow
And all the withering woods confess their woe
While his sad mother frantick with despair
Accus'd the Gods and curs'd each luckless star.
That day, that mournfull day, no chearfull song
With pleasing sound allur'd the rural throng.
The sympathising cattle hung their heads
10   Nor crop'd the tastefull herb, nor trac'd the verdant meads.
Touch'd with thy fate Numidia's lyons roar
And spread their echoing grief from shore to shore.
By Daphnis skill th'Armenian tigers broke
Endur'd the stinging lash, and tamely bore the yoke.
Daphnis with ivy wreath'd the jav'lins round
And trod to Bacchus praise the mystick ground.
As vines the elms, as grapes adorn the vine,   ⎫
As corn the fields, as bulls the herds of kine,   ⎬
So much our splendour was encreas'd by thine. ⎭
20   Now, at thy fall incens'd, the rural Gods
Withdraw their cars and seek the blesst abodes.
In vain the lab'ring hind manures the plain,
The banefull weeds spring up, and choak the grain.
Now each parterre with thorny brakes is fill'd
Where late the lilies mix'd with violets smil'd.
Ye swains! bestrow the ground with leaves and spread
O'er all the warbling founts a cooling shade.
On his dead body let a tomb be plac'd
And be the stone with this inscription grac'd:
30   'Here fairer than his flock the shepherd lyes
Whose fame from earth resounded to the skies.'

Now beauteous Daphnis cloath'd with heav'nly light
Shuns Pluto's Kingdoms and the Realms of Night.
Beneath his feet admires each shining Star,
And sees the Motions of th'Harmonious Sphere.
Pleasure in ev'ry Nymph and Shepherd reigns,
And banish'd Sorrow flies the joyous Plains.
The harmless Wolves no more our Cattle fear,
No toils shall intercept the nimble Deer.
40 Rocks send their acclamations to the Skie,
And Woods and Mountains hail the Deity.
Attend my prayers propitious, hear my vow ⎱
Here have I rais'd four sacred altars, two ⎰
To great Latona's Son, and two to you. ⎰
Two Bowls with oyl and Milk I'll yearly crown,
And pour them on the consecrated Stone.
Then we with wine will drown our troubles, laid
If winter by the fire; if Summer, in the Shade.
Thyrsis while   sings shall   the gods
50 That range Lascivious through the lonesome roads
When to the nymphs the swain due homage pays
Libations we shall pour to Daphnis praise
While Boars the rocks, while Fish the Rivers love,
While Bees shall feed on Thyme, and Birds shall haunt
    the grove
Thou shalt with Bacchus equal honours share,
The Swains shall pay their vows, and thou shalt hear
    their prayer.

Translation of Addison's
Πυγμαιογερανομαχια
The Battle of the Pygmies and Cranes

Feather'd battalions, squadrons on the wing
And the sad fate of Pygmie realms I sing.
Direct O Goddess, my advent'rous song;
In warring colours shew the warring throng;

Teach me to range my troopes in just array }
Whilst beaks and swords engage in bloody fray }
And paint the horrors of the dreadfull day. }
In pompous numbers ancient heroes rise;
Their growing fame re'echoes to the skies.
10 Who hath not heard of Argo's valiant crew?
How great Achilles godlike Hector slew?
How Turnus by Aeneas sword expir'd?
Or how before Nassau the Gallick troops retir'd?
Who has not read the Theban brothers hate?
And wept unhappy Pompey's hapless fate?
I first attempt in never-dying lays
To propagate the Pygmie heroes praise.
While in my verse the shrilling trumpets sound,
I'll sing the chiefs dispensing fate around.
20 In vain from heaven's black concave, like a cloud,
Fresh foes descending glut their swords with blood.
Where radiant Phœbus rising from the sea
Dispells the darkness with his golden ray
In a low vale by rocks that pierce the skies
Guarded from all but winged enemies
In former ages while upheld by fate
Securely flourish'd the Pygmiean state,
The fruitful fields th'industrious people till'd
And with laborious crouds the plains were fill'd.
30 Now, wand'ring o'er the cliffs the traveller
Small bones and mangled bodies scatter'd there
Affrighted views; and looking o'er the plain
With horrour counts the number of the slain.
The victor Cranes the conquer'd realms possess,
Scream in the nests and brood their young in peace.
Not so while long th'undaunted race maintain'd
Against th'invading birds their native land:
Whatever Crane confiding in his might
Dar'd have provok'd a foe to single fight,
40 Soon forth in arms had some bold soldier stood,
Soon had the wrathfull faulchion drank his blood.
Oft from behind they wounded them with darts

Or fix'd the pointed arrows in their hearts.
Whene'er the lab'ring bird with anxious care
Had form'd her nest and plac'd her burthen there,
Some furious soldier would approach that bore
Death in his look, and hands imbru'd in gore
Who to the ground the shatter'd building flung
And crush'd the yet unanimated young.

50 From hence the seeds of discord first arose
The Pygmies thus exasperate their foes.
Hence men and birds promiscuous press the sand
And Death exulting stalk'd along the land.
Not the Mæonian Bard in lofty strain
Sung such a war when in a miry fen
Fiercely contending two vast armies stood
And dy'd their bulrush-spears in mutual blood.
Here with dead mice the marsh was strew'd around;
There frogs crept croaking o'er the swampy ground,

60 Wounded and spent, in vain they strive to rise
Or lift themselves into the wonted skies.
But now alass! the fatall hour drew nigh
In which the Pygmie wept his cruelty.
The injur'd Cranes their murther'd offspring mourn
And with fell rage and secret anguish burn.
When all conspiring leave Mæon's lake
And warm Cäyster's flowing banks forsake
To Mareotis fen the rumour flies
From Isther's flood unnumber'd flocks arise

70 Which whet their beaks, for flight their wings prepare,
Sharpen their claws, and meditate the war.
These when o'er winter's sway, prevail'd the spring
Together rise and shoot upon the wing.
Astonish'd nations view with wild affright
The dark horizon ravish'd from their sight.
Meantime the Pygmies with undaunted hearts
Temper their swords and point their missive darts.
The steely troops embodied closely stand
Their wings extend themselves across the land.

80 Then rises the brave leader of their hosts

Who matchless strength and bulk gygantick boasts,
Of aspect stern for in his face he wears
The prints of claws and honourable scars.
With rage implacable he still persue'd
The feather'd race and thirsted for their blood:
Soon as their young began to draw their breath
He tore them down and trampled them to death.
This forc'd the Cranes to utter dolefull moans,
And Strymon's hollow banks resounded with their groans.
90 But now their cruel enemies draw near
And first a sound invades th'astonish'd ear.
Quickly the Cranes appear before their eyes;
Thick clouds of hostile birds obscure the skies.
Above their heads th'embattled squadrons hung
And scarce the lab'ring air sustain the throng
The fearless Pygmies view them from afar
Rage with disdain, and hope th'approaching war;
Not long they stood, when stooping from their height
The Cranes with beaks and claws provoke the fight.
100 Thick from their wounded wings the feathers fly,
Beneath Pygmæan steel what numbers dye!
Breathless at length they leave th'unfinish'd war
And hang aloft suspended in the air.
But their lost strength and vigour soon return
They clap their wings, and with new fury burn;
Then, swift as thought, by headlong anger driv'n
Descend, impetuous, from the vault of Heav'n.
Their foes the shock sustain in Battle skill'd,
And victory hangs doubtfull o'er the field.
110 Here lies a fowl transfix'd with many a wound
That strugling pants, and rowls her eye-balls round.
There a stout warriour fainting gasps for breath
And grasps the bloody sand involv'd in death.
Swords, arms and wings are scatter'd o'er the plain
On ev'ry side rise mountains of the slain,
Whose mortal wounds pour forth a purple flood,
The plain contested flows with mingled blood.
The valiant Prince with unresisted force

Where'er the battle rages bends his course.
120 That day what legions by his faulchion bled!
His arm alone rais'd bulwarks of the dead.
Before his face the frighted Cranes gave way.
He turn'd awhile the fortune of the day
Till thither an huge bird the tumult drew
Who caught the chief, ev'n in his soldiers view
In his fell claws, then into th' air he springs.
The joyfull Cranes triumphant clap their wings:
While the sad Pygmies mourn with weeping eyes
Their godlike hero strugling in the skies.
130 Now bleeds the war afresh, the Crane from high
Forceful descending strikes his enemy,
Then flies aloft; th'astonish'd warriours feel
The wound, and, furious, wave the shining steel.
The birds elude the stroke with cautious care;
Its useless force the weapon spends in air.
Such was the horrour of the dreadfull fight
As when great Briareus with matchless might
Hurling vast mounts against the realms above
Shook headlong from his throne imperial Jove.
140 In rat'ling storms huge Promontories flie
And Bolts and rocks encounter in the Skie.
At length deform'd with many a grizly wound
Th'enormous Gyants smoke upon the Ground.
O'erpowr'd and faint the Pygmies, scarce sustain
Their foes attacks, and wield their arms with pain.
Part turn their Backs, part seiz'd with wild surprise
Utter sad groans and lamentable cries.
Impending death they strive to 'scape in vain ⎫
For fear retards their flight, the cruell Crane ⎬
150 Scatters their breathless bodies o'er the plain. ⎭
Thus fell the Pygmie state, which long had stood
Secure, and triumph'd oft in hostile blood.
To ev'ry empire bounds the Gods ordain
The limits fix'd they strive to pass in vain;
So by their great decree Assyria fell
And Persia felt the force of Grecian steel;

Not Rome itself that held the world in awe
Could cancell their irrevocable Law.
Now in the Realms below, the Pygmie shades
160   Mix'd with old Heroes trace the flow'ry meads,
And wander sportive o'er th'Elysian plain:
Or if old womens tales may credit gain,
When pale-fac'd Cynthia sheds her silver light
Dispelling the black horrors of the Night,
The Shepherds oft' see little ghosts glide by
And shades of Pygmies swim before their eye.
They call them Fairies; these now free from care
And giv'n to mirth, the Cranes no longer fear,
But move their num'rous arms to Musicks sound,
170   And tread in mystick rings the mossie ground.

Festina Lentè

Whatever course of Life great Jove allots,
Whether you sit on thrones, or dwell in cots,
Observe your steps; be carefull to command
Your passions; guide the reins with steady hand,
Nor down steep cliffs precipitately move
Urg'd headlong on by hatred or by love:
Let Reason with superior force controul
The floods of rage, and calm thy rufled soul.
Rashness! thou spring from whence misfortunes flow!
10   Parent of ills! and source of all our woe!
Thou to a scene of bloodshed turn'st the Ball,
By thee wholl citys burn, wholl nations fall!
By thee Orestes plung'd his vengefull dart
Into his supplicating mothers heart.
Hurry'd to death by thee, Flaminius fell,
And crowds of godlike Romans sunk to hell.
But cautious Fabius from impending fate
Preserv'd the reliques of the Latian state
From bold invaders clear'd th'Italian lands
20   And drove the swarthy troops to their own barren sands.

Upon the Feast of St Simon and St Jude

Of Fields with dead bestrew'd around,
And Cities smoaking on the ground
 Let vulgar Poets sing,
Let them prolong their turgid lays
With some victorious Heroe's praise
 Or weep some falling King.

While I to nobler themes aspire,
To nobler subjects tune my lyre;
 Those Saints my numbers grace
10 Who to their Lord were ever dear,
To whom the church each rolling year
 Her solemn honours pays.

In vain proud tyrants strove to shake
Their faith, or force them to forsake
 The Steps their Saviour trod;
With breasts resolv'd, they follow'd still
Obsequious to his heav'nly will
 Their master and their God

When Christ had conquer'd Hell and fate
20 And rais'd us from our wretched state,
 O prodigy of Love!
Ascending to the skies he shone
Refulgent on his starry throne
 Among the Saints above.

Th'Apostles round the world were sent
Dispensing blessings as they went,
 Thro' all the spacious ball;
Far from their happy native home
They, pleas'd, thro' barb'rous nations roam
30 To raise them from their fall.

Where Atlas was believ'd to bear
The weight of ev'ry rolling sphere,
 Where sev'nmouth'd Nilus roars,
Where the Darkvisag'd Natives fry
And scarce can breath th'infected sky,
 But bless the Northern shoars,

Simon by gen'rous Zeal inspir'd,
With ardent love of virtue fir'd,
 There trod the Lybian sands,
40 Though fierce Barbarians threatend death
And Serpents with their poys'nous breath
 Infest the barren Lands.

Nor there confin'd his active Soul;
But where the Realms beneath the Pole
 In clouds of Ign'rance mourn,
Thither with eager hast he runs
And visits Britain's hardy Sons
 Ah! never to return!

Nor whilst she Simons acts persues
50 Art thou forgotten by the Muse,
 Most venerable Jude!
Where Tigris beats his sounding shore
The haughty Persian in thy gore
 His wrathfull sword imbru'd.

Thrice happy Saints – where do I rove?
Where doth extatick fury move
 My rude unpolish'd song;
Mine unharmonious verse profanes
Those names which in immortal strains
60 Angelick choirs have sung.

To a Young Lady on her Birthday

This tributary verse receive, my fair,
Warm with an ardent lover's fondest pray'r.
May this returning day for ever find
Thy form more lovely, more adorn'd thy mind;
All pains, all cares, may favouring heav'n remove,
All but the sweet solicitudes of love.
May powerful nature join with graceful art,
To point each glance, and force it to the heart.
O then, when conquer'd crowds confess thy sway,
10 When even proud wealth and prouder wit obey,
My fair, be mindful of the mighty trust,
Alas! 'tis hard for beauty to be just.
Those sovereign charms with strictest care employ,
Nor give the generous pain, the worthless joy.
With his own form acquaint the forward fool,
Shewn in the faithful glass of ridicule;
Teach mimick censure her own faults to find,
No more let coquets to themselves be blind,
So shall Belinda's charms improve mankind.

The Young Author

When first the peasant, long inclin'd to roam,
Forsakes his rural seats and peaceful home,
Charm'd with the scene the smiling ocean yields,
He scorns the flow'ry vales and verdant fields;
Jocund he dances o'er the wat'ry way,
While the breeze whispers and the streamers play.
Joys insincere! thick clouds invade the skies,
Loud roars the tempest, high the billows rise,
Sick'ning with fear he longs to view the shore,
10 And vows to trust the faithless deep no more.
   So the young author panting for a name,

And fir'd with pleasing hope of endless fame,
Intrusts his happiness to human kind,
More false, more cruel than the seas and wind.
'Toil on, dull croud, in extacy,' he cries,
'For wealth or title, perishable prize;
'While I these transitory blessings scorn,
'Secure of praise from nations yet unborn.'
This thought once form'd, all counsel comes too late,
20 He plies the press, and hurries on his fate;
Swiftly he sees the imagin'd laurels spread,
He feels th'unfading wreath surround his head;
Warn'd by another's fate, vain youth, be wise,
These dreams were *Settle*'s once and *Ogilby*'s.

The pamphlet spreads, incessant hisses rise,
To some retreat the baffled writer flies,
Where no sour criticks damn, nor sneers molest,
Safe from the keen lampoon and stinging jest;
There begs of heav'n a less distinguish'd lot;
30 Glad to be hid, and proud to be forgot.

*An Ode on a Lady leaving her place
of abode; almost impromptu*

When the departing sun resigns
    The northern shores to clouds and frost
The chill inhabitant repines,
    In half a year of darkness lost.

Cleora thus regretted flies,
    Fair source of wit, and love, and mirth,
Withdraws the influence of those eyes,
    Which gave a thousand pleasures birth.

Not long the happy Russians mourn;
10   Revolving springs their frosts repay.
O would Cleora thus return,
    And bless me with continu'd day.

On a Lady's presenting a Sprig of Myrtle to a Gentleman

What Fears, what Terrors does thy Gift create!
Ambiguous Emblem of uncertain Fate!
The Myrtle, Ensign of supreme Command,
(Consign'd by *Venus* to *Melissa*'s Hand)
Not less capricious than a reigning Fair,
Oft favors, oft rejects the Lover's Care.
In Myrtle Groves oft sings the happy Swain,
In Myrtle Shades despairing Ghosts complain;
The Myrtle crowns the happy Lovers Heads,
10   Th'unhappy Lovers Graves the Myrtle spreads;
Oh! then the Meaning of thy Gift impart,
And cure the throbbings of an anxious Heart;
Soon must this Bough, as you shall fix his Doom,
Adorn *Philander*'s Head, or grace his Tomb.

To Miss Hickman playing on the Spinet

Bright Stella, form'd for universal Reign,
Too well You know to keep the Slaves You gain.
When in Your Eyes resistless Lightnings play,
Aw'd into Love, our conquer'd hearts obey,
And yield, reluctant, to despotick Sway.
But when your Musick sooths the raging pain,
We bid propitious Heav'n prolong your reign,
We bless the Tyrant, and we hug the Chain.

When old Timotheus struck the vocal String,
10   Ambitious Fury fir'd the Grecian King:
Unbounded Projects lab'ring in his Mind,
He pants for room, in one poor World confin'd.
Thus wak'd to rage by Musick's dreadfull Pow'r,
He bids the Sword destroy, the Flame devour.

Had Stella's gentle touches mov'd the Lyre,
Soon had the Monarch felt a nobler fire,
No more delighted with destructive War,
Ambitious only now to please the Fair,
Resign'd his Thirst of Empire to her Charms,
20 And found a Thousand Worlds in Stella's Arms.

Epigram on Colley Cibber

Augustus still survives in Maro's strain,
And Spenser's verse prolongs Eliza's reign;
Great George's acts let tuneful Cibber sing;
For Nature form'd the Poet for the King.

Selections from Irene

PROLOGUE

Ye glitt'ring Train! whom Lace and Velvet bless,
Suspend the soft Sollicitudes of Dress;
From grov'ling Business and superfluous Care,
Ye Sons of Avarice! a Moment spare:
Vot'ries of Fame and Worshippers of Pow'r!
Dismiss the pleasing Phantoms for an Hour.
Our daring Bard with Spirit unconfin'd,
Spreads wide the mighty Moral for Mankind.
Learn here how Heav'n supports the virtuous Mind,
10 Daring, tho' calm; and vigorous, tho' resign'd.
Learn here what Anguish racks the guilty Breast,
In Pow'r dependent, in Success deprest.
Learn here that Peace from Innocence must flow;
All else is empty Sound, and idle Show.

If Truths like these with pleasing Language join;
Ennobled, yet unchang'd, if Nature shine:
If no wild Draught depart from Reason's Rules,
Nor Gods his Heroes, nor his Lovers Fools:

Intriguing Wits! his artless Plot forgive;
20   And spare him, Beauties! tho' his Lovers live.

Be this at least his Praise; be this his Pride;
To force Applause no modern Arts are try'd.
Shou'd partial Cat-calls all his Hopes confound,
He bids no Trumpet quell the fatal Sound.
Shou'd welcome Sleep relieve the weary Wit,
He rolls no Thunders o'er the drowsy Pit.
No Snares to captivate the Judgment spreads;
Nor bribes your Eyes to prejudice your Heads.
Unmov'd tho' Witlings sneer and Rivals rail;
30   Studious to please, yet not asham'd to fail.
He scorns the meek Address, the suppliant Strain,
With Merit needless, and without it vain.
In Reason, Nature, Truth he dares to trust:
Ye Fops be silent! and ye Wits be just!

I i 28–57

LEONTIUS
              The Sons of *Greece*,
Ill-fated Race! So oft besieg'd in vain,
30   With false Security beheld Invasion.
Why should they fear? – That Power that kindly spreads
The Clouds, a Signal of impending Show'rs,
To warn the wand'ring Linnet to the Shade,
Beheld without Concern, expiring *Greece*,
And not one Prodigy foretold our Fate.

DEMETRIUS
A thousand horrid Prodigies foretold it.
A feeble Government, eluded Laws,
A factious Populace, luxurious Nobles,
And all the Maladies of sinking States.
40   When publick Villainy, too strong for Justice,
Shows his bold Front, the Harbinger of Ruin,
Can brave Leontius call for airy Wonders,
Which Cheats interpret, and which Fools regard?
When some neglected Fabrick nods beneath

The Weight of Years, and totters to the Tempest,
Must Heaven dispatch the Messengers of Light,
Or wake the Dead to warn us of its Fall?

LEONTIUS

Well might the Weakness of our Empire sink
Before such Foes of more than human Force;
50 Some Pow'r invisible, from Heav'n or Hell,
Conducts their Armies and asserts their Cause.

DEMETRIUS

And yet, my Friend, what Miracles were wrought
Beyond the Power of Constancy and Courage;
Did unresisted Lightning aid their Cannon,
Did roaring Whirlwinds sweep us from the Ramparts:
'Twas Vice that shook our Nerves, 'twas Vice, Leontius,
That froze our Veins, and wither'd all our Powers.

I ii 50–73

DEMETRIUS

50 Unhappy Lot of all that shine in Courts;
For forc'd Compliance, or for zealous Virtue,
Still odious to the Monarch, or the People.

CALI

Such are the Woes when arbitrary Pow'r,
And lawless Passion, hold the Sword of Justice.
If there be any Land, as Fame reports,
Where common Laws restrain the Prince and Subject,
A happy Land, where circulating Pow'r
Flows through each Member of th'embodied State,
Sure, not unconscious of the mighty Blessing,
60 Her grateful Sons shine bright with ev'ry Virtue;
Untainted with the Lust of Innovation,
Sure all unite to hold her League of Rule
Unbroken as the sacred Chain of Nature,
That links the jarring Elements in Peace.

LEONTIUS

But say, great Bassa, why the Sultan's Anger,
Burning in vain, delays the Stroke of Death?

CALI

Young, and unsettled in his Father's Kingdoms,
Fierce as he was, he dreaded to destroy
The Empire's Darling, and the Soldier's Boast;
70   But now confirm'd, and swelling with his Conquests,
Secure he tramples my declining Fame
Frowns unrestrain'd, and dooms me with his Eyes.

DEMETRIUS

What can reverse thy Doom?

CALI

                                        The Tyrant's Death.

II i 1–37

IRENE

Aspasia, yet pursue the sacred Theme;
Exhaust the Stores of pious Eloquence,
And teach me to repell the Sultan's Passion.
Still at Aspasia's Voice a sudden Rapture
Exalts my Soul, and fortifies my Heart.
The glitt'ring Vanities of empty Greatness,
The Hopes and Fears, the Joys and Pains of Life,
Dissolve in Air, and vanish into Nothing.

ASPASIA

Let nobler Hopes and juster Fears succeed,
10   And bar the Passes of Irene's Mind
Against returning Guilt.

IRENE

                                When thou art absent
Death rises to my View, with all his Terrors;
Then Visions horrid as a Murd'rer's Dreams
Chill my Resolves, and blast my blooming Virtue:
Stern Torture shakes his bloody Scourge before me,
And Anguish gnashes on the fatal Wheel.

ASPASIA

Since Fear predominates in every Thought,
And sways thy Breast with absolute Dominion,
Think on th'insulting Scorn, the conscious Pangs,
20   The future Miseries that wait th'Apostate;
So shall Timidity assist thy Reason,
And Wisdom into Virtue turn thy Frailty.

IRENE

Will not that Pow'r that form'd the Heart of Woman,
And wove the feeble Texture of her Nerves,
Forgive those Fears that shake the tender Frame?

ASPASIA

The Weakness we lament, our selves create,
Instructed from our infant Years to court
With counterfeited Fears the Aid of Man;
We learn to shudder at the rustling Breeze,
30   Start at the Light, and tremble in the Dark;
Till Affectation, rip'ning to Belief,
And Folly, frighted at her own Chimeras,
Habitual Cowardice usurps the Soul.

IRENE

Not all like thee can brave the Shocks of Fate,
Thy Soul by Nature great, enlarg'd by Knowledge,
Soars unencumber'd with our idle Cares,
And all Aspasia but her Beauty's Man.

II iii 1–17

CALI *solus*

How Heav'n in Scorn of human Arrogance,
Commits to trivial Chance the Fate of Nations!
While with incessant Thought laborious Man
Extends his mighty Schemes of Wealth and Pow'r,
And tow'rs and triumphs in ideal Greatness;
Some accidental Gust of Opposition
Blasts all the Beauties of his new Creation,
O'erturns the Fabrick of presumptuous Reason,

And whelms the swelling Architect beneath it.
10 Had not the Breeze untwin'd the meeting Boughs,
And through the parted Shade disclos'd the *Greeks,*
Th'important Hour had pass'd unheeded by,
In all the sweet Oblivion of Delight,
In all the Fopperies of meeting Lovers;
In Sighs and Tears, in Transports and Embraces,
In soft Complaints, and idle Protestations.

III ii 14–33

CALI
At my Command yon' Iron Gates unfold;
At my Command the Sentinels retire;
With all the Licence of Authority,
Through bowing Slaves, I range the private Rooms,
And of To-morrow's Action fix the Scene.

DEMETRIUS
To-morrow's Action? Can that hoary Wisdom
20 Born down with Years, still doat upon To-morrow?
That fatal Mistress of the Young, the Lazy,
The Coward, and the Fool, condemn'd to lose
An useless Life in waiting for To-morrow,
To gaze with longing Eyes upon To-morrow,
Till interposing Death destroys the Prospect!
Strange! that this gen'ral Fraud from Day to Day
Should fill the World with Wretches undetected.
The Soldier lab'ring through a Winter's March,
Still sees To-morrow drest in Robes of Triumph;
30 Still to the Lover's long-expecting Arms,
To-morrow brings the visionary Bride.
But thou, too old to bear another Cheat,
Learn, that the present Hour alone is Man's.

III viii 111–35

IRENE

Ambition is the Stamp impress'd by Heav'n
To mark the noblest Minds, with active Heat
Inform'd they mount the Precipice of Pow'r,
Grasp at Command, and tow'r in quest of Empire;
While vulgar Souls compassionate their Cares,
Gaze at their Height and tremble at their Danger:
Thus meaner Spirits with Amazement mark
The varying Seasons, and revolving Skies,
And ask, what guilty Pow'r's rebellious Hand
120   Rolls with eternal Toil the pond'rous Orbs;
While some Archangel nearer to Perfection,
In easy State presides o'er all their Motions,
Directs the Planets with a careless Nod,
Conducts the Sun, and regulates the Spheres.

ASPASIA

Well may'st thou hide in Labyrinths of Sound
The Cause that shrinks from Reason's powerful Voice.
Stoop from thy Flight, trace back th'entangled Thought,
And set the glitt'ring Fallacy to view.
Not Pow'r I blame, but Pow'r obtain'd by Crime,
130   Angelic Greatness is Angelic Virtue.
Amidst the Glare of Courts, the Shouts of Armies,
Will not th'Apostate feel the Pangs of Guilt,
And wish too late for Innocence and Peace?
Curst as the Tyrant of th'infernal Realms,
With gloomy State and agonizing Pomp.

V vi 1–16

IRENE

Against the Head which Innocence secures,
Insidious Malice aims her Darts in vain;
Turn'd backwards by the powerful Breath of Heav'n.
Perhaps ev'n now the Lovers unpursu'd
Bound o'er the sparkling Waves. Go, happy Bark,

Thy sacred Freight shall still the raging Main.
To guide thy Passage shall th'aerial Spirits
Fill all the starry Lamps with double Blaze;
Th'applauding Sky shall pour forth all its Beams
10 To grace the Triumph of victorious Virtue;
While I, not yet familiar to my Crimes,
Recoil from Thought, and shudder at myself.
How am I chang'd! How lately did Irene
Fly from the busy Pleasures of her Sex,
Well pleas'd to search the Treasures of Remembrance,
And live her guiltless Moments o'er anew!

V xiii 1–15

MUSTAPHA *to* MURZA
What Plagues, what Tortures, are in store for thee,
Thou sluggish Idler, dilatory Slave?
Behold the Model of consummate Beauty,
Torn from the mourning Earth by thy Neglect.

MURZA
Such was the Will of Heav'n – A Band of *Greeks*
That mark'd my Course, suspicious of my Purpose,
Ruch'd out and seiz'd me, thoughtless and unarm'd,
Breathless, amaz'd, and on the guarded Beach
Detain'd me till Demetrius set me free.

MUSTAPHA
10 So sure the Fall of Greatness rais'd on Crimes,
So fix'd the Justice of all-conscious Heav'n.
    When haughty Guilt exults with impious Joy,
    Mistake shall blast, or Accident destroy;
    Weak Man with erring Rage may throw the Dart,
    But Heav'n shall guide it to the guilty Heart.

London: A Poem

IN IMITATION OF THE THIRD SATIRE OF JUVENAL

Quis ineptæ
Tam patiens Urbis, tam ferreus ut teneat se?
Juv. [Sat.i.30–31]

Tho' Grief and Fondness in my Breast rebel,
When injur'd Thales bids the Town farewell,
Yet still my calmer Thoughts his Choice commend,
I praise the Hermit, but regret the Friend,
Resolv'd at length, from Vice and London far,
To breathe in distant Fields a purer Air,
And, fix'd on Cambria's solitary Shore,
Give to St David one *true Briton* more.

For who would leave, unbrib'd, *Hibernia*'s Land,
10 Or change the rocks of *Scotland* for the *Strand*?
There none are swept by sudden Fate away,
But all whom Hunger spares, with Age decay:
Here Malice, Rapine, Accident, conspire,
And now a Rabble rages, now a Fire;
Their Ambush here relentless Ruffians lay,
And here the fell Attorney prowls for Prey;
Here falling Houses thunder on your Head,
And here a female Atheist talks you dead.

While Thales waits the Wherry that contains
20 Of dissipated Wealth the small Remains,
On *Thames*'s Banks, in silent Thought we stood,
Where Greenwich smiles upon the silver Flood:
Struck with the Seat that gave Eliza birth,
We kneel, and kiss the consecrated Earth;
In pleasing Dreams the blissful Age renew,
And call Britannia's Glories back to view;
Behold her Cross triumphant on the Main,
The Guard of Commerce, and the Dread of *Spain*,

Ere Masquerades debauch'd, Excise oppress'd,
30 Or *English* Honour grew a standing Jest.

A transient Calm the happy Scenes bestow,
And for a Moment lull the Sense of Woe.
At length awaking, with contemptuous Frown,
Indignant Thales eyes the neighb'ring Town.

Since Worth, he cries, in these degen'rate Days
Wants ev'n the cheap Reward of empty Praise;
In those curs'd Walls, devote to Vice and Gain,
Since unrewarded Science toils in vain;
Since Hope but sooths to double my Distress,
40 And ev'ry Moment leaves my Little less;
While yet my steady Steps no Staff sustains,
And Life still vig'rous revels in my Veins;
Grant me, kind Heaven, to find some happier Place,
Where Honesty and Sense are no Disgrace;
Some pleasing Bank where verdant Osiers play,
Some peaceful Vale with Nature's Paintings gay;
Where once the harrass'd Briton found Repose,
And safe in Poverty defy'd his Foes;
Some secret Cell, ye Pow'rs, indulgent give.
50 Let — live here, for — has learn'd to live.
Here let those reign, whom Pensions can incite
To vote a Patriot black, a Courtier white;
Explain their Country's dear-bought Rights away,
And plead for Pirates in the Face of Day;
With slavish Tenets taint our poison'd Youth,
And lend a Lye the Confidence of Truth.

Let such raise Palaces, and Manors buy,
Collect a Tax, or farm a Lottery,
With warbling Eunuchs fill a licens'd Stage,
60 And lull to Servitude a thoughtless Age.

Heroes, proceed! What Bounds your Pride shall hold?
What Check restrain your Thirst for Pow'r and Gold?
Behold rebellious Virtue quite o'erthrown,
Behold our Fame, our Wealth, our Lives your own.

To such, a groaning Nation's spoils are giv'n,
When publick Crimes inflame the Wrath of Heav'n:
But what, my Friend, what Hope remains for me,
Who start at Theft, and blush at Perjury?
Who scarce forbear, tho' Britain's Court he sing,
70 To pluck a titled Poet's borrow'd Wing;
A Statesman's Logic, unconvinc'd can hear,
And dare to slumber o'er the *Gazetteer*;
Despise a Fool in half his Pension drest,
And strive in vain to laugh at Clodio's Jest.

Others with softer Smiles, and subtler Art,
Can sap the Principles, or taint the Heart;
With more Address a Lover's Note convey,
Or bribe a Virgin's Innocence away.
Well may they rise, while I, whose Rustic Tongue
80 Ne'er knew to puzzle Right, or varnish Wrong,
Spurn'd as a Beggar, dreaded as a Spy,
Live unregarded, unlamented die.

For what but social Guilt the Friend endears?
Who shares *Orgilio*'s Crimes, his Fortune shares.
But thou, should tempting Villainy present
All *Marlb'rough* hoarded, or all *Villiers* spent;
Turn from the glitt'ring Bribe thy scornful Eye,
Nor sell for Gold, what Gold could never buy,
The peaceful Slumber, self-approving Day,
90 Unsullied Fame, and Conscience ever gay.

The cheated Nation's happy Fav'rites, see!
Mark whom the Great caress, who frown on me!
London! the needy Villain's gen'ral Home,
The Common Sewer of *Paris* and of *Rome*;
With eager Thirst, by Folly or by Fate,
Sucks in the Dregs of each corrupted State.
Forgive my Transports on a Theme like this,
I cannot bear a *French* Metropolis.

Illustrious Edward! from the Realms of Day,
100 The Land of Heroes and of Saints survey;

Nor hope the *British* Lineaments to trace,
The rustic Grandeur, or the surly Grace;
But lost in thoughtless Ease, and empty Show,
Behold the Warriour dwindled to a Beau;
Sense, Freedom, Piety, refin'd away,
Of France the Mimic, and of Spain the Prey.

All that at home no more can beg or steal,
Or like a Gibbet better than a Wheel;
Hiss'd from the Stage, or hooted from the Court,
110   Their Air, their Dress, their Politicks import;
Obsequious, artful, voluble and gay,
On *Britain*'s fond Credulity they prey.
No gainful Trade their Industry can 'scape,
They sing, they dance, clean Shoes, or cure a Clap;
All Sciences a fasting Monsieur knows,
And bid him go to Hell, to Hell he goes.

Ah! what avails it, that, from Slav'ry far,
I drew the Breath of Life in *English* Air;
Was early taught a *Briton*'s Right to prize,
120   And lisp the Tale of Henry's Victories;
If the gull'd Conqueror receives the Chain,
And Flattery prevails when Arms are vain?

Studious to please, and ready to submit,
The supple *Gaul* was born a Parasite:
Still to his Int'rest true, where'er he goes,
Wit, Brav'ry, Worth, his lavish Tongue bestows;
In ev'ry Face a Thousand Graces shine,
From ev'ry Tongue flows Harmony divine.
These Arts in vain our rugged Natives try, ⎞
130   Strain out with fault'ring Diffidence a Lye, ⎬
And get a Kick for awkward Flattery. ⎠

Besides, with Justice, this discerning Age
Admires their wond'rous Talents for the Stage:
Well may they venture on the Mimic's Art,
Who play from Morn to Night a borrow'd Part;
Practis'd their Master's Notions to embrace,

Repeat his Maxims, and reflect his Face;
With ev'ry wild Absurdity comply,
And view each Object with another's Eye;
140 To shake with Laughter ere the Jest they hear,
To pour at Will the counterfeited Tear;
And as their Patron hints the Cold or Heat,
To shake in Dog-days, in *December* sweat.

How, when Competitors like these contend,
Can surly Virtue hope to fix a Friend?
Slaves that with serious Impudence beguile,
And lye without a Blush, without a Smile;
Exalt each Trifle, ev'ry Vice adore,
Your Taste in Snuff, your Judgment in a Whore;
150 Can *Balbo*'s Eloquence applaud, and swear
He gropes his Breeches with a Monarch's Air.

For Arts like these preferr'd, admir'd, carest,
They first invade your Table, then your Breast;
Explore your Secrets with insidious Art,
Watch the weak Hour, and ransack all the Heart;
Then soon your ill-placed Confidence repay,
Commence your Lords, and govern or betray.
By Numbers here from Shame or Censure free,
All Crimes are safe, but hated Poverty.
160 This, only this, the rigid Law persues,
This, only this, provokes the snarling Muse;
The sober Trader at a tatter'd Cloak,
Wakes from his Dream, and labours for a Joke;
With brisker Air the silken Courtiers gaze,
And turn the varied Taunt a thousand Ways.
Of all the Griefs that harrass the Distrest,
Sure the most bitter is a scornful Jest;
Fate never wounds more deep the gen'rous Heart,
Than when a Blockhead's Insult points the Dart.

170 Has Heaven reserv'd, in Pity to the Poor,
No pathless Waste, or undiscover'd Shore?
No secret Island in the boundless Main?

No peaceful Desart yet unclaim'd by Spain?
Quick let us rise, the happy Seats explore,
And bear Oppression's Insolence no more.
This mournful Truth is ev'ry where confest,
Slow rises Worth, by Poverty deprest:
But here more slow, where all are Slaves to Gold,
Where Looks are Merchandise, and Smiles are sold,
180 Where won by Bribes, by Flatteries implor'd,
The Groom retails the Favours of his Lord.

But hark! th'affrighted Crowd's tumultuous Cries
Roll thro' the Streets, and thunder to the Skies;
Rais'd from some pleasing Dream of Wealth and Pow'r,
Some pompous Palace, or some blissful Bow'r,
Aghast you start, and scarce with aking Sight
Sustain th'approaching Fire's tremendous Light;
Swift from pursuing Horrors take your Way,
And Leave your little *All* to Flames a Prey;
190 Then thro' the World a wretched Vagrant roam,
For where can starving Merit find a Home?
In vain your mournful Narrative disclose,
While all neglect, and most insult your Woes.

Should Heaven's just Bolts *Orgilio*'s Wealth confound,
And spread his flaming Palace on the Ground,
Swift o'er the Land the dismal Rumour flies,
And publick Mournings pacify the Skies;
The Laureat Tribe in servile Verse relate,
How Virtue wars with persecuting Fate;
200 With well-feign'd Gratitude the pension'd Band
Refund the Plunder of the begger'd Land.
See! while he builds, the gaudy Vassals come,
And crowd with sudden Wealth the rising Dome;
The Price of Boroughs and of Souls restore,
And raise his Treasures higher than before.
Now bless'd with all the Baubles of the Great,
The polish'd Marble, and the shining Plate,
Orgilio sees the golden Pile aspire,
And hopes from angry Heav'n another Fire.

210   Could'st thou resign the Park and Play content,
     For the fair Banks of *Severn* or of *Trent*;
     There might'st thou find some elegant Retreat,
     Some hireling Senator's deserted Seat;
     And stretch thy Prospects o'er the smiling Land,
     For less than rent the Dungeons of the *Strand*;
     There prune thy Walks, support thy drooping Flow'rs,
     Direct thy Rivulets, and twine thy Bow'rs;
     And, while thy grounds a cheap Repast afford,
     Despise the Dainties of a venal Lord:
220   There ev'ry Bush with Nature's Music rings,
     There ev'ry Breeze bears Health upon its Wings;
     On all thy Hours Security shall smile,
     And bless thine Evening Walk and Morning Toil.

     Prepare for Death, if here at Night you roam,
     And sign your Will before you sup from Home.
     Some fiery Fop, with new Commission vain,
     Who sleeps on Brambles till he kills his Man;
     Some frolick Drunkard, reeling from a Feast,
     Provokes a Broil, and stabs you for a Jest.
230   Yet ev'n these Heroes, mischievously gay,
     Lords of the Street, and Terrors of the Way;
     Flush'd as they are with Folly, Youth and Wine,
     Their prudent Insults to the Poor confine;
     Afar they mark the Flambeau's bright Approach,
     And shun the shining Train, and golden Coach.

     In vain, these Dangers past, your Doors you close,
     And hope the balmy Blessings of Repose:
     Cruel with Guilt, and daring with Despair,
     The midnight Murd'rer bursts the faithless Bar;
240   Invades the sacred Hour of silent Rest
     And leaves, unseen, a Dagger in your Breast.

     Scarce can our Fields, such Crowds at *Tyburn* die,
     With Hemp the Gallows and the Fleet supply.
     Propose your Schemes, ye Senatorian Band,
     Whose *Ways and Means* support the sinking Land;

Lest Ropes be wanting in the tempting Spring,
To rig another Convoy for the K—g.

A single Jail, in Alfred's golden Reign,
Could half the Nation's Criminals contain;
250 Fair Justice then, without Constraint ador'd
Held high the steady Scale, but sheath'd the sword;
No Spies were paid, no *Special Juries* known,
Blest Age! but ah! how diff'rent from our own!

Much could I add, – but see the Boat at hand,
The Tide retiring, calls me from the Land:
Farewel! — When Youth, and Health, and Fortune spent,
Thou fly'st for Refuge to the Wilds of *Kent*;
And tir'd like me with Follies and with Crimes,
In angry Numbers warn'st succeeding Times;
260 Then shall thy Friend, nor thou refuse his Aid,
Still Foe to Vice forsake his *Cambrian* Shade;
In Virtue's Cause once more exert his Rage,
Thy Satire point, and animate thy Page.

To Eliza plucking Laurel in Mr Pope's Gardens

As learn'd *Eliza*, sister of the Muse,
   Surveys with new contemplative delight
Pope's hallow'd glades, and never tiring views,
   Her conscious hand his laurel leaves invite.

Cease, lovely thief! my tender limbs to wound,
   (Cry'd *Daphne* whisp'ring from the yielding tree;)
Were *Pope* once void of wonted candour found,
   Just *Phœbus* would devote his plant to thee.

To Lady Firebrace

TO LADY F—CE AT BURY ASSIZES

At length must *Suffolk*'s beauties shine in vain,
So long renown'd in B—n's deathless strain?
Thy charms at least, fair F—e, might inspire
Some zealous bard to wake the sleeping lyre.
For such thy beauteous mind, and lovely face,
Thou seem'st at once, bright nymph, a Muse and Grace.

To Miss —

ON HER PLAYING UPON THE HARPSICHORD IN A
ROOM HUNG WITH SOME FLOWER-PIECES OF HER
OWN PAINTING

When Stella strikes the tuneful String
In Scenes of imitated Spring,
Where Beauty lavishes her Powers
On Beds of never-fading Flowers;
And Pleasure propagates around
Each Charm of modulated Sound;
Ah! think not, in the dang'rous hour,
The Nymph fictitious as the Flower;
But shun, rash Youth, the gay Alcove,
10 Nor tempt the Snares of wily Love.
    When Charms thus press on every Sense,
What Thought of Flight, or of Defence?
Deceitful Hope, and vain Desire,
Forever flutter o'er her Lyre;
Delighting, as the Youth draws nigh,
To point the Glances of her Eye;
And forming with unerring Art,
New Chains to hold the Captive-Heart.
    But on those Regions of Delight,

20   Might *Truth* intrude, with daring Flight,
      Could Stella, sprightly, fair, and young,
      One Moment hear the Moral Song,
      Instruction with her Flowers might spring,
      And *Wisdom* warble from her String.
          Mark, when from thousand mingled Dyes
      Thou seest one pleasing Form arise;
      How active Light, and thoughtful Shade,
      In greater Scenes each other aid;
      Mark, when the diff'rent Notes agree
30   In friendly Contrariety;
      How Passion's well-accorded Strife
      Gives all the Harmony of Life:
      Thy Pictures shall thy Conduct frame,
      Consistent still, tho' not the same;
      Thy Musick teach the nobler Art,
      To tune the regulated Heart.

To Miss —

ON HER GIVING THE AUTHOR A GOLD AND SILK NET-WORK PURSE OF HER OWN WEAVING

      Tho' gold and silk their charms unite,
      To make thy curious web delight,
      In vain the vary'd work would shine,
      If wrought by any hand but thine;
      Thy hand, that knows the subtler art,
      To weave those nets that catch the heart;
          Spread out by me, the roving coin
      Thy nets may catch, but not confine;
      Nor can I hope, thy silken chain
10   The glitt'ring vagrants shall restrain.
      Why, *Sylvia*, was it then decreed,
      The heart, once caught, should ne'er be freed?

Stella in Mourning

When, lately, *Stella*'s form display'd
The beauties of the gay brocade,
The nymphs, who found their pow'r decline,
Proclaim'd her, not so fair as fine.
'Fate! snatch away the bright disguise,
And let the goddess trust her eyes.'
Thus blindly pray'd the fretful fair,
And fate malicious heard the pray'r.
But brighten'd by the sable dress,
10 As virtue rises in distress,
Since *Stella* still extends her reign,
Ah! how shall envy sooth her pain?
    Th'adoring youth, and envious fair,
Henceforth shall form one common pray'r,
And Love and Hate alike implore
The skies, that *Stella* mourn no more.

An Evening Ode

TO STELLA

Ev'ning, now, from purple wings,
Sheds the grateful gifts she brings;
Brilliant drops bedeck the mead,
Cooling breezes shake the reed;
Shake the reed, and curl the stream,
Silver'd o'er with *Cynthia*'s beam.
Near, the chequer'd, lonely grove
Hears, and keeps thy secrets, Love. –
Stella! thither let us stray,
10 Lightly o'er the dewy way;
Phœbus drives his burning car
Hence, my lovely *Stella*, far;
In his stead, the Queen of Night
Round us pours a lambent light;

Light, that serves but just to show
Breasts that beat, and cheeks that glow.
Let us now, in whisper'd joy,
Ev'ning's silent hours employ;
Silence, best, and conscious shades
20 Please the hearts that Love invades;
Other pleasures give them pain,
Lovers all but Love disdain.

The Vanity of Wealth

AN ODE TO A FRIEND

No more thus brooding o'er yon heap,
With Av'rice painful vigils keep.
Still unenjoy'd the present store,
Still endless sighs are breath'd for more.
O! quit the shadow, catch the prize,
Which not all *India*'s treasure buys!

To purchase heav'n, has gold the pow'r?
Can gold remove the mortal hour?
In life, can *Love* be bought with gold?
10 Are *Friendship*'s pleasures to be sold?
No – all that's worth a wish, a thought,
Fair *Virtue* gives, unbrib'd, unbought.
Cease, then, on trash thy hopes to bind,
Let nobler views engage thy mind.

With *Science* tread the wond'rous way,
Or learn the *Muse*'s moral lay;
In social hours indulge thy soul,
Where *Mirth* and *Temp'rance* mix the bowl.
To virtuous *Love* resign thy breast,
20 And be, by blessing *Beauty*, blest.

Thus taste the feast by Nature spread,
Ere Youth and all its joys are fled;

Come, taste with me the balm of life,
Secure from pomp, and wealth, and strife.
I boast whate'er for man was meant,
In health, and *Stella*, and content:
And scorn, oh! let that scorn be thine!
Mere things of clay, that dig the mine.

The Winter's Walk

Behold my fair, where-e'er we rove,
   What dreary prospects round us rise,
The naked hills, the leafless grove,
   The hoary ground, the frowning skies.

Nor only through the wasted plain,
   Stern winter, is thy force confest,
Still wider spreads thy horrid reign,
   I feel thy pow'r usurp my breast.

Enliv'ning hope, and fond desire,
10   Resign the heart to spleen and care,
Scarce frighted love maintains his fire,
   And rapture saddens to despair.

In groundless hope, and causeless fear,
   Unhappy man! behold thy doom,
Still changing with the changeful year,
   The slave of sunshine and of gloom.

Tir'd with vain joys, and false alarms,
   With mental and corporeal strife,
Snatch me, my *Stella*, to thy arms,
20   And screen me from the ills of life.

Post-Genitis

Cum Lapidem hunc, magni
Qui nunc jacet Incola stagni,

Vel Pede Equus tanget,
Vel Arator vomere franget,

Sentiet ægra Metus,
Effundet Patria Fletus,

Littoraque ut Fluctu,
Resonabunt Oppida Luctu:

Nam fœcunda rubri
10   Serpent per Prata Colubri,

Gramina vastantes,
Flores Fructusque vorantes,

Omnia fœdantes,
Vitiantes, et spoliantes;

Quanquam haud pugnaces,
Ibunt per cuncta minaces,

Fures absque Timore,
Et pingues absque Labore.

Horrida dementes
20   Rapiet Discordia Gentes,

Plurima tunc Leges
Mutabit, plurima Reges

Natio, conversâ
In Rabiem tunc contremet Ursâ

Cynthia, tunc latis
Florebunt Lilia Pratis,

Nec fremere audebit
Leo, sed violare timebit,

Omnia consuetus
30   Populari Pascua lætus.

Ante Oculos Natos
Calcatos et Cruciatos

Jam feret ignavus,
Vetitâque Libidine pravus.

En quoque quod Mirum,
Quod dicas denique dirum,

Sanguinem Equus sugit,
Neque Bellua victa remugit.

To Posterity

Whene'er this Stone, now hid beneath the Lake,
The Horse shall trample, or the Plough shall break,
Then, O my Country! shalt thou groan distrest,
Grief swell thine Eyes, and Terror chill thy Breast.
Thy Streets with Violence of Woe shall sound,
Loud as the Billows bursting on the Ground.
Then thro' thy Fields shall scarlet Reptiles stray,
And Rapine and Pollution mark their Way.
Their hungry Swarms the peaceful Vale shall fright
10 Still fierce to threaten, still afraid to fight;
The teeming Year's whole Product shall devour,
Insatiate pluck the Fruit, and crop the Flow'r:
Shall glutton on the industrious Peasants Spoil,
Rob without Fear, and fatten without Toil.
Then o'er the World shall Discord stretch her Wings,
Kings change their Laws, and Kingdoms change their
    Kings.
The Bear enrag'd th'affrighted Moon shall dread;
The Lilies o'er the Vales triumphant spread;
Nor shall the Lyon, wont of old to reign
20 Despotic o'er the desolated Plain,
Henceforth th'inviolable Bloom invade,
Or dare to murmur in the flow'ry Glade;
His tortur'd Sons shall die before his Face,
While he lies melting in a lewd Embrace;
And, yet more strange! his Veins a Horse shall drain,
Nor shall the passive Coward once complain.

Prologue to Garrick's Lethe

Prodigious Madness of the writing Race!
Ardent of Fame, yet fearless of Disgrace.
   Without a boding Tear, or anxious Sigh,
The Bard obdurate sees his Brother die.
Deaf to the Critick, Sullen to the Friend,
Not One takes Warning, by another's End.
   Oft has our Bard in this disastrous Year,
Beheld the Tragic Heroes taught to fear.
Oft has he seen the indignant Orange fly,
10 And heard th'ill Omen'd Catcall's direful Cry.
Yet dares to venture on the dangerous Stage,
And weakly hopes to 'scape the Critick's Rage.
   This Night he hopes to shew that Farce may charm,
Tho' no lewd Hint the mantling Virgin warm,
That useful Truth with Humour may unite,
That Mirth may mend, and Innocence delight.

An Epitaph on Claudy Phillips, a Musician

Phillips, whose touch harmonious could remove
The pangs of guilty pow'r, and hapless love,
Rest here distress'd by poverty no more,
Find here that calm, thou gav'st so oft before.
Sleep, undisturb'd, within this peaceful shrine,
Till angels wake thee, with a note like thine.

A Translation of the Latin Epitaph on Sir Thomas Hanmer, written by Doctor Freind

Thou, who survey'st these walls with curious eye,
Pause at this tomb – where *Hanmer*'s ashes lie.
His various worth, thro' varied life attend,

And learn his virtues, while thou mourn'st his end.
His force of genius burn'd in early youth,
With thirst of knowledge, and with love of truth;
His learning, join'd with each endearing art,
Charm'd ev'ry ear, and gain'd on ev'ry heart;
Thus early wise, th'endanger'd realm to aid,
10 His country call'd him from the studious shade;
In life's first bloom his publick toils began,
At once commenc'd the senator and man.
In bus'ness dextrous, weighty in debate,
Thrice ten long years he labour'd for the state;
In ev'ry speech persuasive wisdom flow'd,
In ev'ry act, refulgent virtue glow'd;
Suspended faction ceas'd from rage and strife,
To hear his eloquence, and praise his life;
Resistless merit fix'd the senate's choice,
20 Who hail'd him Speaker, with united voice.
Illustrious age! how bright thy glories shone,
When *Hanmer* fill'd the chair, and *Anne* the throne!
Then – when dark arts obscur'd each fierce debate,
When mutual frauds perplex'd the maze of state,
The moderator firmly mild appear'd,
Beheld with love, with veneration heard.
This task perform'd, he sought no gainful post,
Nor wish'd to glitter at his country's cost;
Strict on the right he fix'd his stedfast eye,
30 With temp'rate zeal, and wise anxiety;
Nor e'er from virtue's path was lur'd aside,
To pluck the flow'rs of pleasure, or of pride;
Her gifts despis'd, corruption blush'd and fled,
And fame persu'd him, where conviction led:
Age call'd, at length, his active mind to rest,
With honour sated, and with cares oppress'd;
To letter'd ease retir'd, and honest mirth,
To rural grandeur, and domestick worth,
Delighted still to please mankind, or mend,
40 The patriot's fire yet sparkled in the friend.
Calm conscience then his former life survey'd,

And recollected toils endear'd the shade;
Till nature call'd him to the gen'ral doom,
And virtue's sorrow dignify'd his tomb.

An Ode

Stern winter now, by spring repress'd,
   Forbears the long-continu'd strife,
And nature, on her naked breast,
   Delights to catch the gales of life.

Now, o'er the rural kingdom roves
   Soft Pleasure with her laughing train,
Love warbles in the vocal groves,
   And vegetation paints the plain.

Unhappy! whom to beds of pain
10   Arthritic tyranny consigns,
Whom smiling nature courts in vain,
   Tho' rapture sings, and beauty shines.

Yet, tho' my limbs disease invades,
   Her wings Imagination tries,
And bears me to the peaceful shades,
   Where —'s humble turrets rise.

Here stop, my soul, thy rapid flight,
   Nor from the pleasing groves depart,
Where first great nature charm'd my sight,
20   Where wisdom first inform'd my heart.

Here, let me, thro' the vales, pursue
   A guide, a father, and a friend;
Once more great nature's work review,
   Once more on wisdom's voice attend.

From false caresses, causeless strife,
   Wild hope, vain fear, alike remov'd,
Here let me learn the use of life,
   Then best enjoy'd, when most improv'd.

Teach me, thou venerable bow'r,
30   Cool meditation's quiet seat,
The gen'rous scorn of venal pow'r,
    The silent grandeur of retreat.

When Pride, by guilt, to greatness climbs,
    Or raging factions rush to war,
Here let me learn to shun the crimes
    I can't prevent, and will not share.

But, lest I fall by subtler foes,
    Bright wisdom teach me *Curio*'s art,
The swelling passions to compose,
40   And quell the rebels of the heart.

To Lyce, an elderly Lady

Ye nymphs whom starry rays invest,
    By flatt'ring poets giv'n;
Who shine, by lavish lovers drest,
    In all the pomp of heav'n;

Engross not all the beams on high,
    Which gild a lover's lays,
But as your sister of the sky,
    Let *Lyce* share the praise.

Her silver locks display the moon,
10   Her brows a cloudy show,
Strip'd rainbows round her eyes are seen,
    And show'rs from either flow.

Her teeth the night with darkness dyes,
    She's starr'd with pimples o'er,
Her tongue like nimble lightning plies,
    And can with thunder roar.

But some *Zelinda* while I sing
   Denies my *Lyce* shines,
And all the pens of *Cupid*'s wing
20   Attack my gentle lines.

Yet spite of fair *Zelinda*'s eye,
   And all her bards express,
My *Lyce* makes as good a sky,
   And I but flatter less.

A Song

Not the soft sighs of vernal gales,
The fragrance of the flow'ry vales,
The murmurs of the crystal rill,
The vocal grove, the verdant hill;
Not all their charms, tho' all unite,
Can touch my bosom with delight.

Not all the gems on *India*'s shore,
Not all *Peru*'s unbounded store,
Not all the pow'r, nor all the fame
10 That heroes, kings, or poets claim,
Nor knowledge, which the learn'd approve,
To form one wish my soul can move.

Yet nature's charms allure my eyes,
And knowledge, wealth and fame I prize;
Fame, wealth and knowledge I obtain,
Nor seek I nature's charms in vain:
In lovely *Stella* all combine,
And, lovely *Stella*! thou art mine.

Prologue Spoken by Mr Garrick
at the Opening of the Theatre in Drury-Lane, 1747

When Learning's Triumph o'er her barb'rous Foes
First rear'd the Stage, immortal Shakespear rose;
Each Change of many-colour'd Life he drew,
Exhausted Worlds, and then imagin'd new:
Existence saw him spurn her bounded Reign,
And panting Time toil'd after him in vain:
His pow'rful Strokes presiding Truth impress'd,
And unresisted Passion storm'd the Breast.
    Then Johnson came, instructed from the School,
10 To please in Method, and invent by Rule;
His studious Patience, and laborious Art,
By regular Approach essay'd the Heart;
Cold Approbation gave the ling'ring Bays,
For those who durst not censure, scarce cou'd praise.
A Mortal born he met the general Doom,
But left, like *Egypt*'s Kings, a lasting Tomb.
    The Wits of *Charles* found easier Ways to Fame,
Nor wish'd for Johnson's Art, or Shakespear's Flame;
Themselves they studied, as they felt, they writ,
20 Intrigue was Plot, Obscenity was Wit.
Vice always found a sympathetick Friend;
They pleas'd their Age, and did not aim to mend.
Yet Bards like these aspir'd to lasting Praise,
And proudly hop'd to pimp in future Days.
Their Cause was gen'ral, their Supports were strong,
Their Slaves were willing, and their Reign was long;
Till Shame regain'd the Post that Sense betray'd,
And Virtue call'd Oblivion to her Aid.
    Then crush'd by Rules, and weaken'd as refin'd,
30 For Years the Pow'r of Tragedy declin'd;
From Bard, to Bard, the frigid Caution crept,
Till Declamation roar'd, while Passion slept.
Yet still did Virtue deign the Stage to tread,
Philosophy remain'd, though Nature fled.

But forc'd at length her antient Reign to quit,
She saw great *Faustus* lay the Ghost of Wit:
Exulting Folly hail'd the joyful Day,
And Pantomime, and Song, confirm'd her Sway.
    But who the coming Changes can presage,
40 And mark the future Periods of the Stage? –
Perhaps if Skill could distant Times explore,
New *Behns*, new *Durfeys*, yet remain in Store.
Perhaps, where *Lear* has rav'd, and *Hamlet* dy'd,
On flying Cars new Sorcerers may ride.
Perhaps, for who can guess th'Effects of Chance?
Here *Hunt* may box, or *Mahomet* may dance.
    Hard is his lot, that here by Fortune plac'd,
Must watch the wild Vicissitudes of Taste;
With ev'ry Meteor of Caprice must play,
50 And chase the new-blown Bubbles of the Day.
Ah! let not Censure term our Fate our Choice,
The Stage but echoes back the publick Voice.
The Drama's Laws the Drama's Patrons give,
For we that live to please, must please to live.
    Then prompt no more the Follies you decry,
As Tyrants doom their Tools of Guilt to die;
'Tis yours this Night to bid the Reign commence
Of rescu'd Nature, and reviving Sense;
To chase the Charms of Sound, the Pomp of Show,
60 For useful Mirth, and salutary Woe;
Bid scenic Virtue form the rising Age,
And Truth diffuse her Radiance from the Stage.

The Vanity of Human Wishes

THE TENTH SATIRE OF JUVENAL IMITATED

Let Observation with extensive View,
Survey Mankind from *China* to *Peru*;
Remark each anxious Toil, each eager Strife,
And watch the busy Scenes of crouded Life;
Then say how Hope and Fear, Desire and Hate,
O'erspread with Snares the clouded Maze of Fate,
Where wav'ring Man, betray'd by vent'rous Pride,
To tread the dreary Paths without a Guide;
As treach'rous Phantoms in the Mist delude,
10 Shuns fancied Ills, or chases airy Good.
How rarely Reason guides the stubborn Choice,
Rules the bold Hand, or prompts the suppliant Voice,
How Nations sink, by darling Schemes oppress'd,
When Vengeance listens to the Fool's Request.
Fate wings with ev'ry Wish th'afflictive Dart,
Each Gift of Nature, and each Grace of Art,
With fatal Heat impetuous Courage glows,
With fatal Sweetness Elocution flows,
Impeachment stops the Speaker's pow'rful Breath,
20 And restless Fire precipitates on Death.
     But scarce observ'd the Knowing and the Bold,
Fall in the gen'ral Massacre of Gold;
Wide-wasting Pest! that rages unconfin'd,
And crouds with Crimes the Records of Mankind,
For Gold his Sword the Hireling Ruffian draws,
For Gold the hireling Judge distorts the Laws;
Wealth heap'd on Wealth, nor Truth nor Safety buys,
The Dangers gather as the Treasures rise.
     Let Hist'ry tell where rival Kings command,
30 And dubious Title shakes the madded Land,
When Statutes glean the Refuse of the Sword,
How much more safe the Vassal than the Lord,
Low sculks the Hind beneath the Rage of Pow'r,
And leaves the wealthy Traytor in the *Tow'r*,
Untouch'd his Cottage, and his Slumbers sound,

Tho' Confiscation's Vulturs hover round.
  The needy Traveller, serene and gay,
Walks the wild Heath, and sings his Toil away.
Does Envy seize thee? crush th'upbraiding Joy,
40 Encrease his Riches and his Peace destroy,
Now Fears in dire Vicissitude invade,
The rustling Brake alarms, and quiv'ring Shade,
Nor Light nor Darkness bring his Pain Relief,
One shews the Plunder, and one hides the Thief.
  Yet still one gen'ral Cry the Skies assails
And Gain and Grandeur load the tainted Gales;
Few know the toiling Statesman's Fear or Care,
Th'insidious Rival and the gaping Heir.
  Once more, *Democritus*, arise on Earth,
50 With chearful Wisdom and instructive Mirth,
See motley Life in modern Trappings dress'd,
And feed with varied Fools th'eternal Jest:
Thou who couldst laugh where Want enchain'd Caprice,
Toil crush'd Conceit, and Man was of a Piece;
Where Wealth unlov'd without a Mourner dy'd;
And scarce a Sycophant was fed by Pride;
Where ne'er was known the Form of mock Debate,
Or seen a new-made Mayor's unwieldy State;
Where change of Fav'rites made no Change of Laws,
60 And Senates heard before they judg'd a Cause;
How wouldst thou shake at *Britain*'s modish Tribe,
Dart the quick Taunt, and edge the piercing Gibe?
Attentive Truth and Nature to descry,
And pierce each Scene with Philosophic Eye.
To thee were solemn Toys or empty Shew,
The Robes of Pleasure and the Veils of Woe:
All aid the Farce, and all thy Mirth maintain,
Whose Joys are causeless, or whose Griefs are vain.
  Such was the Scorn that fill'd the Sage's Mind,
70 Renew'd at ev'ry Glance on Humankind;
How just that Scorn ere yet thy Voice declare,
Search every State, and canvass ev'ry Pray'r.
  Unnumber'd Suppliants croud Preferment's Gate,
Athirst for Wealth, and burning to be great;

Delusive Fortune hears th'incessant Call,
They mount, they shine, evaporate, and fall.
On ev'ry Stage the Foes of Peace attend,
Hate dogs their Flight, and Insult mocks their End.
Love ends with Hope, the sinking Statesman's Door
80   Pours in the Morning Worshiper no more;
For growing Names the weekly Scribbler lies,
To growing Wealth the Dedicator flies,
From every Room descends the painted Face,
That hung the bright *Palladium* of the Place,
And smoak'd in Kitchens, or in Auctions sold,
To better Features yields the Frame of Gold;
For now no more we trace in ev'ry Line
Heroic Worth, Benevolence Divine:
The Form distorted justifies the Fall,
90   And Detestation rids th'indignant Wall.
      But will not *Britain* hear the last Appeal,
Sign her Foes Doom, or guard her Fav'rites Zeal;
Through Freedom's Sons no more Remonstrance rings,
Degrading Nobles and controuling Kings;
Our supple Tribes repress their Patriot Throats,
And ask no Questions but the Price of Votes;
With Weekly Libels and Septennial Ale,
Their Wish is full to riot and to rail.
      In full-blown Dignity, see *Wolsey* stand,
100   Law in his Voice, and Fortune in his Hand:
To him the Church, the Realm, their Pow'rs consign,
Thro' him the Rays of regal Bounty shine,
Turn'd by his Nod the Stream of Honour flows,
His Smile alone Security bestows:
Still to new Heights his restless Wishes tow'r,
Claim leads to Claim, and Pow'r advances Pow'r;
Till Conquest unresisted ceas'd to please,
And Rights submitted, left him none to seize.
At length his Sov'reign frowns – the Train of State
110   Mark the keen Glance, and watch the Sign to hate.
Where-e'er he turns he meets a Stranger's Eye,
His Suppliants scorn him, and his Followers fly;
At once is lost the Pride of aweful State,

The golden Canopy, the glitt'ring Plate,
The regal Palace, the luxurious Board,
The liv'ried Army, and the menial Lord.
With Age, with Cares, with Maladies oppress'd,
He seeks the Refuge of Monastic Rest.
Grief aids Disease, remember'd Folly stings,
120 And his last Sighs reproach the Faith of Kings.
   Speak thou, whose Thoughts at humble Peace repine,
Shall *Wolsey*'s Wealth, with *Wolsey*'s End be thine?
Or liv'st thou now, with safer Pride content,
The wisest Justice on the Banks of *Trent*?
For why did *Wolsey* near the Steeps of Fate,
On weak Foundations raise th'enormous Weight?
Why but to sink beneath Misfortune's Blow,
With louder Ruin to the Gulphs below?
   What gave great *Villiers* to th'Assassin's Knife,
130 And fixed Disease on *Harley*'s closing Life?
What murder'd *Wentworth*, and what exil'd *Hyde*,
By Kings protected and to Kings ally'd?
What but their Wish indulg'd in Courts to shine,
And Pow'r too great to keep or to resign?
   When first the College Rolls receive his Name,
The young Enthusiast quits his Ease for Fame;
Through all his Veins the Fever of Renown
Burns from the strong Contagion of the Gown;
O'er *Bodley*'s Dome his future Labours spread,
140 And *Bacon*'s Mansion trembles o'er his Head;
Are these thy Views? proceed, illustrious Youth,
And Virtue guard thee to the Throne of Truth,
Yet should thy Soul indulge the gen'rous Heat,
Till captive Science yields her last Retreat;
Should Reason guide thee with her brightest Ray,
And pour on misty Doubt resistless Day;
Should no false Kindness lure to loose Delight,
Nor Praise relax, nor Difficulty fright;
Should tempting Novelty thy Cell refrain,
150 And Sloth effuse her opiate Fumes in vain;
Should Beauty blunt on Fops her fatal Dart,
Nor claim the Triumph of a letter'd Heart;

Should no Disease thy torpid Veins invade,
Nor Melancholy's Phantoms haunt thy Shade;
Yet hope not Life from Grief or Danger free,
Nor think the Doom of Man revers'd for thee:
Deign on the passing World to turn thine Eyes,
And pause awhile from Letters to be wise;
There mark what Ills the Scholar's Life assail,
160 Toil, Envy, Want, the Patron, and the Jail.
See Nations slowly wise, and meanly just,
To buried Merit raise the tardy Bust.
If Dreams yet flatter, once again attend,
Hear *Lydiat*'s Life and *Galileo*'s End.

Nor deem, when Learning her last Prize bestows
The glitt'ring Eminence exempt from Foes;
See when the Vulgar 'scapes, despis'd or aw'd,
Rebellion's vengeful Talons seize on *Laud*.
From meaner Minds, tho' smaller Fines content
170 The plunder'd Palace or sequester'd Rent;
Mark'd out by dangerous Parts he meets the Shock,
And fatal Learning leads him to the Block:
Around his Tomb let Art and Genius weep,
But hear his Death, ye Blockheads, hear and sleep.

The festal Blazes, the triumphal Show,
The ravish'd Standard, and the captive Foe,
The Senate's Thanks, the Gazette's pompous Tale,
With Force resistless o'er the Brave prevail.
Such Bribes the rapid *Greek* o'er *Asia* whirl'd,
180 For such the steady *Romans* shook the World;
For such in distant Lands the *Britons* shine,
And stain with Blood the *Danube* or the *Rhine*;
This Pow'r has Praise, that Virtue scarce can warm,
Till Fame supplies the universal Charm.
Yet Reason frowns on War's unequal Game,
Where wasted Nations raise a single Name,
And mortgag'd States their Grandsires Wreaths regret
From Age to Age in everlasting Debt;
Wreaths which at last the dear-bought Right convey
190 To rust on Medals, or on Stones decay.
On what Foundation stands the Warrior's Pride?

How just his Hopes let *Swedish Charles* decide;
A Frame of Adamant, a Soul of Fire,
No Dangers fright him, and no Labours tire;
O'er Love, o'er Fear, extends his wide Domain,
Unconquer'd Lord of Pleasure and of Pain;
No Joys to him pacific Scepters yield,
War sounds the Trump, he rushes to the Field;
Behold surrounding Kings their Pow'rs combine,
200 And One capitulate, and One resign;
Peace courts his Hand, but spreads her Charms in vain;
'Think Nothing gain'd, he cries, till nought remain,
On *Moscow*'s Walls till *Gothic* Standards fly,
And all be Mine beneath the Polar Sky.'
The March begins in Military State,
And Nations on his Eye suspended wait;
Stern Famine guards the solitary Coast,
And Winter barricades the Realms of Frost;
He comes, nor Want nor Cold his Course delay; –
210 Hide, blushing Glory, hide *Pultowa*'s Day:
The vanquish'd Hero leaves his broken Bands,
And shews his Miseries in distant Lands;
Condemn'd a needy Supplicant to wait,
While Ladies interpose, and Slaves debate.
But did not Chance at length her Error mend?
Did no subverted Empire mark his End?
Did rival Monarchs give the fatal Wound?
Or hostile Millions press him to the Ground?
His Fall was destin'd to a barren Strand,
220 A petty Fortress, and a dubious Hand;
He left the Name, at which the World grew pale,
To point a Moral, or adorn a Tale.
    All Times their Scenes of pompous Woes afford,
From *Persia*'s Tyrant to *Bavaria*'s Lord.
In gay Hostility, and barb'rous Pride,
With half Mankind embattled at his Side,
Great *Xerxes* comes to seize the certain Prey,
And starves exhausted Regions in his Way;
Attendant Flatt'ry counts his Myriads o'er,
230 Till counted Myriads sooth his Pride no more;

Fresh Praise is try'd till Madness fires his Mind,
The Waves he lashes, and enchains the Wind;
New Pow'rs are claim'd, new Pow'rs are still bestow'd,
Till rude Resistance lops the spreading God;
The daring *Greeks* deride the Martial Shew,
And heap their Vallies with the gaudy Foe;
Th'insulted Sea with humbler Thoughts he gains,
A single Skiff to speed his Flight remains;
Th'incumber'd Oar scarce leaves the dreaded Coast
240 Through purple Billows and a floating Host.
    The bold *Bavarian*, in a luckless Hour,
Tries the dread Summits of *Cesarean* Pow'r,
With unexpected Legions bursts away,
And sees defenceless Realms receive his Sway;
Short Sway! fair *Austria* spreads her mournful Charms,
The Queen, the Beauty, sets the World in Arms;
From Hill to Hill the Beacons rousing Blaze
Spreads wide the Hope of Plunder and of Praise;
The fierce *Croatian*, and the wild *Hussar*,
250 With all the Sons of Ravage croud the War;
The baffled Prince in Honour's flatt'ring Bloom
Of hasty Greatness finds the fatal Doom,
His Foes Derision, and his Subjects Blame,
And steals to Death from Anguish and from Shame.
    Enlarge my Life with Multitude of Days,
In Health, in Sickness, thus the Suppliant prays;
Hides from himself his State, and shuns to know,
That Life protracted is protracted Woe.
Time hovers o'er, impatient to destroy,
260 And shuts up all the Passages of Joy:
In vain their Gifts the bounteous Seasons pour,
The Fruit Autumnal, and the Vernal Flow'r,
With listless Eyes the Dotard views the Store,
He views, and wonders that they please no more;
Now pall the tastless Meats, and joyless Wines,
And Luxury with Sighs her Slave resigns.
Approach, ye Minstrels, try the soothing Strain,
Diffuse the tuneful Lenitives of Pain:
No Sounds alas would touch th'impervious Ear,

270   Though dancing Mountains witness'd *Orpheus* near;
　　　Nor Lute nor Lyre his feeble Pow'rs attend,
　　　Nor sweeter Musick of a virtuous Friend,
　　　But everlasting Dictates croud his Tongue,
　　　Perversely grave, or positively wrong.
　　　The still returning Tale, and ling'ring Jest,
　　　Perplex the fawning Niece and pamper'd Guest,
　　　While growing Hopes scarce awe the gath'ring Sneer,
　　　And scarce a Legacy can bribe to hear;
　　　The watchful Guests still hint the last Offence,
280   The Daughter's Petulance, the Son's Expence,
　　　Improve his heady Rage with treach'rous Skill,
　　　And mould his Passions till they make his Will.
　　　　Unnumber'd Maladies his Joints invade,
　　　Lay Siege to Life and press the dire Blockade;
　　　But unextinguish'd Av'rice still remains,
　　　And dreaded Losses aggravate his Pains;
　　　He turns, with anxious Heart and cripled Hands,
　　　His Bonds of Debt, and Mortgages of Lands;
　　　Or views his Coffers with suspicious Eyes,
290   Unlocks his Gold, and counts it till he dies.
　　　　But grant, the Virtues of a temp'rate Prime
　　　Bless with an Age exempt from Scorn or Crime;
　　　An Age that melts with unperceiv'd Decay,
　　　And glides in modest Innocence away;
　　　Whose peaceful Day Benevolence endears,
　　　Whose Night congratulating Conscience cheers;
　　　The gen'ral Fav'rite as the gen'ral Friend:
　　　Such Age there is, and who shall wish its End?
　　　　Yet ev'n on this her Load Misfortune flings,
300   To press the weary Minutes flagging Wings:
　　　New Sorrow rises as the Day returns,
　　　A Sister sickens, or a Daughter mourns.
　　　Now Kindred Merit fills the sable Bier,
　　　Now lacerated Friendship claims a Tear.
　　　Year chases Year, Decay pursues Decay,
　　　Still drops some Joy from with'ring Life away;
　　　New Forms arise, and diff'rent Views engage,

Superfluous lags the Vet'ran on the Stage,
Till pitying Nature signs the last Release,
310 And bids afflicted Worth retire to Peace.
But few there are whom Hours like these await,
Who set unclouded in the Gulphs of Fate.
From *Lydia*'s Monarch should the Search descend,
By *Solon* caution'd to regard his End,
In Life's last Scene what Prodigies surprise,
Fears of the Brave, and Follies of the Wise?
From *Marlb'rough*'s Eyes the Streams of Dotage flow,
And *Swift* expires a Driv'ler and a Show.
The teeming Mother, anxious for her Race,
320 Begs for each Birth the Fortune of a Face:
Yet *Vane* could tell what Ills from Beauty spring;
And *Sedley* curs'd the Form that pleas'd a King.
Ye Nymphs of rosy Lips and radiant Eyes,
Whom Pleasure keeps too busy to be wise,
Whom Joys with soft Varieties invite
By Day the Frolick, and the Dance by Night,
Who frown with Vanity, who smile with Art,
And ask the latest Fashion of the Heart,
What Care, what Rules your heedless Charms shall save,
330 Each Nymph your Rival, and each Youth your Slave?
Against your Fame with Fondness Hate combines,
The Rival batters, and the Lover mines.
With distant Voice neglected Virtue calls,
Less heard, and less the faint Remonstrance falls;
Tir'd with Contempt, she quits the slipp'ry Reign,
And Pride and Prudence take her Seat in vain.
In croud at once, where none the Pass defend,
The harmless Freedom, and the private Friend.
The Guardians yield, by Force superior ply'd;
340 To Int'rest, Prudence; and to Flatt'ry, Pride.
Here Beauty falls betray'd, despis'd, distress'd,
And hissing Infamy proclaims the rest.
Where then shall Hope and Fear their Objects find?
Must dull Suspence corrupt the stagnant Mind?
Must helpless Man, in Ignorance sedate,

Roll darkling down the Torrent of his Fate?
Must no Dislike alarm, no Wishes rise,
No Cries invoke the Mercies of the Skies?
Enquirer, cease, Petitions yet remain,
350 Which Heav'n may hear, nor deem Religion vain.
Still raise for Good the supplicating Voice,
But leave to Heav'n the Measure and the Choice.
Safe in his Pow'r, whose Eyes discern afar
The secret Ambush of a specious Pray'r.
Implore his Aid, in his Decisions rest,
Secure whate'er he gives, he gives the best.
Yet when the Sense of sacred Presence fires,
And strong Devotion to the Skies aspires,
Pour fourth thy Fervours for a healthful Mind,
360 Obedient Passions, and a Will resign'd;
For Love, which scarce collective Man can fill;
For Patience sov'reign o'er transmuted Ill;
For Faith, that panting for a happier Seat,
Counts Death kind Nature's Signal of Retreat:
These Goods for Man the Laws of Heav'n ordain,
These Goods he grants, who grants the Pow'r to gain;
With these celestial Wisdom calms the Mind,
And makes the Happiness she does not find.

A New Prologue Spoken at the Representation of Comus

Ye patriot Crouds, who burn for *England*'s Fame,
Ye Nymphs, whose Bosoms beat at Milton's Name,
Whose gen'rous Zeal, unbought by flatt'ring Rhimes,
Shames the mean Pensions of *Augustan* Times;
Immortal Patrons of succeeding Days,
Attend this Prelude of perpetual Praise!
Let Wit, condemn'd the feeble War to wage
With close Malevolence, or public Rage;
Let Study, worn with Virtue's fruitless Lore,
10 Behold this Theatre, and grieve no more.

This Night, distinguish'd by your Smile, shall tell,
That never Briton can in vain excel;
The slighted Arts Futurity shall trust,
And rising Ages hasten to be just.
  At length our mighty Bard's victorious Lays
Fill the loud Voice of universal Praise,
And baffled Spite, with hopeless Anguish dumb,
Yields to Renown the Centuries to come.
With ardent Haste, each Candidate of Fame
20 Ambitious catches at his tow'ring Name:
He sees, and pitying sees, vain Wealth bestow
Those pageant Honours which he scorn'd below:
While Crowds aloft the laureat Bust behold,
Or trace his Form on circulating Gold,
Unknown, unheeded, long his Offspring lay,
And Want hung threat'ning o'er her slow Decay.
What tho' she shine with no Miltonian Fire,
No fav'ring Muse her morning Dreams inspire;
Yet softer Claims the melting Heart engage,
30 Her Youth laborious, and her blameless Age:
Hers the mild Merits of domestic Life,
The patient Suff'rer, and the faithful Wife.
Thus grac'd with humble Virtue's native Charms
Her Grandsire leaves her in *Britannia's* Arms,
Secure with Peace, with Competence, to dwell,
While tutelary Nations guard her Cell.
Yours is the Charge, ye Fair, ye Wise, ye Brave!
'Tis yours to crown Desert – beyond the Grave!

Translations of the Mottoes and Quotations in the Rambler

6   *Saturday, 7 April 1750*

Ni vitiis pejora fovens
  Proprium deserat ortum.
[Boethius, III vi]

Unless the soul, to vice a thrall
Desert her own original.

7 Tuesday, 10 April 1750

O qui perpetuâ mundum ratione gubernas,
Terrarum cœlique sator! –
Disjice terrenæ nebulas et pondera molis,
Atque tuo splendore mica! Tu namque serenum,
Tu requies tranquilla piis. Te cernere, finis,
Principium, vector, dux, semita, terminus, idem.
Boethius [III ix]

O thou whose pow'r o'er moving worlds presides,
Whose voice created, and whose wisdom guides,
On darkling man in pure effulgence shine,
And chear the clouded mind with light divine.
'Tis thine alone to calm the pious breast
With silent confidence and holy rest:
From thee, great God, we spring, to thee we tend,
Path, motive, guide, original, and end.

8 Saturday, 14 April 1750

Media inter prælia semper
Sideribus, cœlique plagis, superisque vocavi.
[Lucan, X 185–6]

Amid the storms of war, with curious eyes
I trace the planets and survey the skies.

10 Saturday, 21 April 1750

Posthabui tamen illorum mea seria ludo.
Virg. [Eclog. VII 17]

For trifling sports I quitted grave affairs.

12   Saturday, 28 April 1750

> Miserum parvâ stipe focilat, ut pudibundos
Exercere sales inter convivia possit. –
> Tu mitis, et acri
Asperitate carens, positoque per omnia fastu,
Inter ut æquales unus numeraris amicos,
Obsequiumque doces, et amorem quæris amando.

Lucanus *ad* Pisonem [126–132]

Unlike the ribald, whose licentious jest
Pollutes his banquet and insults his guest;
From wealth and grandeur easy to descend,
Thou joy'st to lose the master in the friend:
We round thy board the cheerful menials see,
Gay with the smile of bland equality;
No social care the gracious lord disdains;
Love prompts to love, and rev'rence rev'rence gains.

17   Tuesday, 15 May 1750

> Ridetque sui ludibria trunci.

[Lucan, IX 14]

And soaring mocks the broken frame below.

21   Tuesday, 29 May 1750

Terra salutiferas herbas, eademque nocentes,
Nutrit; et urticæ proxima sæpe rosa est.

Ovid [*Rem. Amor.* 45]

Our bane and physic the same earth bestows,
And near the noisome nettle blooms the rose.

32   Saturday, 7 July 1750

Leniter ex merito quicquid patiare ferendum est.

[Ovid, *Her.* V 7]

Let pain deserv'd without complaint be borne.

33   Tuesday, 10 July 1750

Quod caret alternâ Requie durabile non est.
Ovid [*Her*. IV 89]

Alternate rest and labour long endure.

39   Tuesday, 31 July 1750

Infelix – nulli bene nupta marito.
Ausonius [*Ep. Her*. XXX]

Unblest, still doom'd to wed with misery.

45   Tuesday, 21 August 1750

Ἥπερ μεγίστη γίγνεται σωτηρία,
Ὅταν γυνὴ πρὸς ἄνδρα μὴ διχοστατῇ,
Νῦν δ' ἐχθρὰ πάντα.
Euripides [*Med*. 14–16]

This is the chief felicity of life,
That concord smile on the connubial bed;
But now 'tis hatred all. –

46   Saturday, 25 August 1750

     Genus, et proavos, et quæ non fecimus ipsi,
Vix ea nostra voco.
Ovid [*Metam*. XIII 140–41]

Nought from my birth or ancestors I claim;
All is my own, my honour and my shame.

48   Saturday, 1 September 1750

     Projecere animam! quam vellent æthere in alto
Nunc et pauperiem, et duros tolerare labores!
[Virg. *Aen*. VI 436–7]

For healthful indigence in vain they pray,
In quest of wealth who throw their lives away.

54 Saturday, 22 September 1750

Tu-ne etiam moreris? Ah! quid me linquis, Erasme,
  Ante meus quam sit conciliatus amor?
J. C. Scaliger [*Epit. in Laude Erasmi*]

Art thou too fall'n? ere anger could subside
And love return, has great *Erasmus* died?

65 Tuesday, 30 October 1750

        Garrit anilis
Ex re fabellas. –
Hor. [*Sat.* II vi 77]

The chearful sage, when solemn dictates fail,
Conceals the moral counsel in a tale.

        χείμαρροι ποταμοὶ κατ' ὄρεσφι ῥέοντες
'Ες μισγάγκειαν συμβάλλετον ὄβριμον ὕδωρ,
Τόνδε τέ τηλόσε δοῦπον ἐν οὔρεσιν ἔκλυε ποιμήν.
[Homer, *Iliad* IV 452–5]

Work'd into sudden rage by wintry show'rs,
Down the steep hill the roaring torrent pours;
The mountain shepherd hears the distant noise.

67 Tuesday, 6 November 1750

Αἱ δ' ἐλπίδες βόσκουσι φυγάδας, ὡς λόγος
Καλῶς βλέπουσιν ὄμμασι, μέλλουσι δέ.
Eurip. [*Phœn.* 396–7]

Exiles, the proverb says, subsist on hope.
Delusive hope still points to distant good,
To good that mocks approach.

71   Tuesday, 20 November 1750

Τὸ ῥόδον ἀκμάζει βαιὸν χρόνον. ἢν δὲ παρέλθῃ,
Ζητῶν εὑρήσεις οὐ ῥόδον, ἀλλὰ βάτον.
[Gk Anthol. XI 53]

Soon fades the rose; once past the fragrant hour,
The loiterer finds a bramble for a flow'r.

81   Tuesday, 25 December 1750

Discite Justitiam moniti –
Virg. [*Aeneid* VI 620]

Hear, and be just.

82   Saturday, 29 December 1750

Omnia *Castor* emit, sic fiet ut omnia vendat.
Mart. [*Epig.* VII xcvii]

Who buys without discretion, buys to sell.

83   Tuesday, 1 January 1751

Nisi utile est quod facias stulta est gloria.
Phædrus [*Fab.* III xvii 12]

All useless science is an empty boast.

85   Tuesday, 8 January 1751

Otia si tollas periere *Cupidinis* arcus
    Contemptæque jacent, et sine luce faces
Ovid [*Remed. Amor.* 139–40]

At busy hearts in vain love's arrows fly;
Dim, scorn'd, and impotent, his torches lie.

89   Tuesday, 22 January 1751

Dulce est disipere in Loco.
Hor. [*Od*. IV xii 28]

Wisdom at proper times is well forgot.

90   Saturday, 26 January 1751

In tenui labor.
Virg. [*Georg*. IV 6]

What toil in slender things!

93   Tuesday, 5 February 1751

    Experiar quid concedatur in illos
Quorum Flaminiâ tegitur cinis atque Latinâ.
Juv. [*Sat*. I 170–71]

More safely truth to urge her claim presumes,
On names now found alone on books and tombs.

96   Saturday, 16 February 1751

Quod si *Platonis* musa personat verum,
Quod quisque discit, immemor recordatur.
Boethius [III xi 15]

Truth in platonic ornaments bedeck'd,
Inforc'd we love, unheeding recollect.

104   Saturday, 16 March 1751

    Nihil est quod credere de se
Non possit. –
Juv. [*Sat*. IV 70–71]

None e'er rejects hyperbolies of praise.

105   Tuesday, 19 March 1751

Animorum
Impulsu, et cæcâ magnâque cupidine ducti.
Juv. [*Sat.* X 350–51]

Vain man runs headlong, to caprice resign'd;
Impelled by passion, and with folly blind.

106   Saturday, 23 March 1751

Non unquam dedit
Documenta fors majora, quam fragili loco
Starent superbi. –
[Seneca, *Troad.* 4–6]

Insulting chance ne'er call'd with louder voice,
On swelling mortals to be proud no more.

111   Tuesday, 9 April 1751

Φρονεῖν γὰρ οἱ ταχεῖς, οὐκ ἀσφαλεῖς.
Sophoc. [*Oed. Tyran.* 617]

Disaster always waits an early wit.

117   Tuesday, 30 April 1751

Quàm juvat immites ventos audire cubantem –
Aut, gelidas hybernus aquas cùm fuderit auster,
Securum somnos, imbre juvante, sequi!
[Tibullus, *Eleg.* I i 45–8]

How sweet in sleep to pass the careless hours,
Lull'd by the beating wind and dashing show'rs!

122   Saturday, 18 May 1751

Nescio qua natale solum dulcedine cunctos
   Ducit.

Ovid [*Pont. Epist.* I iii 35]

By secret charms our native land attracts.

127   Tuesday, 4 June 1751

Cœpisti melius quàm desinis: ultima primis
   Cedunt: dissimiles hic vir, et ille puer.

Ovid [*Her.* IX 23-4]

Succeeding years thy early fame destroy;
Thou, who began'st a man, wilt end a boy.

128   Saturday, 8 June 1751

     Αἰὼν δ᾽ ἀσφαλὴς
Οὐκ ἐγένετ᾽, οὔτ᾽ Αἰακίδα παρὰ Πηλεῖ,
Οὔτε πὰρ᾽ ἀντιθέῳ
Κάδμῳ. λέγονταί γε μὰν βροτῶν
῎Ολβον ὑπέρτατον οἳ
Σχεῖν.

Pind. [*Pyth.* III 153-8]

For not the brave, or wise, or great,
E'er yet had happiness compleat;
Nor *Peleus*, grandson of the sky,
   Nor *Cadmus*, scap'd the shafts of pain,
Though favour'd by the pow'rs on high,
   With ev'ry bliss that man can gain.

129   Tuesday, 11 June 1751

    Nunc, o nunc, Dædale, dixit,
   Materiam, qua sis ingeniosus, habes.
Possidet en terras, et possidet æquora Minos:
   Nec tellus nostræ, nec patet unda fugæ.

Restat iter cœlo: cœlo tentabimus ire.
　Da veniam cœpto, Jupiter alte, meo.
Ovid [*Ars Amat.* II 33–8]

Now *Dædalus*, behold, by fate assign'd,
A task proportion'd to thy mighty mind!
Unconquer'd bars on earth and sea withstand;
Thine, *Minos*, is the main, and thine the land.
The skies are open – let us try the skies:
Forgive, great *Jove*, the daring enterprize.

130　Saturday, 15 June 1751

Non sic prata novo vere Decentia
Æstatis calidæ dispoliat Vapor,
Sævit Solstitio cum medius dies; –
Ut Fulgor teneris qui radiat Genis
Momento rapitur, nullaque non Dies
Formosi Spolium Corporis abstulit.
Res est Forma fugax. Quis sapiens bono
Confidat fragili?
Seneca [*Hippol.* 764–71]

Not faster in the summer's ray
The spring's frail beauty fades away,
Than anguish and decay consume
The smiling virgin's rosy bloom.
Some beauty's snatch'd each day, each hour;
For beauty is a fleeting flow'r:
Then how can wisdom e'er confide
In beauty's momentary pride?

132　Saturday, 22 June 1751

　　Dociles imitandis
Turpibus ac pravis omnes sumus. –
Juv. [*Sat.* XIV 40–41]

The mind of mortals, in perverseness strong,
Imbibes with dire docility the wrong.

135   Tuesday, 2 July 1751

Cœlum non animum mutant.
Hor. [*Epist.* I xi 27]

Place may be chang'd; but who can change his mind?

138   Saturday, 13 July 1751

    tecum libeat mihi sordida rura
Atque humiles habitare casas, et figere cervos.
Virg. [*Eclog.* II 28–9]

With me retire and leave the pomp of courts
For humble cottages and rural sports.

139   Tuesday, 16 July 1751

  Sit quod vis simplex duntaxat et unum.
Hor. [*Ars Poet.* 23]

Let ev'ry piece be simple and be one.

140   Saturday, 20 July 1751

    Quis tam *Lucili* fautor inepte est
Ut non hoc fateatur?
Hor. [*Sat.* I x 2–3]

What doating bigot to his faults so blind,
As not to grant me this, can *Milton* find?

141   Tuesday, 23 July 1751

Hilarisque, tamen cum pondere, virtus.
Stat. [*Silv.* II iii 65]

Greatness with ease, and gay severity.

143   Tuesday, 30 July 1751

Imperet bellante prior, jacentem
   Lenis in hostem.
Hor. [*Carm. Secul.* 51]

Let *Cæsar* spread his conquests far,
Less pleas'd to triumph than to spare.

153   Tuesday, 3 September 1751

Turba Remi sequitur fortunam, ut semper, et odit
Damnatos.
Juv. [*Sat.* X 73]

The fickle crowd with fortune comes and goes;
Wealth still finds followers, and misfortune foes.

156   Saturday, 14 September 1751

Nunquam aliud natura, aliud sapientia dicit.
Juv. [*Sat.* XIV 321]

For wisdom ever echoes nature's voice.

160   Saturday, 28 September 1751

      Inter se convenit ursis.
Juv. [*Sat.* XV 164]

Beasts of each kind their fellows spare;
Bear lives in amity with bear.

161   Tuesday, 1 October 1751

Οἵη γὰρ φύλλων γενεή, τοίηδε καὶ Ἀνδρῶν.
Hom. [*Iliad* VI 146]

Frail as the leaves that quiver on the sprays,
Like them man flourishes, like them decays.

Quantulacunque estis, vos ego magna voco.
[Ovid, *Amor*. III xv 14]

How small to others, but how great to me!

῝Ος ὑπέρτατα δώματα ναίει.
[Hesiod, *Op*. 8]

This habitant th'aerial regions boast.

164 Saturday, 12 October 1751

Vitium, Gaure, Catonis habes.
Mart. [*Epig*. II lxxxix 2]

Gaurus pretends to *Cato*'s fame;
And proves, by *Cato*'s vice, his claim.

168 Saturday, 26 October 1751

Decipit
Frons prima multos, rara mens intelligit
Quod interiore condidit cura angulo.
Phædrus [*Fab*. IV ii 5–7]

The tinsel glitter, and the specious mein,
Delude the most; few pry behind the scene.

Si robora sacra ferirent,
In sua credebant reditturas membra secures.
[Lucan, *Phars*. III 430–31]

None dares with impious steel the grove to rend,
Lest on himself the destin'd stroke descend.

169   Tuesday, 29 October 1751

Thebais, multa cruciata lima,
Tentat, audaci fide, Mantuanæ
  Gaudia famæ.
[Statius, *Sylv.* IV vii 26–8]

Polish'd with endless toil, my lays
At length aspire to *Mantuan* praise.

170   Saturday, 2 November 1751

Confiteor; si quid prodest delicta fateri.
Ovid [*Amor.* II iv 3]

I grant the charge; forgive the fault confess'd.

171   Tuesday, 5 November 1751

Tædet cœli convexa tueri.
Virg. [*Aen.* IV 451]

Dark is the sun, and loathsome is the day.

173   Tuesday, 12 November 1751

Quo Virtus, quo ferat Error.
Hor. [*Ars Poet.* 308]

Now say, where virtue stops and vice begins?

176   Saturday, 23 November 1751

   Naso suspendere adunco.
Hor. [*Sat.* I vi 5]

On me you turn the nose.

178 Saturday, 30 November 1751

Pars Sanitatis velle sanari fuit.
Seneca [*Hyppol.* 248]

To yield to remedies is half the cure.

180 Saturday, 7 December 1751

Ταῦτ' εἰδὼς σοφὸς ἴσθι, μάτην δ 'Επίκουρον ἔασον
  Ποῦ τὸ κενὸν ζητεῖν, καὶ τίνες αἱ μονάδες.

Automedon [Gk Anthol. XI 50]

On life, on morals, be thy thoughts employ'd;
Leave to the schools their atoms and their void.

182 Saturday, 14 December 1751

        Dives qui fieri vult,
Et cito vult fieri.
Juv. [*Sat.* XIV 176–7]

The lust of wealth can never bear delay.

183 Tuesday, 17 December 1751

Nulla fides regni sociis, omnisque Potestas
Impatiens consortis erat.
Lucan [*Phars.* I 92–3]

No faith of partnership dominion owns;
Still discord hovers o'er divided thrones.

188 Saturday, 4 January 1752

        Si te colo, *Sexte*, non amabo.
Mart. [*Epig.* II lv 3]

The more I honour thee, the less I love.

199 Tuesday, 11 February 1752

Decolor, obscurus, vilis, non ille repexam
Cæsariem Regum, nec candida virginis ornat
Colla, nec insigni splendet per cingula morsu;
Sed nova si nigri videas miracula Saxi,
Tunc superat pulchros cultus, et quicquid Eois
Indus Littoribus rubra scrutatur in alga.

Claudianus [XLVIII 10–15]

Obscure, unpriz'd, and dark, the magnet lies,
Nor lures the search of avaricious eyes,
Nor binds the neck, nor sparkles in the hair,
Nor dignifies the great, nor decks the fair.
But search the wonders of the dusky stone,
And own all glories of the mine outdone,
Each grace of form, each ornament of state,
That decks the fair, or dignifies the great.

208 Saturday, 14 March 1752

Ἡράκλειτος ἐγώ. τί με ὦ κάτω ἕλκετ' ἄμουσοι;
  Οὐχ ὑμῖν ἐπόνουν, τοῖς δέ μ' ἐπισταμένοις.
Εἷς ἐμοὶ ἄνθρωπος τρισμύριοι. οἱ δ' ἀνάριθμοι
  Οὐδείς. ταῦτ' αὐδῶ καὶ παρὰ Περσεφόνῃ.

Diog. Laert. [*Vitae* IX i 16]

Be gone ye blockheads, *Heraclitus* cries,
And leave my labours to the learn'd and wise,
By wit, by knowledge, studious to be read,
I scorn the multitude, alive and dead.

Αὐτῶν ἐκ μακάρων ἀντάξιος εἴη ἀμοιβή.
[Dionysius, *Periegesis*, 1186]

Celestial pow'rs! that piety regard,
From you my labours wait their last reward.

The Ant

FROM PROVERBS VI 6

Turn on the prudent Ant, thy heedful eyes,
Observe her labours, Sluggard, and be wise.
No stern command, no monitory voice
Prescribes her duties, or directs her choice,
Yet timely provident, she hastes away
To snatch the blessings of the plenteous day;
When fruitful summer loads the teeming plain,
She gleans the harvest, and she stores the grain.
  How long shall sloth usurp thy useless hours,
10 Dissolve thy vigour, and enchain thy powers?
While artful shades thy downy couch enclose,
And soft solicitation courts repose,
Amidst the drousy charms of dull delight,
Year chases year, with unremitted flight,
Till want, now following fraudulent and slow,
Shall spring to seize thee like an ambush'd foe.

Translations of the Mottoes and Quotations in the Adventurer

Motto for the title-page

Tentanda via est; quâ me quoque possim
Tollere humo, victorque virûm volitare per ora.
Virg. [*Georg.* III 9–10]

On vent'rous wing in quest of praise I go,
And leave the gazing multitude below.

3   Tuesday, 14 November 1752

Scenis decora alta futuris.
Virg. [*Aen.* I 429]

The splendid ornament of future scenes.

7   Tuesday, 28 November 1752

Sit mihi fas audita loqui –
Virg. [*Aen.* VI 266]

What I have heard, permit me to relate.

8   Saturday, 2 December 1752

Durate, et vosmet rebus servate secundis.
Virg. [*Aen.* I 207]

Endure and conquer; live for better fate.

9   Tuesday, 5 December 1752

Ἐν προθύροις θῆκε διδασκαλίην.

Vet. Epigr. [Gk Anthol. XVI 275]

He hung th'instructive symbol o'er his door.

10   Saturday, 9 December 1752

Da, Pater, augustam menti conscendere sedem;
Da fontem lustrare boni; da, luce repertâ,
In Te conspicuos animi defigere visus!
Boeth. [III 9–11]

Give me, O Father! to thy throne access,
Unshaken seat of endless happiness!
Give me, unveil'd, the source of good to see!
Give me thy light, and fix mine eyes on thee!

12 Saturday, 16 December 1752

Magnum pauperies opprobrium jubet
  Quidvis aut facere aut pati.
Hor. [*Od.* III xxiv 42–3]

He whom the dread of want ensnares,
With baseness acts, with meanness bears.

14 Saturday, 23 December 1752

Admonet, et magnâ testatur voce per umbras:
Discite justitiam moniti, et non temnere Divos.
Virg. [*Aen.* VI 619–20]

Ev'n yet his voice from Hell's dread shades we hear –
'Beware, learn justice, and the Gods revere.'

16 Saturday, 30 December 1752

Gratior et pulchro veniens in corpore virtus.
Virg. [*Aen.* V 344]

More lovely virtue, in a lovely form.

18 Saturday, 6 January 1753

Duplex libelli dos est; quod risum movet,
Et quod prudenti vitam consilio monet.
Phædrus [*Fab.* I Prol. 3–4]

A two-fold gift in this my volume lies;
It makes you merry, and it makes you wise.

19 Tuesday, 9 January 1753

Quodcunque ostendis mihi sic, incredulus odi.
Hor. [*Ars Poet.* 188]

The monstrous tale, incredulous I hate.

20 *Saturday, 13 January 1753*

Quid violentius aure tyranni.
Juv. [*Sat.* IV 86]

Rough truth soon irritates a tyrant's ear.

21 *Tuesday, 16 January 1753*

Si genus humanum et mortalia temnitis arma;
At sperate Deos memores fandi atque nefandi.
Virg. [*Aen.* I 542–3]

Of mortal Justice if thou scorn the rod –
Believe and tremble, thou art judg'd of God.

22 *Saturday, 20 January 1753*

Rursus et in veterem fato revoluta figuram.
Virg. [*Aen.* VI 449]

His native form at length by fate restor'd.

23 *Tuesday, 23 January 1753*

Quo fit, ut omnis
Votiva pateat veluti descripta tabellâ
Vita –
Hor. [*Sat.* II i 32–4]

In books the various scenes of life he drew,
As votive tablets give the wreck to view.

24 *Saturday, 27 January 1753*

Longa mora est, quantum noxæ sit ubique repertum,
Enumerare.
Ovid [*Metam.* I 214–15]

The various ills ordain'd to man by fate
Where'er he turns, 'tis tedious to relate.

26 *Saturday, 3 February 1753*

Est ardelionum quædam Romæ natio
Gratis anhelans –
Phædrus [*Fab.* II v 1–3]

Through all the town the busy triflers swarm,
Fix'd without proof, and without int'rest warm.

27 *Tuesday, 6 February 1753*

Νυκτὸς—Αἰθήρτε καὶ Ἡμέρα ἐξεγένοντο.
Hesiod [*Theog.* 124]

From night arose the sun-shine and the day.

28 *Saturday, 10 February 1753*

Cœlo supinas si tuleris manus
Nascente Lunâ, rustica Phidyle;
Nec pestilentem sentiet Africum
Fœcunda vitis –
Hor. [*Od.* III xxiii 1–2, 5–6]

If rustic Phidyle her prayer renews,
    Her artless prayer, when sacred hours return,
Her vines shall droop beneath no blighting dews,
    Nor southern storms her yellow harvests burn.

33 *Tuesday, 27 February 1753*

        Latet anguis in herba.
Virg. [*Eclog.* III 93]

Within the grass conceal'd a serpent lies.

34   Saturday, 3 March 1753

Has toties optata exegit gloria pœnas.
Juv. [*Sat.* X 187]

Such fate persues the votaries of praise.

> Sed quæ præclara et prospera tanti,
Ut rebus lætis par sit mensura malorum.
Juv. [*Sat.* X 97–8]

See the wild purchase of the bold and vain,
Where ev'ry bliss is bought with equal pain!

37   Tuesday, 13 March 1753

Calumniari si quis autem voluerit,
Quod arbores loquantur, non tantum feræ;
Fictis jocari nos meminerit fabulis.
Phædrus [*Fab.* I Prol. 5–7]

Let those whom folly prompts to sneer,
Be told we sport with fable here;
Be told, that brutes can morals teach,
And trees like soundest casuists preach.

40   Saturday, 24 March 1753

Solvite tantis animum monstris,
Solvite, Superi; rectam in melius
Vertite mentem.
Sen. [*Herc. Fur.* 1063–5]

O! save ye Gods, omnipotent and kind,
From such abhor'd chimeras save the mind!
In truth's strait path no hideous monsters roar;
To truth's strait path the wand'ring mind restore.

42 *Saturday, 31 March 1753*

Sua cuique Deus fit dira Cupido.
Virg. [*Aen.* IX 185]

Our lusts are Gods, and what they will is fate.

43 *Tuesday, 3 April 1753*

Mobilitate viget –
Virg. [*Aen.* IV 175]

Its life is motion.

45 *Tuesday, 10 April 1753*

Nulla fides regni sociis, omnisque potestas
Impatiens consortis erit.
Lucan [*Phars.* I 92–3]

No faith of partnership dominion owns;
Still discord hovers o'er divided thrones.

46 *Saturday, 14 April 1753*

Μισῶ μνήμονα Συμπότην.

Prov. Gr. [Plutarch's 'Table Talk']

Far from my table be the tell-tale guest.

50 *Saturday, 28 April 1753*

Quicunque turpi fraude semel innotuit,
Etiamsi verum dicit, amittit fidem.
Phædrus [*Fab.*·I x 1–2]

The wretch that often has deceiv'd,
Though truth he speaks, is ne'er believ'd.

53 Tuesday, 8 May 1753

Quisque suos patimur Manes.
Virg. [*Aen.* VI 743]

Each has his lot, and bears the fate he drew.

54 Saturday, 12 May 1753

　　　Sensim labefacta cadebat
Relligio –
Claudianus [*In Ruf.* I 14–15]

His confidence in heav'n
Sunk by degrees.

56 Saturday, 19 May 1753

　　　Multos in summa pericula misit
Venturi timor ipse mali.
Lucanus [*Phars.* VII 105–6]

How oft the fear of ill to ill betrays!

58 Saturday, 26 May 1753

Te spectem, suprema mihi cùm venerit hora,
　Te teneam moriens deficiente manu.
Tibullus [*Eleg.* I i 59–60]

Before my closing eyes, dear Cynthia, stand,
Held weakly by my fainting trembling hand.

Cynthia decedens, felicius, inquit, amata
　Sum tibi; vixisti dum tuus ignis eram.
Cui Nemesis, quid, ait, tibi sunt mea damna dolori?
　Me tenuit moriens deficiente manu.
Ovid [*Amor.* III ix 55–8]

Blest was my reign, retiring Cynthia cry'd,
Not till he left my breast, Tibullus dy'd.
Forbear, said Nemesis, my loss to moan,
The fainting trembling hand was mine alone.

60   Saturday, 2 June 1753

Jus est et ab hoste doceri.
Ovid [*Metam.* IV 428]

Our foes may teach, the wise by foes are taught.

61   Tuesday, 5 June 1753

Ploravere suis non respondere favorem
Quæsitum meritis –
Hor. [*Epist.* II i 9–10]

Each inly murm'ring at th'unequal meed,
Repines that merit should reward exceed.

62   Saturday, 9 June 1753

O fortuna viris invida fortibus
Quam non æqua bonis præmia dividis.
Seneca [*Hercul. Fur.* 524–5]

Capricious fortune ever joys,
With partial hand to deal the prize,
To crush the brave and cheat the wise.

    rari quippe boni;
[Juvenal, *Sat.* XIII 26]

The good are few.

65   Tuesday, 19 June 1753

Et furiis agitatus amor. –
Virg. [*Aen.* X 872]

Love, which the furies irritate to rage.

66   *Saturday, 23 June 1753*

Nolo virum, facili redimit qui sanguine famam:
  Hunc volo, laudari qui sine morte potest.
Mart. [*Epigr*. I viii 5–6]

Not him I prize who poorly gains
From death the palm which blood disdains;
But him who wins with nobler strife
An unpolluted wreath from life.

67   *Tuesday, 26 June 1753*

Inventas – vitam excoluere per artes.
Virg. [*Aen*. VI 663]

They polish life by useful arts.

68   *Saturday, 30 June 1753*

Nocet empta dolore voluptas.
Ovid [*In fact*, Horace, *Epist*. I ii 55]

How vain the joy for which our pain must pay.

70   *Saturday, 7 July 1753*

Virtus, repulsæ nescia sordidæ,
Intaminatis fulget honoribus;
  Nec sumit aut ponit secures,
    Arbitrio popularis auræ.
Hor. [*Od*. III ii 17–20]

Stranger to folly and to fear,
  With pure untainted honour bright,
Virtue disdains to lend an ear
  To the mad people's sense of right.

74   Saturday, 21 July 1753

Insanientis dum sapientiæ
Consultus erro.
Hor. [*Od*. I xxxiv 2–3]

I mist my end, and lost my way,
By crack-brain'd wisdom led astray.

77   Tuesday, 31 July 1753

        Peccare docentes
Fallax historias movet.
Hor. [*Od*. III vii 19–20]

To taint th'attentive mind she tries
With tales of exemplary vice.

78   Saturday, 4 August 1753

        Propter vitam vivendi perdere causas.
Juv. [*Sat*. VIII 84]

Nor quit for life, what gives to life its worth.

82   Saturday, 18 August 1753

Nunc scio quid sit Amor.
Virg. [*Eclog*. VIII 43]

Now know I what is love.

92   Saturday, 22 September 1753

Cum tabulis animum censoris sumet honesti.
Hor. [*Epist*. II ii 110]

Bold be the critic, zealous to his trust,
Like the firm judge inexorably just.

95   Tuesday, 2 October 1753

Dulcique animos novitate tenebo.
Ovid [*Metam*. IV 284]

And with sweet novelty your soul detain.

104   Saturday, 3 November 1753

Semita certe
Tranquillæ per virtutem patet unica vitæ.
Juv. [*Sat*. X 363]

But only virtue shews the paths of peace.

112   Saturday, 1 December 1753

Has pœnas garrula lingua dedit.
Ovid [*Amor*. II ii 44]
Such was the fate of vain loquacity.

115   Tuesday, 11 December 1753

Scribimus indocti doctique.
Hor. [*Epist*. II i 117]

All dare to write, who can or cannot read.

118   Saturday, 22 December 1753

Animorum
Impulsu, et cæcâ magnaque cupidine ducti.
Juv. [*Sat*. X 350–51]

By blind impulse of eager passion driv'n.

123   Tuesday, 8 January 1754

Jam protervâ
Fronte petet Lalage maritum.
Hor. [*Od.* II v 15–16]

The maid whom now you court in vain,
Will quickly run in quest of man.

124   Saturday, 12 January 1754

Incedis per ignes
Suppositos cineri doloso.
Hor. [*Od.* II i 7–8]

With heedless feet on fires you go,
That hid in treacherous ashes glow.

130   Saturday, 2 February 1754

Qui non est hodie, cras minus aptus erit.
Mart. [*In fact*, Ovid, *Rem. Amor.* 94]

The man will surely fail who dares delay,
And lose to-morrow that has lost to-day.

132   Saturday, 9 February 1754

Ferimur per opaca locorum.
Virg. [*Aen.* II 725]

Driv'n thro' the palpable obscure.

135   Tuesday, 19 February 1754

Latet anguis in herba.
Virg. [*Ecl.* III 93]

Beneath the grass conceal'd, a serpent lies.

136 Saturday, 23 February 1754

> Quis talia fando
> Temperet a lacrimis.
> Virg. [*Aen.* II 6–7]

And who can hear this tale without a tear?

Translations from Boethius: De Consolatione Philosophiæ

II 2

Though countless as the Grains of Sand
That roll at Eurus loud Command;
Though countless as the lamps of night
That glad us with vicarious light;
Fair plenty gracious Queen shou'd pour
The blessings of a golden Show'r
Not all the gifts of Fate combin'd
Would ease the hunger of the mind,
But swallowing all the mighty Store,
10 Rapacity would call for more;
For still where wishes most abound
Unquench'd the thirst of gain is found
In vain the shining Gifts are sent,
For none are rich without content.

II 4

Wouldst thou to some stedfast Seat
Out of Fortune's Pow'r retreat?
Wouldst thou when fierce Eurus blows
Calmly rest in safe Repose?
Wouldst thou see the foaming Main
Tossing rave but rave in vain?
Shun the Mountain's airy Brow,
Shun the Sea-sapp'd Sand below;
Soon th'aspiring Fabric falls,

10 When loud Auster shakes her Walls,
Soon the treachrous Sands retreat,
From beneath the cumbrous Weight;
Fix not where the tempting Height
Mingles Danger with Delight,
Safe upon the rocky Ground,
Firm and low thy Mansion found;
There, mid Tempests loudest Roars,
Dashing Waves and shatter'd Shoars,
Thou shalt sit and smile to see
20 All the World afraid but thee,
Lead a long and peaceful Age,
And deride their utmost Rage.

III 1

The prudent Hind intent on Gain
Must clear the Ground to sow the Grain,
And Ceres richest gifts abound
Where late the rankest Weeds were found;
To him whom painful Tastes annoy
Sweet honey yields a double Joy;
The Tempest gives the Calm delight,
The Morning owes her Charms to night;
And thus the Mind tormented long
10 With wild Vicissitudes of Wrong,
Contemns at length the treachrous toys
And real Happiness enjoys.

III 3

Through Gripus Grounds let rich Pactolus roll,
No golden Sands can satisfy his Soul;
Though Chains of Pearl bow down his pensive Head,
Though a whole Hecatomb his Acres tread,
No wealth his life from weary care can save,
No care his wealth can carry to the grave.

III 4

Vainly the Tyrian Purple bright,
Vainly the Pearl's pellucid white,
The Tyrant Nero strove t'adorn,
Who liv'd our hatred and our Scorn;
His Choice our sacred Seats disgrac'd,
His Conduct Human Kind debased:
If such on Earth can Bliss bestow
Say what is happiness below?

III 5

The Man who pants for ample Sway
Must bid his Passions all obey;
Must bid each wild Desire be still,
Nor yoke his Reason with his Will:
For tho' beneath thy haughty Brow
Warm India's supple Sons should bow,
Tho' Northern Climes confess thy Sway,
Which erst in Frost and Freedom lay
If Sorrow pine or Av'rice crave
10 Bow down and own thyself a Slave.

III 6

All Men throughout the peopled Earth
　From one sublime Beginning spring;
All from one Source derive their Birth
　The same their Parent and their King.

At his Command proud Titan glows,
　And Luna lifts her Horn on high;
His hand this Earth on Man bestows
　And strews with Stars the spangled Sky.

From her high Seats he drew the Soul,
10 　And in this earthly Case confin'd;
To wondring Worlds produc'd the whole,
　Essence Divine with Matter join'd.

Since then alike All Men derive
From God himself their noble Race,
Why should the witless Mortals strive
For vulgar Ancestry and Place?

Why boast their Birth before his Eyes,
    Who holds no human Creature mean;
Save him whose Soul enslav'd to Vice
20   Deserts her nobler Origin.

III 12

Happy he whose Eyes have view'd
The transparent Fount of Good;
Happy whose unfetter'd Mind
Leaves the Load of Earth behind.
Tho' when Orpheus made his Moan
For his lovely Consort gone,
Tho' the Hind approach'd to hear
Where the Lyoness stood near,
And attentive to the Sound
10 Hares forgot the following hound,
Round him danc'd the listning Woods,
Silent Wonder stopt the Floods;
Grief and Madness unrepress'd
Rag'd within the Master's Breast
While t'asswage the Pangs of Love
Verse and Music vainly strove;
Now he sighs to heav'n, and now
Rushes on the Realms below.
There he breath'd his am'rous Fire,
20 *There he touch'd his trembling Lyre,*
Warbling there his softer Sorrows
From his Parent Muse he borrows
Notes to touch each tender Feeling,
Numbers to each Bosom stealing,
Sighs that silent Measure keep,
Groans that grieve and Words that weep.
These the hapless Poet tries

To regain his beauteous Prize;
Nor in vain – the Strings obey,
30 *Love and Music bear the sway,*
Cerberus Rage their Powers disarm,
Stern Alecto feels the Charm,
Tears from fierce Megæra flow,
While attentive to his Woe
Sudden stops Ixion's Wheel,
Hell's fierce Hawk forgets his Meal.
Tantalus astonish'd stood
Scorning now th'o'erflowing Flood,
Till at length stern Pluto cried
40 Conqu'ring Poet take thy Bride!
Purchas'd by thy powerful Song,
All her Charms to thee belong;
Only this Command obey
Look not on her by the way;
Tho' reluctant still refrain,
Till the Realms of Light you gain
But what Laws can Lovers awe?
Love alone to Love is Law:
Just emerging into Light,
50 Orpheus turn'd his eager Sight,
Fondly view'd his following Bride,
Viewing lost and losing died.

To You whose gen'rous Wishes rise
To court Communion with the Skies
    To you the Tale is told;
When grasping Bliss th'unsteady mind
Looks back on what She left behind,
    She faints and quits her hold.

A Reply to Impromptu Verses by Baretti

At sight of sparkling Bowls or beauteous Dames
When fondness melts me, or when wine inflames,
I too can feel the rapture fierce and strong
I too can pour the extemporary song;
But though the number for a moment please,
Though musick thrills, or sudden sallies seize,
Yet lay the Sonnet for an hour aside,
Its charms are fled and all its power destroy'd:
What soon is perfect, soon alike is past:
10 That slowly grows which must for ever last.

Prologue to Goldsmith's The Good Natur'd Man

Prest by the load of life, the weary mind
Surveys the general toil of human kind;
With cool submission joins the labouring train,
And social sorrow loses half its pain:
Our anxious Bard, without complaint, may share
This bustling season's epidemic care.
Like Cæsar's pilot, dignified by fate,
Tost in one common storm with all the great;
Distrest alike, the statesman and the wit,
10 When one a borough courts, and one the pit.
The busy candidates for power and fame,
Have hopes, and fears, and wishes, just the same;
Disabled both to combat, or to fly,
Must hear all taunts, and hear without reply.
Uncheck'd on both, loud rabbles vent their rage,
As mongrels bay the lion in a cage.
Th'offended burgess hoards his angry tale,
For that blest year when all that vote may rail;
Their schemes of spite the poet's foes dismiss,
20 Till that glad night when all that hate may hiss.

This day the powder'd curls and golden coat,
Says swelling Crispin, begg'd a cobbler's vote.
This night our wit, the pert apprentice cries,
Lies at my feet, I hiss him, and he dies.
The great, 'tis true, can charm th'electing tribe;
The bard may supplicate, but cannot bribe.
Yet judg'd by those, whose voices ne'er were sold,
He feels no want of ill persuading gold;
But confident of praise, if praise be due,
30   Trusts without fear, to merit, and to you.

Parodies of Bishop Percy's Hermit of Warkworth

1

I put my hat upon my head
  And walk'd into the Strand,
And there I met another man
  Who's hat was in his hand.

2

The tender infant, meek and mild,
  Fell down upon the stone;
The nurse took up the squealing child,
  But still the child squeal'd on.

3

I therefore pray thee, Renny dear,
  That thou wilt give to me,
With cream and sugar soften'd well,
  Another dish of tea.

Nor fear that I, my gentle maid,
  Shall long detain the cup,
When once unto the bottom I
  Have drank the liquor up.

Yet hear, alas! this mournful truth,
10   Nor hear it with a frown; –
Thou canst not make the tea so fast
  As I can gulp it down.

An Epitaph on William Hogarth

The Hand of Art here torpid lies
  That wav'd th'essential Form of Grace,
Here death has clos'd the curious eyes
  That saw the manners in the face.

If Genius warm thee, Reader, stay,
  If Merit touch thee, shed a tear,
Be Vice and Dulness far away
  Great Hogarth's honour'd Dust is here.

French Distichs

A Calais
Trop de frais.

St Omer
Tout est cher.

Arras
Helas!

A Amiens
On n'a rien.

Au Mouton
Rien de Bon.

Translation from a Pantomime Version of Benserade's Balet de Cassandre

I am Cassander, come down from the Sky,
To tell each Bystander – what none can deny
That I am Cassander come down from the Sky.

Translations from Metastasio

FROM *La Clemenza di Tito*

Would you hope to gain my heart,
Bid your teizing Doubts depart;
He who blindly trusts, will find
Faith from every generous mind;
He who still expects deceit,
Only teaches how to cheat.

FROM *Adriano in Syria*

Grown old in courts, thou art not surely one
Who keeps the rigid rules of ancient honour;
Well skill'd to sooth a foe with looks of kindness,
To sink the fatal precipice before him,
And then lament his fall with seeming friendship:
Open to all, true only to thyself,
Thou know'st those arts which blast with envious praise,
Which aggravate a fault with feign'd excuses,
And drive discountenanc'd virtue from the throne:
10 That leave the blame of rigour to the prince,
And of his every gift usurp the merit;
That hide in seeming zeal a wicked purpose,
And only build upon another's ruin.

Translation of Du Bellay's Epigram on a Dog

To Robbers furious, and to Lovers tame,
I pleas'd my Master, and I pleas'd my Dame.

Translation of the beginning of Rio Verde

Glassy water, glassy water,
  Down whose current clear and strong,
Chiefs confus'd in mutual slaughter,
  Moor and Christian, roll along.

Translation of Benserade's Verses à son Lit

In bed we laugh, in bed we cry,
And born in bed, in bed we die;
The near approach a bed may shew
Of human bliss to human woe.

Translation of a Distich on the Duke of Modena

If at your coming princes disappear,
Comets! come every day – and stay a year.

Burlesque translation of Lines from Lope de Vega's Arcadia

If the Man who Turneps cries
Cry not when his Father dies;
'Tis a Sign that he had rather
Have a Turnep than a Father.

Translation of Lines in Baretti's Easy Phraseology

Long may live my lovely Hetty!
Always young and always pretty!
Always pretty, always young,
Live my lovely Hetty long!
Always young and always pretty;
Long may live my lovely Hetty!

Lines on Thomas Warton's Poems

1

Wheresoe'er I turn my View,
All is strange, yet nothing new;
Endless Labour all along,
Endless Labour to be wrong;
Phrase that Time has flung away,
Uncouth Words in Disarray:
Trickt in Antique Ruff and Bonnet,
Ode and Elegy and Sonnet.

2

Hermit hoar, in solemn cell,
   Wearing out life's evening gray;
Smite thy bosom, sage, and tell,
   Where is bliss? and which the way?

Thus I spoke; and speaking sigh'd;
   Scarce repress'd the starting tear; –
When the smiling sage reply'd –
   Come, my lad, and drink some beer.

Charade on Dr Thomas Barnard

CHARADE!

My first, shuts out Theives from your house or your Room,
My second, expresses a Syrian perfume;
My whole, is a Man in whose converse is shar'd,
The strength of a Bar, and the sweetness of Nard.

To Mrs Thrale on her Thirty-fifth Birthday

   Oft in Danger yet alive
   We are come to Thirty-five;
   Long may better Years arrive,
   Better Years than Thirty-five;

Could Philosophers contrive
Life to stop at Thirty-five,
Time his Hours should never drive
O'er the Bounds of Thirty-five:
High to soar and deep to dive
10 Nature gives at Thirty-five;
Ladies – stock and tend your Hive,
Trifle not at Thirty-five:
For howe'er we boast and strive,
Life declines from Thirty-five;
He that ever hopes to thrive
Must begin by Thirty-five:
And those who wisely wish to wive,
Must look on Thrale at Thirty-five.

Prologue to Hugh Kelly's A Word to the Wise

This night presents a play, which publick rage,
Or right, or wrong, once hooted from the stage;
From zeal or malice now no more we dread,
For English vengeance *wars not with the dead.*
A generous foe regards, with pitying eye,
The man whom fate has laid, where all must lye.
To wit, reviving from its author's dust,
Be kind, ye judges, or at least be just:
Let no resentful petulance invade
10 Th'oblivious grave's inviolable shade.
Let one great payment every claim appease,
And him who cannot hurt, allow to please;
To please by scenes unconscious of offence,
By harmless merriment, or useful sense.
Where aught of bright, or fair, the piece displays,
.Approve it only – 'tis too late to praise.
If want of skill, or want of care appear,
Forbear to hiss – the Poet cannot hear.
By all, like him, must praise and blame be found;

20   At best, a fleeting gleam, or empty sound.
Yet then shall calm reflection bless the night,
When liberal pity dignify'd delight;
When pleasure fired her torch at Virtue's flame,
And mirth was bounty with a humbler name.

Translation of Anacreon's Dove (Ode ix)

Lovely courier of the sky
Whence or whither dost thou fly?
Scatt'ring, as thy pinions play,
Liquid fragrance all the way:
Is it business? is it love?
Tell me, tell me, gentle dove.

'Soft Anacreon's vows I bear,
Vows to Myrtale the fair;
Grac'd with all that charms the heart,
10   Blushing nature, smiling art.
Venus, courted with an ode,
On the bard her dove bestow'd.
Vested with a master's right
Now Anacreon rules my flight:
His the letters which you see,
Weighty charge consign'd to me:
Think not yet my service hard,
Joyless task without reward:
Smiling at my master's gates,
20   Freedom my return awaits,
But the liberal grant in vain
Tempts me to be wild again:
Can a prudent dove decline
Blissful bondage such as mine?
Over hills and fields to roam,
Fortune's guest, without a home,
Under leaves to hide one's head,

Slightly shelter'd, coarsely fed?
Now my better lot bestows
30   Sweet repast, and soft repose;
Now the generous bowl I sip
As it leaves Anacreon's lip,
Void of care, and free from dread
From his fingers snatch his bread,
Then with luscious plenty gay
Round his chamber dance and play,
Or from wine as courage springs,
O'er his face extend my wings;
And when feast and frolic tire,
40   Drop asleep upon his lyre.
This is all; – be quick and go,
More than all thou canst not know;
Let me now my pinions ply,
I have chatter'd like a pye.'

A Song composed for Fanny Burney

She shall sing me a song,
Of two Day's long
The Woodcock and the sparrow;
Our little Dog has bit his Tail
And he'll be Hang'd to-morrow.

An extempore Elegy

Here's a Woman of the Town,
   Lies as Dead as any Nail!
She was once of high renown, –
   And so here begins my Tale.

She was once as cherry plump
   Red her cheek as Cath'rine Pear,
Toss'd her nose, and shook her Rump,
   Till she made the Neighbours stare.

There she soon became a Jilt,
10   Rambling often to and fro'
All her life was naught but guilt,
    Till Purse and Carcase both were low.

But there came a country 'Squire
    He was a seducing Pug!
Took her from her friends and sire,
    To his own House her did lug.

Black her eye with many a Blow,
    Hot her breath with many a Dram,
Now she lies exceeding low,
20   And as quiet as a Lamb.

Epilogue to Horace's Carmen Seculare

Such strains as, mingled with the lyre,
Could Rome with future greatness fire,
Ye Sons of England, deign to hear,
Nor think our wishes less sincere.

May ye the varied blessings share
Of plenteous peace, and prosp'rous war;
And o'er the globe extend your reign,
Unbounded Masters of the main.

On Seeing a Portrait of Mrs Montagu

Had this fair figure which this frame displays,
Adorn'd in Roman times the brightest days,
In every dome, in every sacred place,
Her statue would have breath'd an added grace,
And on its basis would have been enroll'd,
'This is Minerva, cast in Virtue's mould.'

On Hearing Miss Thrale deliberate about her Hat

Wear the Gown, and wear the Hat,
    Snatch your pleasures while they last;
Hadst thou nine Lives like a Cat,
    Soon those nine Lives would be past.

Translations from the Medea of Euripides

1
Err shall they not, who resolute explore
    Times gloomy backward with judicious eyes;
And scanning right the practices of yore,
    Shall deem our hoar progenitors unwise.

They to the dome where smoke with curling play
    Annòunc'd the dinner to the regions round,
Summon'd the singer blythe, and harper gay,
    And aided wine with dulcet-streaming sound.

The better use of notes, or sweet or shrill,
10   By quiv'ring string, or modulated wind;
Trumpet or lyre – to their harsh bosoms chill,
    Admission ne'er had sought, or could not find.

Oh! send them to the sullen mansions dun,
    Her baleful eyes where Sorrow rolls around;
Where gloom-enamour'd Mischief dreads the Sun,
    And Murder, all blood-bolter'd, schemes the wound.

When cates luxuriant pile the spacious dish,
    And purple nectar glads the festive hour,
The guest, without a want, without a wish,
20   Can yield no room to Music's soothing pow'r.

2
The rites deriv'd from ancient days
With thoughtless reverence we praise,
The rites that taught us to combine
The joys of music and of wine,

And bad the feast, the song, and bowl,
O'erfill the saturated soul;
But ne'er the Flute or Lyre apply'd
To cheer despair, or soften pride,
Nor call'd them to the gloomy cells
10   Where Want repines, and Vengeance swells,
Where Hate sits musing to betray,
And Murder meditates his prey.
To dens of guilt and shades of care
Ye sons of Melody repair,
Nor deign the festive dome to cloy
With superfluities of joy.
Ah, little needs the Minstrel's pow'r
To speed the light convivial hour;
The board with varied plenty crown'd
20   May spare the luxuries of sound.

A Short Song of Congratulation

Long-expected one and twenty
Ling'ring year, at last is flown,
Pomp and Pleasure, Pride and Plenty
Great Sir John, are all your own.

Loosen'd from the Minor's tether,
Free to mortgage or to sell,
Wild as wind, and light as feather
Bid the slaves of thrift farewel.

Call the Bettys, Kates, and Jennys
10   Ev'ry name that laughs at Care,
Lavish of your Grandsire's guineas,
Show the Spirit of an heir.

All that prey on vice and folly
Joy to see their quarry fly,
Here the Gamester light and jolly
There the Lender grave and sly.

Wealth, Sir John, was made to wander,
Let it wander as it will;
See the Jocky, see the Pander,
20 Bid them come, and take their fill.

When the bonny Blade carouses,
Pockets full, and Spirits high,
What are acres? what are houses?
Only dirt, or wet or dry.

If the Guardian or the Mother
Tell the woes of wilful waste,
Scorn their counsel and their pother,
You can hang or drown at last.

Verses modelled on Pope

While many a merry tale, and many a song,
Chear'd the rough road, we wish'd the rough road long,
The rough road then returning in a round,
Mock'd our impatient steps, for all was fairy ground.

On the Death of Dr Robert Levet

Condemn'd to hope's delusive mine,
    As on we toil from day to day,
By sudden blasts, or slow decline,
    Our social comforts drop away.

Well tried through many a varying year,
    See LEVET to the grave descend;
Officious, innocent, sincere,
    Of ev'ry friendless name the friend.

Yet still he fills affection's eye,
10   Obscurely wise, and coarsely kind;
Nor, letter'd arrogance, deny
    Thy praise to merit unrefin'd.

When fainting nature call'd for aid,
  And hov'ring death prepar'd the blow,
His vig'rous remedy display'd
  The power of art without the show.

In misery's darkest caverns known,
  His useful care was ever nigh,
Where hopeless anguish pour'd his groan,
20   And lonely want retir'd to die.

No summons mock'd by chill delay,
  No petty gain disdain'd by pride,
The modest wants of ev'ry day
  The toil of ev'ry day supplied.

His virtues walk'd their narrow round,
  Nor made a pause, nor left a void;
And sure th'Eternal Master found
  The single talent well employed.

The busy day, the peaceful night,
30   Unfelt, uncounted, glided by;
His frame was firm, his powers were bright,
  Tho' now his eightieth year was nigh.

Then with no throbbing fiery pain,
  No cold gradations of decay,
Death broke at once the vital chain,
  And free'd his soul the nearest way.

Translations of Roy's Verses on Skaters

I

O'er Ice the rapid Skaiter flies,
  With Sport above and Death below;
Where Mischief lurks in gay Disguise,
  Thus lightly touch and quickly go.

2

O'er crackling ice, o'er gulphs profound,
    With nimble glide the skaiters play;
O'er treacherous pleasure's flow'ry ground
    Thus lightly skim, and haste away.

Translation of Horace Odes IV vii (Diffugere nives)

The snow dissolv'd no more is seen,
The fields, and woods, behold, are green,
The changing year renews the plain
The rivers know their banks again
The spritely Nymph and naked Grace
The mazy dance together trace.
The changing year's successive plan
Proclaims mortality to Man.
Rough Winter's blasts to Spring give way
Spring yields to Summer's sovereign ray
Then Summer sinks in Autumn's reign
And Winter chills the World again
Her losses soon the Moon supplies
But wretched Man, when once he lies
Where Priam and his Sons are laid
Is nought but Ashes and a Shade.
Who knows if Jove who counts our Score
Will toss us in a morning more?
What with your friend you nobly share
At least you rescue from your heir.
Not you, Torquatus, boast of Rome,
When Minos once has fix'd your doom,
Or Eloquence, or splendid birth
Or Virtue shall replace on earth.
Hyppolytus unjustly slain
Diana calls to life in vain,
Nor can the might of Theseus rend
The chains of hell that hold his friend.

A Selection from Johnson's Latin Poems

Aurora est Musis Amica

Cum caput Hesperiis attollit Phœbus ab undis,
    Atque Æthra ambigua pallida luce rubet;
Harmonia tellus completur lata, per agros
    Curas mulcentes dulcè [qu]eruntur aves.
Rorem, qui segetes, geniali et gramina succo
    Nutrit manè, putes esse Heliconis aqua,
Tunc vati facilem se præbet Apollo, Sybillæ
    Vix majore Deus corda furore quatit.
Carmine præbentur bellantia Numina digne
10   Assurgitque epicis Pagina docta modis.
Hinc annis panguntur Delenda Poemata nullis
    Queis majus pretium sæcula lapsa dabunt.
Quid mirum cum saxa movet statuasque tacentes
    Ignis quem Phœbi naribus efflat equus,
Quos pulsata sonos edit lyra pollice, primis
    [Percussa] a radiis Memnonis ora dabant.

Dawn is a Friend to the Muses

When Phœbus lifts his head from the Western waves and
pale Æthra blushes with uncertain light, the broad earth is
full of harmony; through the fields the birds complain
sweetly, soothing their cares. You would think that the dew,
which feeds the crops and the grass with its pleasant
moisture, was from the water of Helicon. It is then that
Apollo presents himself readily to the bard; the god strikes
the heart of the Sybil with hardly a greater madness. In
verse warring divinities are worthily presented and the
learned page surges in epic strains. Hence poems that no
years shall destroy are brought to the light and the passing
ages will give them a greater value. What is strange in
this when the fire that the horse of Phœbus breathes
from his nostrils moves rocks and mute statues, and those
sounds that the lyre, smitten with the thumb, gives forth,

the mouth of Memmon used to utter at the first dawn-
rays?

Verses on the Death of His Mother

At tu quisquis eris, miseri qui cruda poetæ
    Credideris fletu funera digna tuo,
Hæc postrema tibi sit flendi causa, fluatque
    Lenis inoffenso vitaque morsque gradu.

But you, whoever you be, who deemed the early death
of an unhappy poet worthy of your tears, may this be
for you the last cause you have for weeping, and may
life and death glide gently on with unstumbling pace.

Γνωθι σεαυτον

(POST LEXICON ANGLICANUM AUCTUM ET
EMENDATUM)

Lexicon ad finem longo luctamine tandem
Scaliger ut duxit, tenuis pertæsus opellæ
Vile indignatus Studium, nugasque molestas
Ingemit exosus, scribendaque lexica mandat
Damnatis pœnam pro pœnis omnibus unam.
    Ille quidem recte, sublimis, doctus, et acer,
Quem decuit majora sequi, majoribus aptum,
Qui veterum modo facta ducum, modo carmina vatum,
Gesserat et quicquid Virtus, Sapientia quicquid
10 Dixerat, imperiique vices, cœlique meatus,
Ingentemque animo seclorum volverat orbem.
    Fallimur exemplis; temere sibi turba scholarum
Ima tuas credit permitti, Scaliger, iras.
Quisque suum nôrit modulum; tibi, prime virorum

Ut studiis sperem, aut ausim par esse querelis
Non mihi sorte datum, lenti seu sanguinis obsint
Frigora, seu nimium longo jacuisse veterno,
Sive mihi mentem dederit Natura minorem.
    Te sterili functum cura, vocumque salebris
20 Tuto eluctatum spatiis Sapientia dia
Excipit æthereis, Ars omnis plaudit amica

Linguarumque omni terra discordia concors
Multiplici reducem circumsonat ore magistrum.
    Me, pensi immunis cum jam mihi reddor, inertis
Desidiæ sors dura manet, graviorque labore
Tristis et atra quies, et tardæ tædia vitæ
Nascuntur curis curæ, vexatque dolorum
Importuna cohors, vacuæ mala somnia mentis.
Nunc clamosa juvant nocturnæ gaudia mensæ
30 Nunc loca sola placent, frustra te, Somne, recumbens
Alme voco, impatiens noctis metuensque diei.
Omnia percurro trepidus, circum omnia lustro
Si qua usquam pateat melioris semita vitæ,
Nec quid agam invenio; meditatus grandia cogor
Notior ipse mihi fieri, incultumque fateri
Pectus, et ingenium vano se robore jactans.
Ingenium, nisi materiem Doctrina ministret,
Cessat inops rerum, ut torpet, si marmoris absit
Copia Phidiaci fœcunda potentia cœli.
40 Quicquid agam, quocunque ferar, conatibus obstat
Res angusta domi, et macræ penuria mentis.
    Non Rationis opes Animus nunc parta recensens
Conspicit aggestas, et se miratur in illis
Nec sibi de gaza, præsens quod postulet usus
Summus adesse jubet celsa dominator ab arce
Non operum serie, seriem dum computat ævi,
Præteritis fruitur, lætos aut sumit honores
Ipse sui judex, actæ bene munera vitæ
Sed sua regna videns, loca nocte silentia late
50 Horret, ubi vanæ species, umbræque fugaces,
Et rerum volitant raræ per inane figuræ.

Quid faciam? tenebrisne pigram damnare senectam
Restat? an accingar studiis gravioribus audax?
Aut, hoc si nimium est, tandem nova lexica poscam?

Know Thyself
(After the revision and correction of the English Dictionary)

When Scaliger after long struggle finally finished his dictionary, thoroughly bored with the slender achievement, indignant at the worthless study and the troublesome trifles, he groaned in hatred, and prescribed writing dictionaries for condemned criminals, one punishment in place of all other punishments.

He was right indeed, that sublime, learned and sharp-witted man; who was fit for greater works and should have attempted greater tasks; who had treated now the deeds of ancient generals, now the poems of ancient bards; and whatever Virtue, whatever Wisdom had uttered; and had unravelled with his intellect the vicissitudes of empire, the movements of the heavens, and the great cycle of the ages.

We are deceived by examples; the lowest mob of scholars rashly believes that your anger is allowed to them also, Scaliger. Let each man know his capacity. It was not granted me by fate that I should hope to be your equal in scholarship, first of men, or dare to be your equal in complaints, whether because the chills of sluggish blood or lying too long in idleness stand in the way, or because Nature has given me too small a mind.

Once you were quit of your fruitless toil, once you had safely struggled through the rough roads of words, divine Wisdom received you into the reaches of clear upper air; every Art gave you its friendly applause; and the discord of tongues in every land, now reconciled, with manifold voices sounded around you, the master who led them back from exile.

As for me, though now freed from my task, I am become my own master, the harsh lot of slothful idleness awaits me, and black and gloomy leisure, more burdensome than any labour, and the tedium of sluggish living. Worries beget worries, and a pestering company of troubles harass me, and the bad dreams of an empty mind. Now the noisy enjoyments of late-night dinners are my delight, now solitary places are my pleasure; in vain, kindly Sleep, I call on you, as I lie down, impatient of the night and fearful of the day. In trembling I rush through everything, I wander round everything, to see if anywhere a path to a better life opens up. But I find not what I am to do, meditating on grand schemes, and I am forced to know myself better and confess to an uncouth heart and a mind that boasts of itself with empty strength. A mind, unless Learning provides it material, idles destitute, just as when the supply of marble is wanting, the fertile power of Phidias' chisel languishes. Whatever I do, wherever I am taken, my narrow means and the poverty of a meagre mind block my endeavours.

The Heart, now reviewing its gains, does not see the wealth of Intellect accumulated and admire itself in them, nor does the almighty master from his high tower command the presence of what daily life demands for itself from the treasure; it does not enjoy, as it counts the serried years, its serried works, things of the past, nor, its own judge, does it accept gratifying honours, the rewards of a well-spent life; but seeing its own kingdom, it shudders at the wide regions silent in night, where empty appearances and fleeting shadows and thin shapes of things flit through the void.

What shall I do? Is it left to me to condemn my sluggish old age to darkness? Or should I gird myself boldly for weightier studies? Or, if this is too much, should I at last ask for – new dictionaries?

Skia,
An Ode on the Isle of Skye

Ponti profundis clausa recessibus,
Strepens procellis, rupibus obsita,
Quam grata defesso virentem
Skia sinum nebulosa pandis.

His cura credo sedibus exulat;
His blanda certe pax habitat locis:
Non ira, non mœror quietis
Insidias meditatur horis.

At non cavata rupe latescere,
10 Menti nec ægræ montibus aviis
Prodest vagari, nec frementes
E scopulo numerare fluctus.

Humana virtus non sibi sufficit,
Datur nec æquum cuique animum sibi
Parare posse, ut Stoicorum
Secta crepet nimis alta fallax.

Exæstuantis pectoris impetum,
Rex summe, solus tu regis arbiter,
Mentisque, te tollente, surgunt,
20 Te recidunt moderante fluctus.

Enclosed in the deep recesses of the sea, howling with
gales, beset by rocks, how welcome, misty Skye, do you
open your green bay to the weary traveller. Care, I do
believe, is exiled from these regions; gentle peace surely
dwells in these places: no anger, no sorrow plans traps
for the hours of rest. But it is no help to a sick mind to
hide in a hollow crag or wander through trackless
mountains or count the roaring waves from a rock.
Human virtue is not sufficient unto itself, nor is the
power granted each man to secure for himself an
untroubled mind, as the over-proud Stoic sect deceit-
fully boasts. Thou, almighty King, govern, sole arbiter,

the onrush of the stormy heart and, when Thou raise
them, the waves of the mind surge up and, when Thou
calm them, they fall back.

Ode, De Skia Insula

Permeo terras, ubi nuda rupes
Saxeas miscet nebulis ruinas,
Torva ubi rident steriles coloni
     Rura labores.

Pervagor gentes, hominum ferorum
Vita ubi nullo decorata cultu
Squallet informis, tugurîque fumis
     Fœda latescit.

Inter erroris salebrosa longi,
10 Inter ignotæ strepitus loquelæ,
Quot modis mecum, quid agat, requiro,
     Thralia dulcis.

Seu viri curas, pia nupta, mulcet,
Seu fovet mater sobolem benigna,
Sive cum libris novitate pascit
     Sedula mentem;

Sit memor nostri, fideique merces
Stet fides constans, meritoque blandum
Thraliæ discant resonare nomen
20   Littora Sciæ.

Scriptum in Skiâ.   Sept 6

Ode, from the Isle of Skye

I journey through a land where the naked crags mingle rocky ruins in mists, where the forbidding fields deride the farmer's fruitless labours. I wander among clans where the life of fierce men, dignified by no culture, is but ugly squalor, and the foul smoke of a hut can hardly be seen. Amid the rough stretches of long wandering, amid the din of an unknown tongue, in how many ways I ask myself, How fares sweet Thrale? Whether, as a dutiful wife, she soothes her husband's cares, whether, as kindly mother, she tends her young one, whether with her books she industriously feeds her mind with novelty, may she remember me, and in her fidelity let her pay tribute to fidelity, and deservedly let the shores of Skye learn to re-echo the sweet name of Thrale.

Insula Sancti Kennethi

Parva quidem regio, sed relligione priorum
　　Nota, Caledonias panditur inter aquas;
Voce ubi Cennethus populos domuisse feroces
　　Dicitur, et vanos dedocuisse deos.
Huc ego delatus placido per cœrula cursu
　　Scire locum volui quid daret ille novi.
Illic Leniades humili regnabat in aula,
　　Leniades magnis nobilitatus avis:
Una duas habuit casa cum genitore puellas,
10　　Quas Amor undarum fingeret esse deas:
Non tamen inculti gelidis latuere sub antris,
　　Accola Danubii qualia sævus habet;
Mollia non deerant vacuæ solatia vitæ,
　　Sive libros poscant otia, sive lyram.
Luxerat illa dies, legis gens docta supernæ
　　Spes hominum ac curas cum procul esse jubet.

Ponti inter strepitus sacri non munera cultus
    Cessarunt; pietas hic quoque cura fuit:
Quid quod sacrifici versavit femina libros,
20   Legitimas faciunt pectora pura preces.
Quo vagor ulterius? quod ubique requiritur hic est;
    Hic secura quies, hic et honestus amor.

On the Island of Saint Kenneth

A small place indeed, but one famous for the religion of its earlier settlers, it lies open amid Caledonian waters; a place where Kenneth is said to have tamed fierce clans with his voice and untaught them their false gods. Borne hither through the blue seas with a fair voyage, I wished to know what new was happening in that place. There Maclean ruled in a humble hall, Maclean ennobled by his great forebears. One house sheltered with their father two maidens, whom Love might imagine goddesses of the waves. Yet these were no uncouth people hiding in cold caves such as the savage dweller by the Danube has; the soft comforts of a life of ease were not wanting, whether leisure should require books or the lyre. That day had dawned when the race of men learned in the law of heaven bids men's hopes and cares begone. Amid the roaring of the sea the offices of holy religion did not cease; here too piety was of concern. What of the fact that a woman turned the priest's pages? Pure hearts make prayers lawful. Where further do I wander? What is sought everywhere is here: here is carefree rest and here is honourable love.

On losing the power of Speech

Summe Pater, quodcunque tuum de corpore Numen
  Hoc statuat, precibus Christus adesse velit:
Ingenio parcas, nec sit mihi culpa rogâsse,
  Qua solum potero parte, placere tibi.

Nocte, inter 16 et 17 Junii 1783

Almighty Father, whatever Thy Divinity decrees con-
cerning this body, may Christ be willing to hear my
prayers: spare my mind, and let it not be an offence in
me to ask to please Thee with the only faculty with
which I can do so.

Night, between 16 and 17 June 1783

In Rivum a Mola Stoana Lichfeldiæ diffluentem

Errat adhuc vitreus per prata virentia rivus,
  Quo toties lavi membra tenella puer;
Hic delusa rudi frustrabar brachia motu,
  Dum docuit blanda voce natare pater.
Fecerunt rami latebras, tenebrisque diurnis
  Pendula secretas abdidit arbor aquas.
Nunc veteres duris periêre securibus umbræ,
  Longinquisque oculis nuda lavacra patent.
Lympha tamen cursus agit indefessa perennis,
10 Tectaque qua fluxit, nunc et aperta fluit.
Quid ferat externi velox, quid deterat ætas,
  Tu quoque securus res age, Nise, tuas.

By the river, the confluence at Stowe Mill, Lichfield

Still wanders through green meadows the glassy stream,
wherein as a boy I so often bathed my tender limbs;
here I frustrated my deluded arms with unpractised

movements, while my father, with gentle voice, taught me to swim. The branches made coverts and the bending trees hid the water from sight with their daytime darkness. Now the old shadows have perished beneath hard axes, and the bathing place lies exposed to distant eyes. But the untiring water continues its perennial course, and where it flowed hidden, now, though open, it flows still. You also, Nisus, heedless of what swift time brings from outside or what it wears away, do what is yours to do.

Prayer

Summe Deus, cui cæca patent penetralia cordis;
　Quem nulla anxietas, nulla cupido fugit;
Quem nil vafrities peccantum subdola celat;
　Omnia qui spectans, omnia ubique regis;
Mentibus afflatu terrenas ejice sordes
　Divino, sanctus regnet ut intus amor:
Eloquiumque potens linguis torpentibus affer,
　Ut tibi laus omni semper ab ore sonet:
Sanguine quo gentes, quo secula cuncta piavit,
10　Hæc nobis Christus promeruisse velit!

Dec. 5, 1784

Almighty God, to Whom the hidden innermost places of the heart lie open; Whom no anxiety, no desire escapes; from Whom the cunning knavery of sinners hides nothing; Who, seeing all things, rulest all things everywhere; by Thy divine inspiration cast out from our minds earthly filthiness, that holy love may reign within. Bring to languid tongues potent speech so that praise to Thee may sound always from every mouth: by the Blood with which He redeemed all nations and all ages may Christ consent to merit these gifts for us.

A Selection from Johnson's Contributions to the Poems of other Writers

Johnson freely helped other writers with their work
and it can never be conclusively known exactly how much
of such work remains undiscovered. This appendix
contains a selection of his contributions to poems by others.

Lines in Hawkesworth's Tragedy

Thy mind which Voluntary doubts molest
Asks but its own permission to be blest.

Anna Williams: On the Death of
Stephen Grey, FRS

THE AUTHOR OF THE PRESENT DOCTRINE OF
ELECTRICITY

Long hast thou born the burthen of the day,
Thy task is ended, venerable Grey!
No more shall Art thy dext'rous hand require
To break the sleep of elemental fire;
To rouse the pow'rs that actuate Nature's frame,
The momentaneous shock, th'electrick flame,
The flame which first, weak pupil of thy lore,
I saw, condemn'd, alas! to see no more.

Now hoary Sage, pursue thy happy flight,
10 With swifter motion haste to purer light,
Where Bacon waits with Newton and with Boyle
To hail thy genius, and applaud thy toil;
Where intuition breaks through time and space,
And mocks experiment's successive race;
Sees tardy Science toil at Nature's laws,
And wonders how th'effect obscures the cause.

Yet not to deep research or happy guess
Is ow'd the life of hope, the death of peace.
Unblest the man whom philosophick rage
20 Shall tempt to lose the Christian in the Sage;
Not Art but Goodness pour'd the sacred ray
That cheer'd the parting hour of humble Grey.

Anna Williams: The Excursion

With serious joy th'enlighten'd soul
Surveys a part, admires the whole;
Nor always silently surveys,
But, fir'd by gratitude to praise,
In holy confidence is blest,
And calmly waits eternal rest.

Oliver Goldsmith: The Traveller, 1764
LINES 420, 429–34 AND 437–8

420 To stop too fearful, and too faint to go;
. . . . . .
How small, of all that human hearts endure,
430 That part which laws or kings can cause or cure.
Still to ourselves in every place consign'd,
Our own felicity we make or find:
With secret course, which no loud storms annoy,
Glides the smooth current of domestic joy.
[The lifted ax, the agonizing wheel,
Luke's iron crown, and Damien's bed of steel,]
To men remote from power but rarely known,
Leave reason, faith, and conscience all our own.

Oliver Goldsmith: The Deserted Village, 1770
LINES 427–30

That trade's proud empire hastes to swift decay,
As ocean sweeps the labour'd mole away;
While self dependent power can time defy,
As rocks resist the billows and the sky.

Hannah More: Sir Eldred of the Bower, 1776

PART I

2

Where gliding *Tay* her stream sends forth,
  To feed the neighbouring wood . . .

6

And every deed of lofty worth
  Is but a claim for more.

8

When *merit* raised the sufferer's name,
  He show'r'd his bounty *then*;
And those who cou'd not prove that claim,
  He succour'd still as *men*.

11

Yet if the passions storm'd his soul,
  By jealousy led on,
The whirlwind rage disdain'd controul
  And bore his virtues down.

18

The birds their vernal notes repeat,
  And glad the thick'ning grove,
And feather'd partners fondly greet
  With many a song of love.

33

For wisdom by a father's care,
  Was found in every field.

37

While the sweet-scented rose shall last,
  And boast its fragrant power,
When life's imperfect day is past,
  And beauty's shorter hour.

40
When sailing thro' the cloudless air,
  She sheds her silver light.

41
So Birtha shone! But when she spoke
  The Muse herself was heard –

45
The virgin blush which speads her cheek,
  With Nature's purest dye,
And all those dazzling beams which break,
  Like Morning, from her eye.

46
And still his raptur'd eye pursued,
  And feasted on the sight.

49
My scorn has oft the dart repell'd
  Which guileful beauty threw,
But goodness heard, and grace beheld,
  Must every heart subdue.

50
Quick on the ground her eyes were cast,
  And now as quickly rais'd: –
Her father haply that way past,
  On whom she trembling gaz'd.

PART II

3
Together did we learn to bear
  The casque and ample shield.

66
And dying Birtha close he found
  In brother's blood imbrued.

Verses by Frances Reynolds

As late disconsolate in pensive mood,
I sat revolving Life's vicissitude
Oft sigh'd to think how Youth had pass'd away,
And saw with sorrow Hopes diminish'd ray,
View'd the dark scene with melancholy gaze
Should Fate to helpless Age prolong my Days
Yet whilst I linger in the middle way
Where Life's high vigour verges to decay
Sure Nature acts, I cry'd, by wondrous Laws
10 She prompts resistance yet all hope withdraws ...

The springing grass, the circulating air
Each common bounty prompts to praise and prayer.

George Crabbe: The Village, 1783
LINES 15–20

On Mincio's banks, in Cæsar's bounteous reign,
If Tityrus found the golden age again,
Must sleepy bards the flattering dream prolong,
Mechanick echoes of the Mantuan song?
From Truth and Nature shall we widely stray,
Where Virgil, not where Fancy, leads the way?

*A Transcript of the Original Manuscript
of* The Vanity of Human Wishes

The Vanity of Human Wishes

Let Observation with extensive view
O'erlook Mankind from China to Peru
    ~~eager~~
Explore each ~~restless~~ anxious toil each eager Strife
And all the busy Scenes of Crouded Life
    hot
Then say how ~~fierce~~ desire and raging Hate
Oerspred with snares·the clouded Maze of Fate
Where wav'ring Man betray'd by vent'rous pride
To tread the dang'rous paths without a Guide
As treach'rous Phantoms in the mist delude
10 Shuns fancied ills or chases airy Good
How rarely Reason guides the hasty choice
Rules the bold hand or prompts the Suppliant voice
    Nations sink
How ~~Families~~ by darling Schemes opprest
When Vengeance listens to the Fools Request
Fate wings with ev'ry wish th'afflictive dart
      grace
Each Gift of Nature and each ~~charm~~ of art
With fatal Heat impetuous Courage glows
With fatal Sweetness Elocution flows
Impeachment Stops the Speaker's pow'rful breath
20 And restless Enterprize impells to death.
   unobserv'd
But ~~unregarded~~ the Skilful and the bad
Fall in
~~Amidst~~ the gen'ral Massacre of Gold
Widewasting Pest that rages unconfin'd
And crouds with crimes the records of mankind
    his Sword
For Gold ~~the Hireling~~ the hireling Ruffian draws
For Gold the Hireling Judge distorts the Laws
Wealth heapd on Wealth nor truth nor safety buys
The danger gathers as the treasures rise.

Th~~ee~~ll Hist'ry
~~Historians tell~~ tell where rival Kings command
~~From dubious titles~~

30 ~~And Statutes glean~~ And dubious title shakes the madded
      Land
When Statutes glean the refuse of the Sword,
How much more safe the Vassal than the Lord
Low Sculks the Hind beneath the rage of Pow'r
And leaves the b~~r~~onny Traytor in the Tow'r
Untouch'd
~~Secure~~ his Cottage, and his Slumbers sound
Though Confiscations Bloodhounds yelp around
   The needy Traveller secure and gay
Walks the wild Heath, and sings his toil away
Dos Envy seize thee crush th'upbraiding joy

40 Encrease his Riches, and his peace destroy
New fears in dire vicissitude invade
The Rustling Brake alarms and quiv'ring Shade
Nor light nor Darkness bring his pain relief
One shews the plunder, and one hides the thief.
        the
Yet still the Gen'ral Cry ~~from on~~ Skies assail
And Gain and
~~Assails the Skies~~ Greatness load the tainted Gales
Few know the toiling Statesmans fear or Care
Th'insidious Rival and the gaping Heir
Once more Democritus arise on Earth

50 With chearf Wisdom, and instructive mirth
See Motley Life in modern trappings drest
        new born
And Feed with ~~Change of~~ Fools th'eternal Jest
Thou who couldst laugh where want enchain'd Caprice
Toil crushd Conceit, and man was of a piece,
Where wealth unlov'd without a mourner dy'd
And scarce a sycophant could feed on pride,
Where ne'er was ~~heard~~ the form of mock debate
Or seen ~~the~~ a new made Mayor's unweeldy State
Where change of Fav'rites made no change of laws

60 And senates heard before they judg'd a cause
Where blasted Patriots never shrunk to peers
Nor annual Tax was rais'd by annual fears.
How would thou shake at
~~Evn low built towns they~~ Britain's modish tribe
Dart the quick taunt
~~And unexhausted laughter~~ and edge the piercing Gibe
Attentive Truth and Nature to descry
And pierce each scene with philosophic eye
To thee were solemn toys or empty Shew
The Robes of pleasure and the veils of woe
All aid the farce and all thy mirth maintain
Whose joys are causeless, or whose Griefs are vain
   Such was the Sorn that fill'd the Sages mind
70 Renew'd at ev'ry Glance on Humankind
How just that Scorn ere yet thy voice declare
Search ev'ry State and canvass ev'ry prayer.
   Unnumber'd Suppliants croud preferment's Gate
Athirst for wealth
~~All fir'd with hope~~ and panting to be great
Delusive Fortune hears th'incessant Call
They mount they shine, evaporate and fall
On evry Stage the foes of peace attend,
Hate dogs their flight, and insult mocks their End
Love ends with Hope the Sinking Statesmans door
Pours in
80 ~~Shews pour~~ the morning Worshiper no more
   For growing names the weekly Scribler lies
To
~~For~~ growing wealth the Dedicator flies.
     Room
From every ~~Wall~~ descends the painted face
    the bright
That hung ~~on high~~ Palladium of the place
And smok'd in Kitchens or in Auctions sold
To better Features yields the frame of Gold
For now no more we trace in ev'ry Line
Heroick worth Benevolence divine

But find the form distorted by the fall
  why should odious
90 And ~~hiss the Dauber~~ Ruin dawb the Wall.
But will not Britain Hear the last appeal
        Fav'rites
Sign her foes doom or g[uar]d her ~~Patriots~~ zeal
Through Freedoms Sons no more remonstrance rings
Degrading nobles, and controling Kings
Our Supple Tribes repress their patriot throats
And ask no question but the price of votes
With weekly Libels, and septennial ale
Their wish is full to riot and to rail
    ~~State~~ Dignity see
 In Fullblown ~~Powr see mighty~~ Wolsey stand
100 Law in his Voice, and Fortune in his Hand
     Realm
To him the Church the ~~State~~ their pow'rs resign
Through him the Rays of royal bounty shine
Turn'd by his nod the stream of Honour flows
His Smile alone Security bestows
Still to new heights his restless wishes towr
Claim leads to Claim, and powr advances Powr
Till Conquest
~~Till conquest~~ unresisted ceasd to please
And Rights Submitted left him none to seize
At length his Sovreign frowns the train of State
110 Mark the Keen Glance, and watch the sign to hate
Where'r he turns he meets a Strangers eye
His Supplians Scorn him, and his Followers fly
What then availd the pride of awful State
The golden Canopy the glittring plate
   regal
The ~~pompous~~ Palace the luxurious Board
The livried Army, or the menial Lord
With age, with cares, with maladies opprest
He seeks the refuge of monastic rest
Grief and Disease, remember'd folly Stings
120 And his last words reproach the faith of Kings

              thoughts at humble
Speak thou whose ∧ peace repine,
Shall Wolseys wealth, with Wolseys end be thine
      livst thou
Or ~~statesmens~~ now with safer Pride content
      wealthiest Landlord
The ~~Wisest Justice~~ on the Bank of Trent
    ~~w~~
For why did Wolsey by the Steeps of Fate
On weak foundations raise th'enormous weight
Why but ﬁto sink beneath misfortunes blow
With louder Ruin to the Gulphs below
[What gave great Villiers to th Assassins Knife
130 ~~W~~ And fix'd Disease on Harley's closing life
What murderd Wentworth and what exile Hyde
By Kings protected and to Kings allied
        ir   indulg'd
What but the wish ∧   in Courts to shine
And pow'r too great to keep or to resign?
   When first the College Rolls receive his name
The Young Enthusiast quits his ease for fame
Quick fires his breast
~~Each act betrays~~ the fever of renown
Caught from the strong Contagion of the Gown
~~On Isis banks he waves, from noise withdrawn~~
~~In sober state th'imaginary Lawn~~
O'er Bodley's Dome his future Labours spread
140 And Bacon's Mansion trembles o'er his head.
Are these thy views, proceed illustrious Youth
And Virtue guard thee to the throne of Truth
Yet should thy ~~fate~~ Soul indulge the gen'rous Heat
Till Captive Science yields her last Retreat
Should Reason guide thee with her brightest Ray
And pour on misty Doubt resistless day
Should no false kindness lure to loose delight
Nor Praise relax, nor difficulty fright
Should tempting Novelty thy cell refrain
150 And Sloth's bland opiates shed their fumes in vain

Should Beauty blunt on fops her fatal dart
Nor claim the triumph of a letter'd heart
~~SNor~~ Should no Disease thy torpid veins invade
Nor Melancholys Spectres haunt thy Shade
     hope
Yet ~~dream~~ not Life from Grief or Danger free,
Nor think the doom of Man revers'd for thee
Deign   passing   to
~~Turn~~ on the ∧ world ~~awhil~~ turn thine eyes
And pause awhile from Learning to be wise
There mark what ill the Scholar's life assail
        the

160 Toil envy Want ~~an~~ Garret and the Jayl
    See Nations slowly wise, and meanly just,
    To buried merit raise the tardy Bust.
    Dreams
If ~~Hope~~ yet flatter once again attend
Hear Lydiats life and Galileo's End.
     deem when
  Nor ~~think though~~ Learning her last prize bestow
   e
Th~~at~~ glittering Eminence exempt from Foes
See when the Vulgar scape despis'd or aw'd
Rebellions vengeful Talons seize on Laud
From meaner minds though smaller fines content

170 The plundred palace or sequestred Rent
Mark'd out by dang'rous parts he meets the schock
And fatal Learning leads him to the Block
Around his Tomb let art and Genius weep
But hear his death ye ~~Block~~heads, hear and sleep
  The festal Blazes, the triumphal show
The ravish'd Standard, and the Captive Foe
The Senate's thanks, the Gazette's pompous tale
With force resistless o'er the Brave prevail
Such
~~These~~ Bribes the rapid Greek o'er Asia whirl'd
  Such

180 For ~~these~~ the steady Romans shook the world,

                    such
For these in distant lands the Britons shine
And stain with blood the Danube or the Rhine
Such pow'er has praise that virtues scarce can ~~do~~ warm
Till Fame supplies the universal charm
Yet Reason ~~blush~~ Frowns on War's unequal Game
Where wasted Nations raise a single name
                    their Grandsires
And mortgaged States ~~their former~~ wreaths regret
From age to age in everlasting
~~Their Grandsires Glories~~   debt
Wreaths which at last
~~Great souls whose natu~~ the dear bought Right convey
190 To Rust on Medals or on Stones decay.
                                        pride
    On what Foundation stands the Warrior's ~~fame~~
How just his Hopes let Swedish Charles decide
A frame of Adamant a soul of Fire
No dangers fright him, and no labours tire.
O'er Love o'er Fear extends his wide domain
Unconquer'd Lord of pleasure and of pain
No joys to him pacific Scepters yield
War sounds the trump he rushes to the field
In vain Surrounding Kings their pow'rs combine
200 See One capitulate and one resign.
Peace courts his Hand, her Fondness he disdains
                                    till
Think nothing gain'd, he cries ~~th~~ nought remains
On Moscows walls till Gothic Standards fly
And all is mine beneath the polar Sky
The march begins in military State
And Nations ~~wait~~ on his eye suspended wait
Stern Famine guards the solitary Coast
And Winter barricades the realms of frost
He comes nor want nor cold his course delay
210 Hide blushing Glory, hide Pultowa's day
The ~~y~~vanquish'd Hero leaves his broken bands

　　　　shews
And hides his miseries in distant lands.
Condemn'd a needy Supplicant to wait
While Ladies interpose, and slaves debate
But did not Chance at length her errour mend
Did no Subverted Empire mark his end
Did rival Monarchs give the fatal wound
Or Hostile Millions press him to the Ground
His Fall was destin'd to a barren Strand
　　　　petty
220　A nameless Fortress, and a nameless hand
He left the name at which the world grew pale
To paint a moral, or adorn a tale.

All Times their Scenes of pompous Woes afford
From Persia's Tyrant to Bavaria's Lord,
In gay Hostility, and barb'rous pride
With half Mankind embattled on his Side
Great Xerxes comes to seize the certain prey
And starves exhausted regions in his way
Attendant Flatt'ry counts his myriads o'er
230　Till counted Myriads sooth his pride no more
　　　　Fresh
　　New praise is tried till Madness fires his mind
The waves he lashes and enchains the wind
New Pow'rs are claimed new pow'rs are still bestow'd
Till rude resistance lops the spreading God
The daring Greeks deride the martial Shew
And heap their vallies with the gaudy foe
Th'insulted Sea with humbler thought he gains
A single Skiff to Speed his flight remains
Th'incumberd Oar scarce leaves the dreaded Coast
240　Through purple Billows and a floating Host.

The bold Bavarian in a luckless hour
Tries the dread summits of Cesarean pow'r
[W]ith unexpected Legions pow'rs away
[An]d sees defenceless realms receive his sway

Short sway for Austria spreads her mournful Charms
The Queen the Beauty sets the world in arms
From hill to hill the Beacons rousing blaze
Spreads wide the hope of plunder and of praise
    fierce Croatian
The ~~sons of Ravage~~ and the wild Hussar
250 And all the son of ravage croud the war
The baffled Prince in honours flattring bloom
Of hasty greatness finds the hasty doom
His foes derision and his subjects blame
And steals to Death from anguish and from Shame

Enlarge my Life with multitude of Days
In health, in Sickness thus the Suppliant
Hides from himself his State and shuns to know
That Life protracted is protracted woe
Time hovers o'er impatient to destroy
260 And ~~sto~~huts up all the passages of Joy
In vain their gifts the bounteous seasons pour
The Fruit autumnal and the vernal flowr
With listless eyes the Dotard views the store
He views and wonders why they please no more
  ~~Th~~ Now
  ~~tasted tast~~ pall the tastless meats and joyless wines
[An]d Luxury with Sighs her slave resigns
Approach ye minstrels try the soothing Strain
      tuneful
And yield the ~~soothing~~ lenitives of pain.
The Notes unfelt would strike th'impervious ear
270 Though dancing Mountains witness'd Orpheus near
Nor lute nor Lyre his feeble pow'rs attend
Nor sweeter musick of a virtuous friend
But everlasting dictates croud his tongue
      or
Perversely grave ~~and~~ positively wrong
The still returning tale and ling'ring Jest
~~Still rise the long tran~~

Perplex the fawning Neice and pamper'd Guest
~~The dull Conjecture~~
While growing hopes ~~re~~ scarce awe the gath'ring Sneer
    scarce a Legacy
And ~~Guests are brib'd~~ can bribe to hear
    watchful
The ~~treachrous G~~ Guests still hints the last offence
280 The ~~ruinous~~ Daughter's insolence the Son's expence
Improve his heady rage with treach'rous skill
And mould his passions till they make his will.

Unnumberd Maladies ~~his~~ each joint invade
Lay siege to life and press the dire blockade
But unextinguish'd Av'rice still remains
And dreaded losses aggravate his pains
He turns with anxious heart and cripled hands
His bonds of Debt, and Mortgages of Lands
Or views his Coffers with suspicious eyes
290 Unlocks his Gold and counts it till he dies.

But grant, the virtues of a temp'rate prime
Bless with an age exempt from scorn or crime
An Age that melts in unperceived decay
And glides in modest innocence away
Whose peaceful day benevolence endears
Whose night congratulating Conscience cheers
    gen'ral
The ~~common~~ fav'rite as the gen'ral Friend
Such Age the is, and who could wish its end

Yet evn on this, her ~~loa~~ loads Misfortune flings
    press   weary   hanging
300 To ~~loade~~ the ~~lingring~~ Minutes ~~weary~~ wings
New Sorrow rises as the day returns
~~Each passing day some cause of sorrow sends~~
                Daughter mourns
A Sister Sickens or a ~~Child offends~~
Now kindred merit fills the mournful Bier

Now lacerated Friendship claims a tear
Year chases Year Decay persues decay
Still drops some Joy from withring life away
New forms She sees whom different views engage
And lags superfluous on th' incumbred
~~And chearless treads the desolated~~ stage
Till pitying Nature signs the last release
310 And bids afflicted worth retire to peace
But few there are whom hours like these await
Who set unclouded in the Gulphs of Fate
From Lydia's Monarch should the search descend
By Solon caution'd to regard his end
In Lifes last Scene what prodigies surprise
Fears of the brave
~~The Wise man's Follies~~ and follies of the wise
From Marlbrough's eyes the Streams of dotage flow
And Swift expires a Driv'ler and a Show.

The teeming Mother anxious for her race
320 Begs for each Birth the fortune of a face
Yet Vane could tell what ills from Beauty spring
And Sedley curs'd the form that pleasd a King
Ye Nymphs of rosy lips and radiant eye
Whom pleasure keeps too busy to be wise
Whom joys in soft vicissitudes invite
By day the frolick and the dance by night
Who frown with vanity who smile ~~by~~ with art
And ask the latest fashion of the Heart
              what rules your heedless charms shall save
What care ~~your charms from wretchedness~~
330 Each Nymph your rival and each youth your Slave
      n envious
A ~~Rivals~~ Breasts with certain Mischief glow
And slaves, the Maxim tells, are always foes.
Against your Fame with Fondness Hate combines
The Rival batters, and the Lover mines
With distant voice neglected Virtue calls
Less heard and less the faint Remonstrance falls

Tir'd with contempt ~~She at~~ She quits the Slippry reign
And Pride and Prudence take her seat in vain

pass

In croud at once where none the ~~fort~~ defend
The harmless freedom and the private Friend

by

The Guardians yield with force resistless plied
340 By Intrest Prudence and by Flatt'ry Pride

falls betray'd despis'd distress'd

Here Beauty'~~s drops her pomp betray~~
And shout Infamy proclaims the rest

Where then shall Hope and fear their Objects find

becalm

Must dull Suspence ~~still e~~ the stagnant Mind
Must helpless Man in ignorance sedate
Swim darkling down the current of his fate
Must no dislike
~~Enquirer cease~~ alarm no wishes rise
No cries attempt the mercies of the skies
~~Which Heavn may hear~~
Enquirer cease, petitions yet remain
350 Which Heavn may hear, nor deem Religion vain
For Blessing, raise the supplicating voice
But leave to Heavn the measure and the choice
Safe in his Pow'r whose eyes discern´afar
The secret ambush of a Specious pray'r
Implore his aid, in his decisions rest
And hope with humble confidence the best
Yet with the sense of sacred presence prest
When strong
~~If Aspirations~~ Devotion fills thy glowing breast
Pour
~~Breat~~ forth thy fervours for a ~~Soul re~~ mind

healthful

360 Obedient Passions and a will resignd

which scarce

For Love ~~whose grasp Creation~~ collective Man can fill,

For Patience Sov'reign o'er transmuted ill,
For Hope that panting for a happier seat
Thinks Death kind Nature's signal of Retreat
These goods for Man the laws of Heav'n ordain
These Goods he grants who grants the pow'r to gain
With these celestial Wisdom calms the mind
And makes the Happiness she do's not find

Notes

The following notes include both textual and explanatory notes, together with a general note on the sources of the text. Variant readings are recorded, but the record is not complete: only variants which have seemed to be of substantive significance are listed. They will, however, give the reader a fair indication of the kinds of changes which Johnson was accustomed to make in his work as it developed.

Mythological and proper names have been collected into a separate list following the notes (p. 239). Johnson alluded freely to classical mythology and literature and it would have been an undue burden on the explanatory notes to repeat an identification at each incidence. By removing them from the body of the notes it is hoped that the learned reader will not be irritated and the forgetful one will easily be able to remind himself.

Frequent reference has been made to a number of standard books. To avoid lengthy repetitions their titles have been abbreviated as follows:

Dict. *A Dictionary of the English Language*, by Samuel Johnson, A.M., 1755.
Letters *The Letters of Samuel Johnson*, ed. R. W. Chapman, 3 vols., Oxford, 1952.
Life *The Life of Samuel Johnson, LL.D.*, by James Boswell, ed. G. B. Hill, revised L. F. Powell, 6 vols., Oxford, 1934–64. (To facilitate the use of other editions I have usually supplied the date of any passage.)
Poems *The Poems of Samuel Johnson*, ed. David Nichol Smith and Edward L. McAdam, Jr, Oxford, 1941.
Thraliana *Thraliana, The Diary of Mrs Hester Lynch Thrale*, ed. K. C. Balderston, 2 vols., 2nd. edn, Oxford, 1951.
Works VI The Yale Edition of the *Works of Samuel Johnson: Poems*, ed. E. L. McAdam, Jr, and G. Milne, vol. 6, New Haven, 1964.

Other abbreviations are:
Y   Yale Papers.
GM   Gentleman's Magazine.

ON A DAFFODILL

According to Edmund Hector, Johnson's schoolfellow, who sent copies of Johnson's early verse to Boswell, this was the first of his compositions and was written between his fifteenth and sixteenth years, i.e. in 1724-5. The subject suggests spring, probably of 1725, when Johnson was fifteen and a half. According to Hector: 'As it was not characteristick of the Flower He never much lik'd it.'

Text from Hector's copies sent to Boswell in 1785 and 1791; *Works* VI 3-4.

10   *And*] May *in 1791 copy*

17   *Cleora* probably a fiction, but see *An Ode on a Lady leaving her place of abode* (p. 51), and *Rambler* 15. The name recurs in the *Adversaria* or notebook, quoted by Sir John Hawkins: 'I near dull – Cleora, a lady dreaded for her elegance and knowledge, came by chance; I shone.'

TRANSLATIONS OF HORACE: *Odes* I xxii (*Integer vitæ*)

Hector told Boswell that '*Integer vitae* was translated at school.' That is, at Lichfield Grammar School, most probably as an exercise. Johnson told Boswell that Horace's Odes 'were the compositions in which he took most delight, and it was long before he liked his Epistles and Satires'.

First version from Hector's copy, published by Boswell in the *Life*, 1791. *Poems* 65-8; *Works* VI, 73-4.

5   *Tho'*] *misread by Hector as* Thro'

6   *torrid*] *misread by Hector as* horrid

21   *burning line*   the Equator, popularly supposed too hot for human life.

The second version is a revision, published in the *GM* in 1743, and revised again and published in William Duncombe's *Horace in English Verse*, 1757. The changes are slight, but the two together illustrate the kind of polishing to which Johnson often subjected his compositions. *Poems* 66-7; *Works* VI, 74-5.

AN ODE ON FRIENDSHIP

Boswell records that this poem was 'written ... at a very early period, as Mr Hector informs me, and inserted in the *Gentleman's Magazine* of this year (1743)'. The theme seems to reflect Johnson's reaction to his departure in 1725 from Lichfield Grammar School, and his consequent leaving his friend Hector behind.

Copy by Hector now at Yale (Y); published in the *GM* July 1743 (*GM* 43); revised and included in Anna Williams's *Miscellanies* (1766). *GM* 43 omitted stanza 6; it was restored in 1766, but then stanza 5 was dropped. A later appearance of an early text was contributed by 'B.W.' to *GM* June 1785 (*GM* 85). The text of 1766 is the final authority and is here followed, with stanza 5 supplied from *GM* 43. *Poems* 97–100; *Works* VI, 71–2.

1 *peculiar* 'belonging to any one with exclusion of others'; *Dict. Gift*] boon Y, *GM* 43, *GM* 85

5 *unknown among*] a stranger to Y, *GM* 85
unknown because a love which is based on preference will be unknown in a state of universal bliss and benevolence. See last stanza.

6 *Rage and hot*] Rage and wild Y; thousand wild *GM* 43, *GM* 85

7] savage and the human *GM* 43

8] Inflame with unrelented Y; Torments alike with raging *GM* 43; Inflames alike with raging *GM* 85

9 *Gleam*] gloom *GM* 43

11 *lambent*] milder Y. Literally, 'flame-like', but see *An Evening Ode*, note to line 14 (p. 203, below).

13 *guiltless* without shame or tinge of immorality.

15 *Monarch*] tyrant *GM* 43

18 *us*] me *GM* 85

22] sister minds Y

23 *Pleasures*] charms as Y

25] Oh must thine ardours Y; Nor shall thine ardours *GM* 43; Oh, must their ardours *GM* 85

26 *happier*] blissful Y, *GM* 43, *GM* 85

TRANSLATION OF PART OF THE DIALOGUE BETWEEN HECTOR AND ANDROMACHE

Probably written whilst Johnson was a pupil at Stourbridge School from Whitsuntide 1726 until nearly the end of the same year. The allusions to Hector perhaps include a reference to his Lichfield friend.

The original of this poem was lent to Boswell by the nephew of John Wentworth, Johnson's Stourbridge schoolmaster, and transcribed by James Ross, Boswell's servant (see Introduction, p. 16 above). The Ross transcript contains a few errors which have been silently corrected: 3 scaen, 7 E ..., 8 Hypopla ..., 10 scource, 27 live, 42 Provock'd, 90 hand, 92 affrighed. *Poems* 74–5; *Works* VI, 17–21.

This passage was translated by Dryden and by Pope in his *Iliad*, but Johnson owes surprisingly little to both.

9 *lovely boy* Astyanax, his son, thrown by Achilles to his death from the walls of Troy.

33 *elms* funeral trees.

60 *kind* 'favourable; beneficent'; *Dict.*

82 *Beneath Hyperia's waters* as a slave carrying water for domestic use.

AN EPILOGUE TO *The Distrest Mother*

Hector is again the source of this piece, so that it was perhaps written whilst Johnson was at home before going up to Oxford in 1728. Hector told Boswell that 'some Young Ladies in Lich. had a mind to act *The Distress'd Mother*, for whom he wrote the *Epilogue* and gave it me to convey privately to them'. *The Distrest Mother*, 1712, by Ambrose Philips (the original 'Namby-Pamby'), was an adaptation of Racine's *Andromaque*.

From Hector's transcript at Yale. *Poems* 83–4; *Works* VI, 37–8.

14 *myrtle* the plant sacred to Venus and love (see p. 52).

18 *vapours, spleen, and tears* 'Diseases caused by flatulence or by diseased nerves; hypochondriacal maladies; melancholy'; *Dict.* Ailments supposedly confined to ill-tempered girls.

23 *tort'ring whalebones* corsets.

TRANSLATION OF HORACE: 'EPODE THE 2ᵈ (*Beatus ille*)'

Probably written at Stourbridge School, 1726. The subject suggests that it is a school exercise.

The original manuscript (in the Hyde Collection), in Johnson's youthful handwriting, is signed. A working draft, it bears the marks of rewriting and is not entirely legible (lines 20, 41–2). *Poems* 71–3; *Works* VI, 8–10. Original readings are recorded below.

1 Also the first line of Ambrose Philips's translation of an ode by Sappho, and of verses by 'Theophilus' in *GM*, October 1739.

4 *Nectar* the drink of the gods.

10 *from*] for *orig.*

11 *boist'rous*] Northern.

17–18 A traditional method of growing vines, described by Virgil in Georgic II.

27–8] Rewards the fav'ring Deities,
          That grant his Prayers, and hear his cries.

29 *spreading*] venerable
    Ilex the holm-oak.

39–40] The foaming Boar he then with op'ning hounds
        And twisted toils [etc.]

40 *twisted toils* nets. *Toil* 'any net or snare, woven or meshed';
Dict.

43 *springes* 'A gin; a noose which fastened to any elastick body
catches by a spring or jerk'; *Dict.*

45] Such Pleasures quickly would

56 *studied*] various

57–62 *No fish . . . supply*] Whate'er the swarthy Lybian boasts
                          Whate'er from India spicy coasts
                          Driv'n hither by inclement skies
                          I once admir'd, I'd then despise:
                          The painted meads and Forrests nigh
                          Can more delicious food supply.

61 *forrests*] fields

67 *How pleas'd*] Joyfull

69 *How pleas'd beholds his*] He sees the wearied

70 *faintly* 'without strength of body'; *Dict.*

79 *sets it out* (compare Lat. *ponere*: to put, also to lend) lends his
money at interest. (This usage is not in Johnson's *Dict.*)

TRANSLATION OF HORACE: EPODE xi

Probably written whilst Johnson was at Stourbridge School, 1726.
    This poem survives in a transcript by James Ross. Two scribal
errors in the transcript, now at Yale, are emended: 7 chip'd, and 26
quite. *Works* VI, 10–12.

12 *scandall* 'Offence given by the faults of others. Reproachful
aspersion; opprobrious censure; infamy'; *Dict.*

TRANSLATION OF HORACE: *Odes* II ix

Probably written whilst Johnson was at Stourbridge School, 1726.
    Transcript by James Ross, now at Yale, was published by Boswell in
the *Life*. Poems 67–8; *Works* VI, 12–13. Three readings are emended:
1 viel (though this spelling is represented in Johnson's own manu-
script of Horace *Odes* II xx 11 (p. 39)), 17 of, 21 roll's.

5 *Armenian shores* the shores of the Caspian Sea.

11 *care* usually amended to *cares*, but the plural seems unnecessary.

13 *Grecian sage* Nestor.

23 Boswell emended to *Romans'*, but *Roman's* is correct as Horace is
speaking of Augustus only.

TRANSLATION OF HORACE: *Odes* II xiv (*Eheu fugaces*)

Probably written whilst Johnson was at Stourbridge School, 1726.

The original manuscript, signed 'Sam: Johnson', is in the Johnson Birthplace Museum at Lichfield, but there is also a transcript by James Ross at Yale, which associates the composition with Stourbridge. *Poems* 68-9; *Works* VI, 13-14.

Compare Isaac Watts's hymn 'Awake our Souls' (1707), ll. 11-12: 'While endless years / Their everlasting circles run.'

10   *haughty King below*   Pluto, god of the Underworld.

24   *Cypress*   a funeral and mourning tree. See Browne, *Urne Buriall*, IV: 'in strewing their Tombs the Romans affected the Rose, the Greek Amaranthus and Myrtle; that the Funerall pyre consisted of sweet fuell, Cypresse, Firre, Larix, Yewe, and trees perpetually verdant.'

TRANSLATION OF HORACE: *Odes* II xx

Probably written whilst Johnson was at Stourbridge School, 1726.

The original manuscript, signed 'Sam: Johnson', is in the Hyde Collection, but a transcript by James Ross, at Yale, links the piece with Stourbridge. *Poems* 69-70; *Works* VI, 14-15.

2   *double-form'd*   both a poet and a swan.

8   *Nectar*   the drink of the gods.

11   *plumes*   feathers.

12   *Swan*   a bird sacred to Apollo, god of music and poetry. Swans are supposed to sing just before they die: the quality of the song is assumed from its rarity and occasion.

TRANSLATION OF VIRGIL: PASTORAL I

Probably written whilst Johnson was at Stourbridge School, 1726.

From a transcript by James Ross, which associates the piece with Stourbridge. *Poems* 64-5; *Works* VI, 5.

1   How] Now *Boswell*

6   This line is a direct translation of the corresponding line in Virgil, of which Johnson said: 'All the modern languages cannot furnish so melodious a line as *Formosam resonare doces Amarillida silvas*.'

9   *firstlings*   first-born. Compare *Genesis* iv 4: 'And Abel, he brought of the firstlings of his flock. . . . And the Lord had respect unto Abel and to his offering.'

12   *unequall reeds*   the Pan pipes, consisting of short reed pipes of varying length, each tuned to a particular note.

13   *admiration*   '*Admire* – to regard with wonder; generally in a good sense'; *Dict.*

24 *lefthand* sinister.

crows traditionally birds of ill-omen.

25 *dismal* derived by Minsheu (*Dictionary*, 1617) from Lat. *dies mali*, evil days. It is already noticeable how even in this early piece Johnson employs etymological meanings to enrich his language.

TRANSLATION OF VIRGIL: PASTORAL V

Probably written whilst Johnson was at Stourbridge School, 1726.

Part of the poem survives in a manuscript fair copy, signed 'Sam: Johnson', in the Hornby Library, Liverpool (lines 32–52). The whole (except for ll. 53–6) is given in a transcript by James Ross, and so is probably a Stourbridge composition. The four lines omitted by Ross are on the verso of Johnson's manuscript, and it seems that Ross simply failed to turn the leaf over. The four lines missing from the manuscript (49–52) were at the foot of the leaf and have perhaps been cut away.

Johnson gave his opinion of Virgil's Pastorals in his *Adventurer*, 92 (22 September 1753).

10 *trac'd* '*Trace* – to follow by the footsteps; to mark out ... to walk over'; *Dict.*

24 *parterre* formal flower-bed.

34 *admires* '*Admire* – to regard with wonder; generally in a good sense'; *Dict.*

39 *toils* nets or snares. '*Toil* – any net or snare, woven or meshed'; *Dict.*

49 Ross left the blanks where he could not read the original, and the original of this line is now missing. Virgil's lines were: 'Cantabunt mini Damoctas et Lyctius Aegon: / Saltantes Satyres imitabitur Alphesiboens' (72–3).

TRANSLATION OF ADDISON'S Πυγμαιογερανομαχια
THE BATTLE OF THE PYGMIES AND CRANES

Probably written whilst Johnson was at Stourbridge School, 1726.

Two portions (lines 97–117, and 140–70) exist in Johnson's manuscript at Yale, where also is a transcript of the whole by James Ross. Some scribal errors in Ross have been emended: 11 Achillis, 64 of spring, 89 St ymons, 130 Crane. Part in *Poems* 75–7; whole in *Works* VI, 21–7.

In his Life of Addison, Johnson wrote: 'Three of his Latin poems are upon subjects on which, perhaps, he would not have ventured to have written in his own language. *The Battle of the Pigmies and Cranes*; *The Barometer*; and *a Bowling Green*. When the matter is low or scanty, a dead language, in which nothing is mean because nothing is familiar, affords great conveniences; and by the sonorous magnificence of Roman syllables, the writer conceals penury of thought and want of novelty, often from the reader, and often from himself' (para. 11, 1781).

1 *squadrons* '1. A body of men drawn up square; 2. A part of an army; a troop; 3. Part of a fleet; a certain number of ships'; *Dict.*

2 *Pygmy* 'A dwarf; one of a nation fabled to be only three spans high, and after long wars to have been destroyed by cranes'; *Dict.*

41 *faulchion* 'A short crooked sword; a cymetar [scimitar]'; *Dict.*

45 *burthen* '*Burden*; properly written burthen'; *Dict.* See note to l. 64.

47 *imbru'd* '*Imbrue* – to steep; to soak; to wet much or long'; *Dict.* The modern equivalent *imbue* struck Johnson with uncertainty, and he commented: '*Imbue*: This word which seems wanted in our language, has been proposed by several writers, but not yet adopted by the rest.' He defined it as 'To tincture deep; to imbibe or soak with any liquor or die [dye]'; *Dict.*

49 *crush'd* originally *kill'd.* Johnson told Steevens: 'When I was a young man, I translated Addison's Latin Poem on the Battle of the Pigmies and the Cranes, and I must plead guilty to the following couplet:

Down from the guardian boughs the nests they flung,
And kill'd the yet unanimated young.

And yet I trust I am no blockhead. I afterwards changed the word *kill'd* into *crush'd*.'

54f Alluding to the crypto-Homeric poem *The Battle of the Frogs and the Mice* (*Batrachomyomachia*).

64 *murther'd* 'The etymology requires that it should be written as it anciently often was, *murther*; but of late the word itself has commonly, and its derivatives universally, been written with *d*'; *Dict.* (1755).

71 *meditate* 'To plan; to scheme; to contrive'; *Dict.*

79 *wings* of an army drawn up for battle.

98 *stooping* as a hawk 'stoops' on its prey.

FESTINA LENTÈ

It has been suggested that the choice of subject for this poem reflects some perception of Johnson's character by his Stourbridge schoolmaster, John Wentworth. If the suggestion is right then the exercise was probably prescribed towards the end of Johnson's stay in that school, late in 1726. The mastery of enjambement and control of the caesura also suggest a maturing skill.

The original manuscript, signed 'Sam: Johnson', is in the Hyde Collection; a transcript by James Ross associates its composition with Stourbridge. *Poems* 77–8; *Works* VI, 15.

11 *Ball* in the sense of a dance.

UPON THE FEAST OF ST SIMON AND ST JUDE

The mastery of a distinct verse-form (also used by Smart in his *Song to David*, 1763) suggests a late period in Johnson's school career, and the commemoration of the two saints makes it likely that the poem was written for 28 October 1726.

The original manuscript, signed 'Sam: Johnson', is in the Hyde Collection; a transcript by James Ross associates its composition with Stourbridge. *Poems* 78–80; *Works* VI, 15–17.

3 *vulgar* popular or common.
27 See Addison's Hymn:

The spacious firmament on high . . .
What though in solemn silence all
Move round the dark terrestrial ball . . .

54 *imbru'd* see *Pygmies and Cranes*, note to l. 47.

56 *extatick fury* the rage of inspiration; *furor poeticus*.

TO A YOUNG LADY ON HER BIRTHDAY

Boswell records that 'Mr Hector informs me that this was made, almost impromptu, in his presence'. After leaving Stourbridge Johnson spent about a year at home in Lichfield, when this piece was probably composed, in 1727.

From a transcription made by Hector and sent to Boswell, now at Yale. The association with Hector suggests that it was written at Lichfield, not Stourbridge. *Poems* 80; *Works* VI, 36.

7 *graceful*] grateful *in Boswell's published text*
14 *generous* 'Noble of mind; magnanimous; open of heart'; *Dict.* Compare Lat. *generosus*: noble, from *genus*: race, hence, a man of distinguished birth and descent.

THE YOUNG AUTHOR

Hector told Boswell: '*The Young Author* was wrote in his 20th Year', i.e. 1729. The poem seems to reflect something of Johnson's disillusionment on leaving Oxford prematurely in December 1729, and was perhaps written on that occasion.

First printed in the *GM* July 1743. Hector had an earlier version (*H*), of which he sent a transcript to Boswell, who used it in the *Life* (*B*). The *GM* is the authoritative revision. *Poems* 81–2; *Works* VI, 72–3. The whole poem may be compared with lines 135 ff. of *The Vanity of Human Wishes* (p. 86).

2   *seats*] sports *H, B*
3   *Charm'd*] Pleas'd *H, B*
4   ] verdant meads and flowry vales *H, B*
5   ] Then dances jocund *H, B*
7   *insincere* 'Sincere – 1. Unhurt, uninjured; 2. Pure, unmingled; 3. Honest, undissembling, uncorrupt'; *Dict.*
6 ∧7   ] Unbounded prospects in his bosom roll,
            And future millions lift his rising soul;
            In blissful dreams he digs the golden mine,
            And raptured sees the new-found ruby shine. *H, B*
8   ] Loud roar the billows, high the waves arise *H, B*
11   *for a name*] after fame *H, B*
12   ] And the long honours of a lasting name *H, B*
18   *nations*] ages *H, B*
20   *plies the*] flies to *H, B*
25   *pamphlet* 'A small book; properly a book sold unbound and only stitched'; *Dict.* On 25 April 1778 Johnson corrected Boswell's misrepresentation of the meaning of this word (*Life*, III, 319).
27   *damn, nor*] snarl, no *H, B*
28   *keen*] tart *H, B*
     lampoon 'A personal satire; abuse; censure written not to reform but to vex'; *Dict.*

AN ODE ON A LADY LEAVING HER PLACE OF ABODE

Hector sent a copy to Boswell, and noted that the original bore the date 1731.

From Hector's transcript at Yale. *Works* VI, 38–9. Compare Dryden's *A Song to a Fair Young Lady going out of Town in the Spring.*

5   *Cleora*   see *On a Daffodill*, note to l. 17.

ON A LADY'S PRESENTING A SPRIG OF MYRTLE
TO A GENTLEMAN

The original manuscript, which Hector sent to Boswell, bore the date 1731. Hector also recounted the story of the composition of the piece: 'The true history (which I could swear to) is as follows: Mr Morgan

Graves, the elder brother of a worthy Clergyman near Bath, with whom I was acquainted, waited upon a lady in this neighbourhood, who at parting presented him the branch. He shewed it me, and wished much to return the compliment in verse. I applied to Johnson, who was with me, and in about half an hour dictated the verses which I sent to my friend.' This was in rebuttal of Anna Seward's contention that Johnson had himself addressed the verses to Lucy Porter, who later became his stepdaughter.

The manuscript has not been seen since 1875. The poem was first published in Dodsley's *Museum* in 1747, and by Boswell in the *Life* (*B*). *Poems* 92–5; *Works* VI, 79–80.

1   *Fears*] hopes *B*
5   *Fair*   a fair or beautiful person
6   ] Now grants and now rejects a lover's prayer *B*
7   *Groves*] shades *B*
12   *cure*] ease *B*

TO MISS HICKMAN PLAYING ON THE SPINET

Dorothy Hickman was a connection of Johnson's by marriage. In the summer of 1731 he spent some time in the home of her father, Gregory Hickman, who helped in Johnson's unsuccessful attempt to obtain a post as teacher at Stourbridge School. Dorothy was in her eighteenth year during Johnson's visit; she married in 1734.

From the original manuscript, undated. It was given by Johnson to Dorothy; now in the Hyde Collection. *Poems* 96–7; *Works* VI, 39–40.

9ff Compare Dryden, *Alexander's Feast; Or, the Power of Musique. An Ode in Honour of St Cecilia's Day, 1697.*
10   *Ambitious* the MS is not certain here; the word could be *Ambitions*.
12   Alexander the Great often complained that there were no more worlds left for him to conquer.

EPIGRAM ON COLLEY CIBBER

From January 1730 until March 1732 Johnson was at home in Lichfield and a member of a circle of bright young people of his own age: the Aston girls, young Henry Hervey, from time to time Edmund Hector, and, almost as president, Gilbert Walmesley.

The epigram on Cibber, though the satire is applicable to all of Cibber's Birthday Odes to King George, would certainly have amused such a group. I place it here soon after Cibber's appointment to the laureateship in 1730.

From the version which Johnson dictated to Boswell at Blackshiels on 21 November 1773, and as published in the *Life* (I 149, V 404). *Poems* 114; *Works* VI, 69–70.

SELECTIONS FROM *Irene*

Irene, Johnson's only play, was written in large part whilst he was schoolmastering at Edial in 1736. After long delays and setbacks it was produced by David Garrick (who played Demetrius) at Drury Lane on 6 February 1749, under the title of *Mahomet and Irene*. It ran for a total of nine nights, and was published on 16 February.

The story of *Irene* was taken primarily from *The Generall Historie of the Turks*, by Richard Knolles, first published in 1603. (See D. Nichol Smith, 'Irene', *Essays and Studies*, XIV (1929), B. Moran, 'The Irene Story and Dr Johnson's Sources', *Modern Language Notes*, LXXI (1956), and B. H. Bronson, *Johnson and Boswell*, 1944.) *Poems* 233–377; *Works* VI, 109–239.

Irene, a beautiful Greek Christian, with her attendant Aspasia (said to be modelled on Johnson's wife), is the beloved prisoner of the Turkish Emperor, Mahomet. Other Greek prisoners, Demetrius and Leontes, conspire with the disaffected Cali Bassa, who plans to murder Mahomet, to escape together with Aspasia (beloved by Demetrius) and Irene. Irene is dazzled by the prospect of becoming Mahomet's Empress; but she is seen as a danger to the Turkish state by Mahomet's courtiers, who fear that she will turn him from his warlike expansion. The conspiracy of Cali is betrayed, the Greeks escape, but Irene, though innocent, is executed.

Though the major part of the play was prepared at Edial, it is clear from the various notes and drafts (in the British Museum and the Hyde Collection) that Johnson worked at it over many years. It is here placed in 1736, but an equally strong case might be made for dating it to 1749, the year of final production and publication. The text is from the first edition; later editions were not revised.

Though it was not, comparatively, a success, Johnson gained almost three hundred pounds from it. He endured its contemporary reception (Garrick noted that it 'went off very well for 4 Acts, the 5th Hiss'd generally' on the first night – when Irene was strangled on stage) with stoicism – 'like the Monument' as he said – but he turned up to the first night in a fancy red waistcoat.

The passages selected illustrate the moral tone of the argument. Below are extracts from the draft notes, which will give some idea of the development of his thoughts and expression.

Prologue.   Almost certainly written for the performance, and so dating
from 1748. There are parallels (e.g. 9–14) with *The Vanity of Human
Wishes.*

16   Quoted in *Dict.* to illustrate 'Ennoble'.

23   *Cat-calls* 'A squeaking instrument, used in the playhouse to
condemn plays'. *Dict.*

27–8   Quoted in *Dict.* to illustrate 'Prejudice'.

31   See *Rambler* 32 (7 July 1750) 'Patience and submission are very
carefully to be distinguished from cowardice and indolence. We are
not to repine, but we may lawfully struggle.'

I i   28–57

'Though no Comets or prodigies foretold the ruin of Greece signs which
Heavn must by another Miracle enable us to understand, yet might it be
foreknown by tokens no less certain by the vices which allways bring
it on.' *Draft*

56   'Vice the Harbinger of Ruin'; *Draft*

I ii   50–73

'Cali Bassa relates the Original Cause of Mahomets hatred of him his
persuasion of Amurath to resume the crown which hatred he makes
the reason of his Correspondence with Greek Emperour that he might
have a retreat in his Necessity here he launches into the misery of
absolute Governments, where if a Man serves his Country counterfeit
Plots and false Suspicions, then breaks out into the Praises of that
Country (after having blam'd the Eastern Tyranny) which he has heard
of in the North

Where King and People own one common Law
    one common Interest, mutual duties
And feel one happiness and one Misfortune.

Where Swain smiles over his little fields, his rising harvest his feeding
flocks, and says these are mine, and gathers his children about him and
portions out to them the acquisitions of his Industry.' *Draft*

55   *any Land*   'amidst the roarings of the Northern Main'; *Draft*,
a romanticized allusion to Britain.

57   The image is of the circulation of the blood, discovered by
Harvey in the seventeenth century. Johnson refers to his anachronism
in *Rambler* 140 (20 July 1751): 'a later writer has put Harvey's doctrine
of the circulation of the blood into the mouth of a Turkish statesman,
who lived near two centuries before it was known to philosophers or
anatomists.'

61 Johnson's praise of Tory conservatism is equally anachronistic as Britain, in Cali's time, was engaged in the Wars of the Roses.

63 *Chain of Nature* a popular eighteenth-century view, that the Universe was a harmonious unity in which everything occupied its proper place in a hierarchical scale between God and inanimate things, was often known as the 'Great Chain of Nature' (see A. O. Lovejoy, *The Great Chain of Being*, 1936).

II i 1-37

'To make Aspasia and Irene name each other'; *Draft*. 'Aspasia encourages Irene to persist in the Faith animates her with the Love of Virtue.' *Draft*

5ff] 'When The Mind disentangled from the Senses

Expands the boundless Scenes of Future Being.' *Draft*

8] 'Fade [Glide] from the sight, and Vanish into nothing.' *Draft*

20 *Apostate* To become Mahomet's Empress Irene would have to renounce her Christianity and accept Islam. Johnson was always deeply disturbed by changes of religion, and much of the vehemence of his quarrel with Mrs Thrale on her marriage to Piozzi stemmed from his expectation of her acceptance of Roman Catholicism.

24 *Nerves* muscles, i.e. physical (not mental) strength. 'It is used by the poets for sinew or tendon'; *Dict*.

26 See *Rambler* 34 (14 July 1750) on 'The uneasiness and disgust of female cowardice'.

III ii 14-33

Charles Burney reported that this passage was received with most applause at the first performance.

'To morrow Strike – Does [then] that experienc'd Wisdom

That Hoary Head, that Head which hungry fate

Marks for his own still doat upon to Morrow

That fatal mistress of the Young the lazy

The coward and the fool, condemn'd to lose

An useless life in waiting for to morrow

To gaze with longing eyes upon to morrow

Till interposing Death destroys (denys) (Darkness bars) the prospect.

The wily Sorc'ress (b)wears a thousand forms,

And various charms displays to various eyes

The Merchant sees her with wealh, the lover with his Mistress &c

The weary Soldier – Still sees to Morrow dressed in robes of triumph

Wealh in her hand, and olive on her brow.

Arsanes tells that persuing to morrow is like following the meteors of a fen where

The traveller persues the (flatt'ring) wandring splendor
Still courting his embrace and still eluding
And as he seems to seize the insidious Phantom that dances before
him he sinks for ever' *Draft*

III viii 111-35
'Aspasia endeavours to dissuade Irene from complying with Mah. but
in vain they argue long.' *Draft*
111ff Johnson described ambition as 'a noble passion' (*Life* III,
39; 12 April 1776), and compare his *Life of Boerhaave* (*GM*, 1739,
para. 26).
112 *Heat*] fire *Draft*
114 ∧ 115] Then pleas'd, and conscious of Superiour Greatness
            And Strength proportioned to the task of Ruling *Draft*
116] They give the Nations Laws, and view serene
        The subject World, familiar to Dominion. *Draft*
121 *nearer to Perfection*] of superiour Nature *Draft*
124] Prescribes the dreadful Comet's flaming path
        Rolls on the Sun, and Regulates the Spheres. *Draft*

V vi 1-16
'[Irene] wonders she could think she would leave Turkey's Empire
to share her [Aspasia's] necessities and bear her lofty Mien she then
goes and seeing the Bark going, acknowledges providence, and wishes
herself with them.' *Draft*
5ff] Go Happy Bark, thy sacred Freight secures thee
        – Th'Eternal Lamps –
        To Guide thy passage shall the [Starry] Aerial Spirits
            Fav'ring Sky
        Fill all the Starry Lamps with double Blaze [Radiance].
        The' [Applauding] Wondring Sky shall shine with Decorations
        To grace the triumphs of victorious Virtue.
                I see the distant Vessel
        Dance o'er the Sparkling Waves – Go happy Bark
        Persue thy course through boiling Eddies,
        Insidious Sands, rough Rocks, and whirling Gulphs
        Thy sacred freight of Innocence and Truth
        Shall [still] the whirle, and bid the Rock subside. *Draft*

V xiii 1-15
'Mustapha examines the Messenger who tells him that he was stopd
by Leontius and that Heavn's Justice proceeds through dark paths.
Laborious maze – imputed guilt.' *Draft*

2 Quoted in *Dict.* to illustrate 'Idler'.
10 ff] Mustapha observ's the Justice of Heav'n that Man
　　　　[And Mortals trace th'Almighty's path in vain]
　　　　By vice or passion driv'n
　　　　Is but the executioner of Heavn – or Instrument
　　　　When erring Fury throws the random dart
　　　　Heav'n turns its point upon the guilty Heart
　　　　Behold Irene – o'erthrown
　　　　By crimes abhord, and treasons not her own
　　　　Eternal Justice (well th'Eternal Mind) thus her doom decreed
　　　　And in the traytress bad th'Apostate bleed *Draft*

LONDON: A POEM

According to Johnson's own note on the fragment of surviving manuscript draft, *London* was published on 12 May 1738.

The poem is strictly called an 'Imitation', not a translation, of which Johnson wrote to Cave: 'part of the beauty of the performance (if any beauty be allow'd it) consisting in adapting Juvenals Sentiments to modern facts and Persons' (see Mary Lascelles, 'Johnson and Juvenal', in *New Light on Johnson*, Yale University Press, 1959). In this respect the poem was therefore something of a challenge to Pope, who was the supreme contemporary 'imitator' of Horace. Pope inquired after the anonymous author and was told 'that his name was Johnson, and that he was some obscure man; Pope said "He will soon be *deterré*."'

The draft of lines 99–106, 147–50, 198–263 is in the Hyde Collection. The second folio edition of 1738 was revised, and further revisions are found in Dodsley's *Collection of Poems* (1748), and again in the version included in Johnson's *Works* (1787). Text from the first edition, incorporating subsequent authoritative readings from second edition (2), Dodsley (*D*) and Works (*W*). Poems 7–23; *Works* VI, 45–61.

The poem exhibits an eager nationalism characteristic of the anti-Walpolean Tories, recalling the great days and expansionism of English history, but balancing against it Johnson's personal view of life as a state in which much is to be endured and little to be enjoyed.

Epigraph 'For who can be so tolerant of this monstrous city, who so iron-willed as to contain himself?'
2 *Thales* identified by Sir John Hawkins in his *Life of Johnson* (1787) with Richard Savage. Boswell denied the identification and controversy continues. Thales is the equivalent of Juvenal's Umbricius, who quitted Rome in disgust.

5] Who now resolves 1, 2, *D*

8 *true Briton* perhaps an allusion to the short-lived (1723-4) periodical essay of that name, conducted by the profligate Duke of Wharton, president of the 'Hell-Fire Club', arch-Tory and anti-Walpolean, who was exiled in 1729.

16 *fell* 'Cruel; barbarous; inhuman'; *Dict.* This line is quoted in the *Dict.* to illustrate the word 'prowl'.

18 *female Atheist* unidentified. An example of unbearable loquacity.

19 *Wherry* 'A light boat used on rivers'; *Dict.*

20 Quoted in *Dict.* to illustrate 'Dissipate'.

23 *Eliza* 'Queen Elizabeth born at Greenwich' – Johnson's note in *D.* Johnson was lodging at 6 Castle Street, Greenwich when he composed this poem. See *Letters* I, 10.

29 *Excise* 'A hateful tax levied upon commodities, and adjudged not by the common judges of property, but wretches hired by those to whom excise is paid'; *Dict.* Johnson's antipathy to the excise and its administrators perhaps dates from the indictment of his father by the Lichfield officer in 1725 for 'using ye Trade of a Tanner', to which he had never served an apprenticeship (*Life* I, 36 n).

38 *Science* knowledge generally.

50 The blanks have never been filled: the verse requires monosyllabic names such as Cave or Pope.

51 *Pensions* 'An allowance made to any one without an equivalent. In England it is generally understood to mean pay given to a state hireling for treason to his country'; *Dict.* State pensions were freely granted by Walpole to reward his adherents. When Johnson himself was awarded a pension in 1762 this definition was naturally turned against him, but he never altered it.

53 See 'These leave the Sense, their Learning to display / And those explain the Meaning quite away.' Pope, *Essay on Criticism*, 116-17.

54 'The invasions of the Spaniards were defended in the houses of Parliament' – Johnson's note in *D.* Captain Robert Jenkins's ear had been cut off in a skirmish with the Spaniards in 1731; he produced it before the House of Commons in March 1738 and so provoked the declaration of war on Spain in 1739. Young Pitt was one of the foremost advocates of war, and Johnson here adopts his view that Walpole was an appeaser.

56 Quoted in *Dict.* to illustrate 'Truth'.

58 Government lotteries were frequent throughout the century.

59 *Eunuchs* the *castrati*, Italian male sopranos.

a licens'd D] our silenc'd 1, 2, *W.* 'The licensing act was then lately made – Johnson's note in *D.* The Act was passed in 1737 and Johnson satirized its censorship of the stage in his *A Compleat Vindication of the Licensers of the Stage* (1739).

65 *a groaning . . . giv'n* 2, *D*] the Plunder of a Land is giv'n 1, *W*

72 *Gazetteer* 'The paper which at that time contained apologies for the Court' – Johnson's note in *D*. The *Daily Gazetteer*, founded in 1735, was the organ of Walpole's government.

74 *Clodio W*] *H—y*'s 1, 2, *D*. Clodio implies a lame man. H—y is usually identified with John, Lord Hervey (Pope's 'Sporus' and 'Lord Fanny'), but a more plausible suggestion is that the Rev. John 'Orator' Henley was intended, described by Pope as 'Preacher at once, and Zany of thy age' (*Dunciad*, III 206).

84 *Orgilio* the name implies pompous pride. Compare lines 194–209.

94 *Sewer W*] Shore 1, 2, *D*. The meaning is the same: '*Shore*: A drain; properly *sewer*'; *Dict*.

98 *French* Johnson condemns France and the French just as Juvenal attacked Greece and the Greeks, but by attacking France he also expressed opposition to Walpole's foreign policy of an alliance with France under Cardinal Fleury.

106 Quoted in *Dict*. to illustrate 'Mimick'.

108 *Gibbet* a gallows.

   Wheel breaking the body on a wheel was the French method of capital punishment.

114 *Clap* gonorrhoea. Venereal diseases were often known as the French diseases.

122 *Flattery prevails . . . vain? W*] What their Armies lost, their Cringes gain? 1, 2] And flattery subdues when arms are vain? *D*

124 *supple* 'Flattering; fawning; bending.' *Dict*.

   Parasite 'One that frequents rich tables, and earns his welcome by flattery'; *Dict*.

131 *get W*] gain 1, 2, *D*

143 *Dog-days* From about 3 July to 11 August, when the Dog Star Sirius is in the ascendant, and the weather was supposed to be commonly close and unhealthy.

148 *Exalt each* 1, 2, *D*, *W*] Praise every *orig. MS, but there corrected*

149 *Your . . . your* 1, 2, *D*, *W*] His . . . his *MS*

150] Who dwell on Balbos courtly mien *MS*

   Balbo a stammerer.

161 *snarling Muse* the Muse of Satire.

168 *gen'rous* see *To a Young Lady on her Birthday*, note to line 14 (p. 189).

172 *Main* 'The ocean; the great sea, as distinguished from bays or rivers'; *Dict*.

173 'The Spaniards at this time were said to make claim to some of our American provinces' – Johnson's note in *D*. They claimed Georgia; see notes on lines 54 and 98 above.

174 *Seats* 'Seat: Situation; site'; *Dict*.

187 *tremendous* Johnson is always careful of etymology. Lat. *tremere* to tremble, hence that which causes to tremble.

194 'This was by Hitch a Bookseller justly remarked to be no picture of modern manners, though it might be true of Rome' – Johnson's note in *D*. Charles Hitch was one of the publishers of Johnson's translation of Lobo's *Voyage to Abyssinia* (1753), and of his *Plan of a Dictionary* (1747).

198–9] With servile grief dependent nobles sigh / And swell with tears the prostituted eye. *MS*

198 *servile* 2, *D*] venal 1, *W*

201 *begger'd* 'Beggar: It is more properly written *begger*; but the common orthography is retained, because the derivatives all retain the *a*.' *Dict*.

202 *See! . . . builds*] From every part *MS*
     gaudy 'Showy; splendid; pompous; ostentatiously fine.' *Dict*.

203 *Dome* a building (Lat. *domus*, a house).

204 *Boroughs* electoral districts, some of which, being virtually uninhabited, were 'rotten', since where there were no voters the owner of the land could nominate the Member of Parliament.

208 *Orgilio*] Sejano *MS*. Sejanus was the ambitious favourite of Tiberius, who struck him down ruthlessly when his schemes were discovered.

209 Fire insurance was possible in 1739.

210 *Play*] Court *MS*. Play, in the sense of the Theatre.

211 *Severn* the river represented an approximate boundary with Wales, whither Thales was bound; Trent was the traditional boundary between the north and the south of England. Johnson's birthplace, Lichfield, is not far from the Trent. Both rivers were sufficiently far from London to be virtuous, without being lost in the savage regions beyond.

212 Quoted in *Dict*. to illustrate 'Elegant'.

214 *smiling*] fruitfull *MS*
     Prospects views. 'Sir, let me tell you, the noblest *prospect* which a Scotchman ever sees, is the high road that leads him to England' (*Life* I 425, 6 July 1763).

215 *Dungeons* cellars and basements.

216 *Walks*] shades *MS*

217 *twine*] plan *MS*

218 *grounds*] beds *MS*, 1, 2, *D*; i.e. the cultivated parts of a garden.

220] On ev'ry bush there artless music sings *MS*

224 *at Night*] the streets *MS*

227 *Brambles* 'taken in popular language, for any rough prickly shrub'; *Dict.* The phrase is proverbial for extreme impatience: 'To sit (or stand) on thorns', M. P. Tilley, *Dict. of Proverbs* (1950) T. 239.

228 *frolick*] gamesome *MS*

231 Quoted in *Dict.* to illustrate 'Terror'.

232] youth confused with wine *MS*. See Milton, '... When night / Darkens the Streets, then wander forth the Sons / Of Belial, flown with Insolence and Wine.' *Paradise Lost* I, 500–502.

234 *Afar they mark*] Mark from afar *MS*

    Flambeau 'A lighted torch'; *Dict.* Carried by a nobleman's escort.

240 Quoted in *Dict.* to illustrate 'Rest'.

241 *leaves W*] *plants* 1, 2, *D*] plants his dagger in your slumbring breast *MS*

242 *Scarce ... Fields*] Well may we fear *MS*

    Tyburn the place of public execution in London, near Marble Arch.

243] Lest scarce the exhausted [? fields] should rope supply *MS*

    Fleet here, the Navy, not the old Fleet prison.

245 *Ways and Means* still a Parliamentary term for the methods of raising money.

247 'The nation was discontented at the visits made by the king to Hanover' – note in *W*. George II made frequent visits to Hanover at public expense, supposedly to see his mistresses.

    rig There is a slight verbal play here: '*Riggish* – from *rig*, an old name for a whore'; *Dict.*

251] Sustain'd the ballance, but resign'd the sword *MS*, 1, 2] ... deep'd the sword *D*] ... sheath'd *W*. *deep'd* is a nonce word: there is no reason to suspect *W*.

252 *Spies*] bribes *MS*

    Special Juries of which the members were qualified by substantial properties, tended to be repressive and were frequently employed to obtain convictions for sedition.

257 *Wilds Weald* (or *Wold*) meaning woodland was popularly confused with *wild*, meaning fierce or untamed. Johnson did not confound them in his Dictionary.

262 *Rage* 'Vehemence of mind'; *Dict.* Here specifically *furor poeticus*, or strong inspiration. See *Upon the Feast of St Simon and St Jude*, note to line 56 (p. 189).

TO ELIZA PLUCKING LAUREL IN MR POPE'S GARDENS

Published in the *GM* in August 1738, and signed 'Urbanus'.

Boswell mentioned 'English verses to her [Elizabeth Carter]' without further details. The Latin, of which these lines are a rendering, was, attributed to Johnson by Croker in 1831. Text from *GM. Poems* 105-6; *Works* VI, 61-2. (For the signature 'Urbanus' see below, p. 248.) In July 1738 Mrs Carter wrote to Mrs Underdown, describing a visit made 'this week' to Twickenham where she walked in Pope's garden and saw 'The Lawrels ... interspers'd about with the most agreeable wildness' (see G. I. Hampshire, *Notes and Queries*, June 1972). The visit made a strong impression and may well have been the provocation of Johnson's verses.

7 *candour* 'Sweetness of temper; purity of mind; openness; in-genuity; kindness'; *Dict.*

TO LADY FIREBRACE

Published in the *GM* in September 1738, and mentioned in a letter from Johnson to Cave: 'The verses on Lady Firebrace may be had when you please, for you know that such a subject neither deserves much thought nor requires it.' In the same magazine in 1785 John Nichols supplied the following note: 'This lady was Bridget, 3d daughter of Philip Bacon, esq; of Ipswich, and relict of Philip Evers, esq; of that town. She became the second wife of sir Cordell Firebrace, the last baronet of that name (to whom she brought a fortune of 25,000£), July [actually October] 26, 1737. Being again left a widow in 1759, she was a third time married, April 7, 1762, to William Campbell, esq; uncle to the present Duke of Argyle; and died July 3, 1782.' She was born in 1699 and was in her thirty-ninth year when the poem appeared.

Though Johnson had no immediate connection with Bury St Edmunds or its Assizes, his friend Henry Hervey Aston, son of the Earl of Bristol, certainly did. Johnson met Hervey (who was stationed there as a cornet of dragoons) in Lichfield in 1728; Hervey's marriage to Catherine Aston and reunion with Johnson in London in 1737 cemented their friendship, which continued until Hervey's death.

From *GM. Poems* 106-7; *Works* VI, 62.

Title] *Bury* Bury St Edmunds.
2 *B—n* W. Bryan (see A. L. Reade, *Johnsonian Gleanings*, VI (1933), pp. 154-6).

TO MISS — ON HER PLAYING UPON THE HARPSICHORD

This is one of a group of poems which survive in a transcription made for Henry Hervey Aston (see pp. 16, 201). The others are: 'Net-work Purse' (p. 70), 'Stella in Mourning' (p. 71) and 'The Winter's Walk' (p. 73). The period of Johnson's greatest intimacy with Hervey was from 1737 to 1743, and these poems are arbitrarily placed here in the 1738-9 group. The references to 'Stella', though mere poetic fiction, provide a community of allusion with other poems of the period.

First printed in Dodsley's *Museum* in November 1747, the Hervey transcript derives from this version. Revised again by Johnson for inclusion in Anna Williams's *Miscellanies* (1766). *Poems* 120-21; *Works* VI, 77-8.

Title] To the Hon. Miss Carpenter *Museum*

5-6   Quoted in *Dict.* as 'Anon', to illustrate 'Modulate'.

7   *hour*] Bower *Mus.*

13   *Deceitful Hope*   Hope is elsewhere 'groundless' (*Winter's Walk* 13, p. 73) and 'delusive' (Motto of *Rambler* 67, p. 97, and *Death of Levet* 1, p. 139), though *Rambler* 203 (25 February 1752) describes it as 'the chief blessing of man.'

14   *flutter*] flatter *Mus.*

18   *Chains to hold*] Tortures for *Mus.*

21   *Could*] Wou'd *Mus.*

29-32   Compare Pope: 'Hence diff'ring Passions more or less in- flame, / As strong, or weak, the Organs of the Frame; / And hence one Master Passion in the breast, / Like Aaron's Serpent, swallows up the rest.' (*Essay on Man*, ii. 119-22).

31-2   Quoted in *Dict.* and attributed to 'Johnson', to illustrate 'Strife'.

TO MISS — ON HER GIVING THE AUTHOR A GOLD AND SILK NET-WORK PURSE

Published in the *GM* in May 1747 and signed *** (see p. 206, below), but also among the earlier Hervey transcripts (see above).

The Hervey transcript (*H*) is based on the *GM* version, which was finally revised by Johnson for inclusion in Anna Williams's *Miscellanies* (1766). *Poems* 119; *Works* VI, 82.

Title] Miss Carpenter *H*

2 *thy*] the *GM*
7 *Spread out by me*] Spread for their prey *GM, H*
8 *catch*] snare *GM, H*
10 *glitt'ring vagrants*   coins.

STELLA IN MOURNING

Published in the *GM* in May 1747 and signed ******* (see p. 206, below), but also present in the Hervey transcripts (see p. 202, above).

Text from *GM*, with slight variant in Hervey transcript (*H*). *Poems* 122; *Works* IV, 82–3.

5 *Fate! snatch*] Fate Snatch'd *H*

AN EVENING ODE

Published in the *GM* in January 1750. Arbitrarily associated here with the Hervey–Stella poems of 1738–9.

All versions derive from the *GM*, January 1750, including that in *Scots Magazine*, September 1754, addressed to Delia. Attributed to Johnson in Pearch's *Collection* (1770), but doubted by both *Poems* 389–90 and *Works* VI, 369.

1 *purple* 'Red tinctured with blue. . . . In poetry, red'; *Dict.*
2 *grateful* 'Pleasing; acceptable; delightful; delicious'; *Dict.*
7 *chequer'd* 'Variegated or diversified, in the manner of a chessboard, with alternate colours, or with darker and brighter parts'; *Dict.*
14 *lambent* 'Playing about; gliding over without harm'; *Dict.*

THE VANITY OF WEALTH

Published in the *GM* in February 1750, but arbitrarily associated here with the Hervey–Stella poems of 1738–9. Compare Horace *Odes* II xviii.

From the *GM*, February 1750. Attributed to Johnson in Pearch's *Collection* (1770), but doubted by both *Poems* 391–2 and *Works* VI, 370–71.

8 *the mortal hour*   the hour of death.
15 *Science* 'Any art or species of knowledge'; *Dict.*
28 *dig the mine*   for gold.

THE WINTER'S WALK

Published in the *GM* in May 1747 and signed ******* (see p. 206, below), and present in the Hervey transcripts.

From *GM*, May 1747, which is the foundation of the Hervey transcript (*H*). A revised version was published in F. Fawkes and W. Woty (eds.), *The Poetical Calendar*, 1763 (*P*). *Poems* 122–4; *Works* VI, 83–4.

2 *prospects* views. See note on line 214 of *London* (p. 199, above).
11 *Scarce ... fire* Love, frightened by the appearance of Winter, can hardly keep his fire burning (i.e. maintain his ardour).
20 *And screen ... life P*] And hide me from the sight of life *GM*, *H*] For there are all the Joys of Life *H* (alternative). Boswell considered that the *GM* version was more characteristic of Johnson, for 'A horrour at life in general is more consonant with Johnson's habitual gloomy cast of thought' (*Life* I, 179–80, 1747). Croker pointed out that 'Johnson's habitual horror was not of *life* but of *death*'.

POST-GENITIS

This supposed inscription on a stone said to be discovered in Norfolk forms the basis of Johnson's early political piece: *Marmor Norfolciense* (*The Norfolk Marble*), published in April 1739. The supposed prophecy is translated and ironically explained in an attack on Walpole's policies.

From: *Marmor Norfolciense: or, an Essay on an Ancient Prophetical Inscription, in Monkish Rhyme, Lately Discover'd near Lynn in Norfolk* (1739). The Latin is the alleged inscription, the English is Johnson's own translation of it. A copy in Manchester Central Library corrects, in Johnson's own handwriting, the erroneous 'Calceatos' (line 32). *Poems* 108–11; *Works* VI, 64–7.

TO POSTERITY

6 *Ground* the shore.
7 *scarlet Reptiles* red-coats; the soldiers of the standing or professional army. The Tory view was that a regular army was a Whiggish (and Walpolean) device to enslave the people, for such an army was responsible directly to the Crown and to the party in power, and not to the people and Parliament.
16 *change their Kings* Johnson's fear of civil war and revolution coloured much of his political thinking (see D. J. Greene, *The Politics of Samuel Johnson*, 1960, pp. 26–34).
17 *Bear* Russia.
   Moon Turkey.
18 *Lilies* France.
19 *Lyon* Britain.

21 *inviolable Bloom* the lily, emblem of purity. Peace with France was an important factor in Walpole's policy; see *London*, note to line 98 (p. 198).

23 *tortur'd Sons* sufferers, like Captain Jenkins, from the cruelties of the Spaniards. See *London*, note to line 54.

24 *lies melting . . . Embrace* see *London*, note to line 247.

25 *Horse* the White Horse, emblem of the House of Hanover.

PROLOGUE TO GARRICK'S *Lethe*

The unique manuscript copy bears a note in Garrick's handwriting: 'Prologue by Mr Sam: Johnson for *Lethe* when first it was wrote for Drury Lane at Giffard's Benefit.' Henry Giffard's benefit night was 15 April 1740.

Garrick was the author of *Lethe*, though in 1740 he was working in London in partnership with his brother Peter in the wine trade. He made his stage début the following year at Ipswich in Giffard's touring company. Text from the unique copy in the Folger Shakespeare Library. *Works* VI, 67.

3 *Tear*] fear *Works*

4 *Bard* poet; here Garrick himself.

9 *the indignant*] the idignant *MS*] the poignant *Works*

10 *Catcall* 'A squeaking instrument used in the playhouse to condemn plays'; *Dict.*

14 *mantling* blushing; '*Mantle*: To ferment; to be in sprightly agitation'; *Dict.*

AN EPITAPH ON CLAÚDY PHILLIPS

First published in the *GM* in September 1740. Phillips was an itinerant Welsh violinist who, despite some success on a tour of Europe, died in poverty in 1732. He is buried in St Peter's, Wolverhampton.

The signature 'G' in the *GM* of September 1740 has led some to attribute the lines to Garrick, but there is no doubt of Johnson's authorship. It was revised for inclusion in Anna Williams's *Miscellanies* (1766). All other versions, and they are numerous, derive from these two authorities. *Poems* 111–13; *Works* IV, 68–9.

Though Johnson was occasionally contemptuous of music, he wrote: 'The delight which Music affords seems to be one of the first attainments of rational nature; wherever there is humanity, there is modulated sound' (Burney's *Commemoration of Handel*, 1785). William Seward recorded his saying that music 'was the only sensual pleasure without vice'.

Title] An Epitaph upon the celebrated Claudy Philips (the name is variously spelt), Musician, who died very poor. *GM*

4 *Find here*] Here find *GM*

A TRANSLATION OF THE LATIN EPITAPH ON
SIR THOMAS HANMER

This is the first of a group of six poems published in the *GM* in May 1747, each signed ***. The attribution of all six to Johnson is confirmed by John Ryland, nephew of John Hawkesworth, at that time editor of the poetry section of the magazine (see *The Times Literary Supplement*, 11 September 1937, p. 656). The poems are: 1. *Epitaph on Hanmer*, 2. *To Miss — . . . Net-Work Purse* (p. 70, above), 3. *Stella in Mourning* (p. 71, above), 4. *The Winter's Walk* (p. 73, above), 5. *An Ode* (p. 78, above) and 6. *To Lyce* (p. 79, above). The association with Henry Hervey (p. 202, above) and the dating of some of these pieces to 1738-9 is not nullified by their publication together in 1747, since Hervey seems to have adapted the poems to his own use, and Johnson was always willing to help his friends with occasional pieces (see *A Sprig of Myrtle*, p. 190, above). The authenticity of these poems is challenged by A. Sherbo, 'Samuel Johnson and certain poems in the May 1747 *Gentleman's Magazine*', *Review of English Studies*, XVII (1966).

This poem is based on a Latin epitaph by Robert Freind, who had been Hanmer's tutor, but it is not a translation, and scarcely even a 'paraphrase', a description added to the title on the first appearance of the poem in the *GM*.

The version in the May 1747 *GM* was lightly revised for inclusion in Anna Williams's *Miscellanies* (1766). *Poems* 116-18; *Works* VI, 80-82.

Title] . . . Or rather a Paraphrase *GM*
1-2 *these walls* the original Latin epitaph is in Hanmer Church, Flintshire.
   at] on *GM*
9 *endanger'd* by Jacobitism, France and the Netherlands.
16 *refulgent* 'Bright; shining; glittering; splendid'; *Dict.*
31 *lur'd*] turn'd *GM*
37 *letter'd ease* the editing of Shakespeare, published as the 'Oxford' edition in 1744, which was censured by Johnson in his *Miscellaneous Observations on Macbeth* in 1745, though Hanmer was more kindly dealt with in the *Preface* to Johnson's own edition of Shakespeare in 1765.

AN ODE

Published in the *GM* in May 1747 and signed *** (see p. 206, above).
Text from the *GM*, May 1747. *Poems* 124–6; *Works* VI, 84–6.

7–8 Quoted in *Dict.* as 'Anonymous' to illustrate 'Vegetation'.
10 *Arthritic tyranny* 'The Author being ill of the Gout'; note in
GM. Johnson did not suffer from gout until late in life. Boswell asks:
'May not this, however, be a poetical fiction? Why may not a poet
suppose himself to have the gout, as well as suppose himself to be in
love . . . ?' (*Life* I, 179 '1747').
16 — the place is presumably a poetic fiction, though the next
stanza shows that it is the poet's birthplace; although 'Lichfield' is
metrically possible, *humble turrets* have no application.
22 *father* If Johnson's, notice that Michael Johnson is similarly
celebrated as a friendly instructor in *In Rivum a Mola Stoana* (p. 154).
27 *use of life* a recurrent preoccupation for Johnson was the 'Choice
of Life' (*Rasselas*), or the preparation of some comprehensive system
by which life could safely be regulated. His diaries abound with reso-
lutions and abortive programmes of self-reform.
32 *retreat* Johnson was generally contemptuous of escapists from
the struggles of life. But see *Irene* Prologue, note to line 31 (p. 193).

TO LYCE, AN ELDERLY LADY

Published in the *GM* in May 1747 and signed *** (see p. 206, above).
Because the poem is a free rendering of Horace; *Odes* IV xiii, it has
been suggested that it was originally a schoolboy exercise, but John-
son translated Horace at several periods of his life (see p. 229, below).
Text from the *GM*, May 1747. *Poems* 126–7; *Works* VI, 86–7.

A SONG

Published in the *GM* in June 1747.
Text from the *GM*, June 1747. Attributed to Johnson in Pearch's
Collection (1770). Doubted by both *Poems* 388, and *Works* VI, 367–8.
7 *India's shore* precious stones were supposed to be cast up on the
coasts of India.
8 *Peru's unbounded store* the gold of the Incas.

PROLOGUE SPOKEN BY MR GARRICK

Drury Lane Theatre was opened under Garrick's management on
15 September 1747. Of his composition, Johnson said: 'The whole

... was composed before I threw a single couplet on paper ... I did not afterwards change more than a word in it, and that was done at the remonstrance of Garrick. I did not think his criticism just, but it was necessary he should be satisfied with what he was to utter.'

The Prologue, and the Epilogue (which was by Garrick), spoken on the occasion, were published in a quarto pamphlet which is the prime authority for the text. *Poems* 49-53; *Works* VI, 87-90.

6 Bennet Langton suggested that Johnson was, in this line, echoing Shakespeare's '— She will outstrip all praise / And make it halt behind her' (*Tempest* IV, i 10-11). *Life* IV 25, '1780'.

9 *Johnson* Ben Jonson's name was often so spelt.

12 *essay'd*] assail'd *Dodsley's Collection*, 1748.

16 The Pharaohs were supposed entombed in the famous Pyramids.

17 In the reign of Charles II, the so-called 'Restoration' theatre was notoriously licentious.

23-4 Quoted in *Dict.* to illustrate 'Pimp'.

36 *Faustus* A popular subject for the farces which were commonly played as after-pieces, or 'second-features'.

48 See Boethius III i 10 (p. 123, above).

50 *Bubbles* not only delusory playthings, but also financial gambles.

59 *chase* here, chase away.

61 Quoted in *Dict.* as 'Anon.' to illustrate 'Scenick'.

THE VANITY OF HUMAN WISHES

The first edition was published on 9 January 1749. Johnson's habit of mental composition makes it difficult to trace the genesis of his work, but the manuscript of an earlier version probably dates from 1748. It bears out Johnson's own statements on his method of composition: 'I have generally had them in my mind, perhaps fifty at a time, walking up and down in my room; and then I have written them down, and often from laziness, have written only half lines. I have written a hundred lines in a day. I remember I wrote a hundred lines of *The Vanity of Human Wishes* in a day.' He also told George Steevens: 'I wrote the first seventy lines ... in the course of one morning, in that small house beyond the church at Hampstead.'

From the first edition of 1749 (*1*), revised for inclusion in Dodsley's *Collection*, 1755 (*D*). A copy, now lost, of the 1749 edition with manuscript alterations by Johnson, was followed in Johnson's *Works*, 1787 (*W*). The alterations were copied out by James Boswell, Jr, into his own copy of Johnson's *Poetical Works* (1789), which is now in the

National Library of Australia. The complete manuscript of the whole poem in a slightly earlier version is in the Hyde Collection; and a transcript of it is printed in Appendix 3. *Poems* 25-48; *Works* VI, 90-109.

The embittered frustration of Juvenal, exiled by Domitian, whose own hatreds provide the motive and the matter of his satires, finds no parallel in Johnson's Imitations. Where the model indulges a destructive rage against the evils Juvenal had known, Johnson (no less outraged by wrong) exhibits the endurance of one who has come to terms with the deeper concerns of human life. Characteristically he expresses that profound tolerance in Christian terms which transcend the narrow aspiration for 'mens sana in corpore sano' of Juvenal.

10 *airy* Wanting reality; having no steady foundation in truth or nature; vain; trifling': *Dict.*

15-16 Suffering is attendant on every wish, every gift, etc.

30 *madded* from *to mad*, meaning 'To be mad; to be furious'; *Dict.*

31 *Statutes* fiscal laws, or taxation.

34 *wealthy*] bonny *1*. An allusion, later dropped, to the Scots Jacobite lords: the Earls of Cromartie and Kilmarnock, and Lords Balmerino and Lovat. Cromartie was pardoned; the rest were executed. Despite Lovat's reprehensible character, Johnson disapproved of the executions.

36 *hover*] clang *1* (Clang: 'Scream'; *Dict.*).

41 *Now W*] New *1*, D

42 *Brake* 'A thicket of brambles or thorns'; *Dict.*

45 *one*] the *1*. Despite this, mankind clamours for Gain and Grandeur and every breeze carries the sound of their cries.

63 *descry 1, W*] decry D

72 *canvass* 'To sift or examine'; *Dict.*

73 See Swift's *To Doctor D—l—y, on the Libels writ against Him*, 1730, line 93: 'croud about Preferment's Gate.' (Parallel pointed out in *Review of English Studies* XI (1960), 413.)

78 Quoted in *Dict.* to illustrate 'Dog'.

84 *Palladium* a celebrated statue of Pallas, the talisman and safeguard of the city of Troy.

97 *Libels* Lat. *libellus*, a little book, hence a pamphlet (see *The Young Author*, note on line 25, p. 790 above); the common vehicle of controversy.

Septennial Parliaments were elected every seven years from 1716 until 1910. 'At the end of every seven years comes the Saturnalian season, when the freemen of Great Britain may please themselves with the choice of their representatives' (Johnson, *The Patriot*, 1774, para. 2). See also *Life* II, 73, 30 September 1769.

Ale the common means for persuading voters. See Hogarth's caricatures of the progress of an election, especially 'Canvassing for votes' (in the British Museum).

97-8 Quoted in *Dict.* as 'Anon.' to illustrate 'Septennial'.

99 *full-blown* in full bloom, as a flower; 'blown' derives from *bloom*, and not from *blow* (to move the air).

99 ff See Shakespeare's representation of Wolsey in *Henry VIII*, II ii and III ii.

103-4 Present in *1* and *W*, not in *D*.

113 *At once is lost* D] Now drops at once *1*, *W*

115 Quoted in *Dict.* as 'Anon.' to illustrate 'Luxurious'.

118 *Monastic Rest* Wolsey, after his fall from grace, retired to Cawood, the old palace of the Archbishops of York, before he was finally arrested in 1530. Cawood was not a monastery.

120 See Shakespeare, *Henry VIII*, III ii, 'O, how wretched / Is that poor man that hangs on Princes' favours.'

124 *The wisest Justice*] The richest Landlord *1*

   Trent see *London*, note on line 211 (p. 199, above).

125 *near the Steeps*] by the Steps *1*

   Steeps precipices.

129 *Knife* In *Rambler* 168 Johnson deprecated the use of this word in *Macbeth*: 'We do not immediately conceive that any crime of importance is to be committed with a *Knife*.'

135ff Compare with *The Young Author* (p. 50, above), and Burton, *Anatomy of Melancholy*, I ii 3 xv.

136 *Enthusiast* a pejorative term. 'One of hot imagination, or violent passions'; *Dict.* A fanatic, or 'extremist'.

137 *Through all his Veins* D] Resistless burns *1*, *W*

138 *Burns Johnson's MS correction given to Boswell* (Bodleian)] Caught *1*, *W*] Spreads *D*

Boswell pointed out the repetition of 'spread' (139) and said: 'I thought this alteration not only cured the fault, but was more poetical, as it might carry an allusion to the shirt by which Hercules was inflamed' (*Life*, III 357-8, 19 May 1778). Nessus's shirt, soaked in his own poisoned blood, was donned by Hercules, who died as a result.

139 *Dome* a building (Lat. *domus*, a house).

140 *Bacon's Mansion* 'There is a tradition, that the study of friar Bacon, built in an arch over the bridge, will fall, when a man greater than Bacon shall pass under it'; note in *D*. Roger Bacon's study was the gatehouse of Grandpoint, or Folly Bridge, in Oxford.

143   *gen'rous*   see *To a Young Lady on her Birthday*, note to line 14 (p. 189, above).

144   *Science*   all learning and knowledge.

148   Quoted in *Dict.* to illustrate 'Relax'.

150   ] And Sloth's bland Opiates shed their Fumes in vain *1*

Sloth   one of the Seven Deadly Sins. Johnson was always alert to his indulgence in it. In his Diary for October 1729 he noted: 'Desidiae valedixi . . .' (I bade farewell to Sloth . . .), and thereafter he repeatedly resolved to 'rise early' and to avoid 'idleness' and 'intemperate sleep'. On 5 September 1784, three months before his death, he again resolved 'to shun idleness'.

154   *Melancholy*   literally, the black bile, once thought to produce the condition. 'A gloomy, pensive, discontented temper'; *Dict.* Today we should call it 'depression'.

158   *Letters*] Learning *1*, *W*

160   *Patron*] Garret *1*. The change to 'Patron' was made about the time of the publication of the *Dictionary* in 1755, shortly after Johnson had repudiated Chesterfield's patronage. '*Patron*: Commonly a wretch who supports with insolence, and is paid with flattery'; *Dict.*

161–2   Quoted in *Dict.* to illustrate 'Just'.

162   *tardy Bust*   erected in memory of Milton (d. 1674) in Westminster Abbey, in 1737.

165   *last*] lost *1*

167   *'scapes W*] 'scap'd *1*] 'scape *D*; *'scapes* is odd in requiring 'the Vulgar' to be singular, but it is supported by James Boswell Jr's transcription of Johnson's corrections.

171   *Parts*   'Qualities; powers; faculties, or accomplishments'; *Dict.*

177   *the Gazette*   here, any newspaper; but see *London*, note to line 72 (p. 198, above).

179   *the rapid Greek*   Alexander the Great.

182   *Danube or the Rhine*   alluding to the campaigns of John Churchill, Duke of Marlborough, and to the war of 1743–8 (see p. 244).

187   *Wreaths*   here triumphal, not funeral.

188   *Debt*   The National Debt, in 1747, was computed at £69½ million. Johnson viewed it with more equanimity later when he told Dr Maxwell that 'It was an idle dream to suppose that the country could sink under it' (*Life* II 127, '1770').

192   *Swedish Charles*   Charles XII of Sweden (see below, p. 240). See Johnson's *Adventurer* 99 (16 October 1753), 'The last royal projectors with whom the world has been troubled, were Charles of Sweden and the Czar of Muscovy . . .' (para. 10).

195   *Fear*] Force *1*

195–6   Quoted in *Dict.* to illustrate 'Lord'.

196   Quoted in *Dict.* to illustrate 'Unconquered'.

200   Frederick IV of Denmark capitulated in 1700, and Augustus II of Poland abdicated in 1706.

201   Quoted in *Dict.* to illustrate 'Peace'.

203   *Gothic* here, Swedish, though then (as now) common for Teutonic.

204   *be*] is *1*

205   Quoted in *Dict.* to illustrate 'March'.

208   'General Winter' is popularly said to be the greatest commander in the Russian armies.

209   *nor . . . nor 1, W*] not . . . and *D*

214   *Ladies interpose* perhaps an allusion to Catherine, Empress of Peter the Great, who influenced his conduct of the war against Charles XII.

220   Charles XII was killed at the siege of Frederikshald in 1718, supposedly by a stray shot from his own forces.

222   *point* the *MS* (see p. 174) reads 'paint', which certainly balances 'adorn', but every printed text has 'point'. In the *Life of Shenstone*, para. 10, is the phrase 'point his prospects'. The usage is not exemplified in *Dict.* Both may be misreadings of 'paint'.

224   *Persia's Tyrant* Xerxes I (see below, p. 249).

   Bavaria's Lord Charles Albert, Elector of Bavaria (see p. 249).

229   *Myriads* Gk. μυρίος, countless.

232   Xerxes' bridge of boats across the Hellespont was wrecked by storms, and on his return he ordered chains to be thrown into the sea and the waves to be whipped in punishment. This action of Xerxes is again mentioned in Johnson's *Adventurer* 137 (26 February 1754), '. . . to call upon mankind to correct their manners, is, like Xerxes, to scourge the wind or shackle the torrent' (para. 6), and in his 'Preface' to his *Dictionary* (1755), '. . . sounds are too volatile and subtile for legal restraints; and to enchain syllables, and to lash the wind, are equally the undertakings of pride, unwilling to measure its desires by its strength' (para. 85).

234   *spreading God* the Hydra

236   *gaudy* 'Showy; splendid; pompous; ostentatiously fine'; *Dict.*

237   See note to line 232, above.

239–40   According to Mrs Thrale, Johnson said that this was his favourite couplet from all his writings.

241   *bold Bavarian* again, Charles Albert, Elector of Bavaria (see below, p. 241).

245   *Austria* Maria Theresa (see below, p. 244).

249 *Croatian* Austrian colonists of Croatia formed irregular troops owing allegiance to the rulers of Austria. They had been a byword for savagery even earlier, see Dryden: 'And grin and whet like a Croatian band' (*The Medal*, line 240).

Hussar strictly a Hungarian light cavalryman, but originally a free-booter, from Lat. *cursus*, a raid, hence *cursarius*, a raider, and so also 'Corsair', a pirate.

250 *With W*] And *1*, D

255ff On old age, see also Johnson's *Rambler*, nos. 41, 50, 69.

266 *Luxury* 'Voluptuousness; addictedness to pleasure'; *Dict.*

268 *Diffuse W*] And yield *1*, D

Lenitives 'Any thing medicinally applied to ease pain'; *Dict.*

279 *last* latest, most recent.

283 *his Joints*] each Joint *1*

291 *Prime* 'The spring of life; the height of health, strength or beauty'; *Dict.*

291–8 Mrs Piozzi reported that Johnson had his own mother in mind in writing this passage; Sarah Johnson died at the age of ninety in January 1759.

293 *with W*] in *1*, D

298 *shall W*] could *1*, D

304 Quoted in *Dict.* to illustrate 'Lacerate'.

308 Compare *Rambler* 207 (10 March 1752), entitled, 'The Folly of continuing too long upon the Stage'.

312 *set ... in* 'To put in a way to begin'; *Dict.*; i.e. who set out in.

313 *Lydia's Monarch* Croesus

330–31] An envious Breast with certain Mischief glows, / And Slaves, the Maxim tells, are always Foes. *1*

332 *batters ... mines* both refer to methods of attacking a besieged town.

338 Quoted in *Dict.* to illustrate 'Private'.

340 *To ... to W*] By ... by *1*, D

341 *Here 1, W*] Now D

345 *sedate* unruffled, calm.

346 *darkling* in the dark; 'a word merely poetical'; *Dict.*

Roll ... Torrent] Swim ... Current *1*. See Motto of *Rambler* 105 (p. 100, above).

348 *invoke W*] attempt *1*, D

357 *Yet when ... fires*] Yet with ... prest *1*

358 *And ... to the Skies aspires*] When ... fills thy glowing Breast *1*

361 *which ... fill* The sense of this particularly elliptical phrase

seems to be: which all human love cannot equal. Literally, which all mankind can hardly fill up the measure of.

362   Quoted in *Dict.* to illustrate 'Transmute'.

364   *Counts*] Thinks *1*

A NEW PROLOGUE SPOKEN AT THE REPRESENTATION OF *Comus*

Published as 'A New Prologue spoken by Mr Garrick, Thursday April 5, 1750. At the Representation of *Comus*, for the Benefit of Mrs Elizabeth Foster, Milton's Grand-Daughter, and only surviving Descendant.'

Mrs Foster was the youngest daughter of Deborah, Milton's youngest daughter. She outlived her children and died in 1754.

From the folio edition, 1750. *Poems* 53-8; *Works* VI, 239-41.

4   *Pensions*   see *London*, note to line 51 (p. 197, above).

Augustan   the rule of Augustus Caesar was notable for literature and the patronage of authors such as Horace and Virgil. The name was applied especially by the writers of the reign of Queen Anne (1702-14) to themselves, and hence was often used to describe authors such as Addison, Pope, Swift and their contemporaries.

23   *Bust*   printed as 'Dust', but corrected by hand in most copies.

24   *circulating Gold*   commemorative medals.

28   Compare with '. . . my celestial patroness, who deigns / Her nightly visitation unimplored, / And dictates to me slumbering; or inspires / Easy my unpremediated verse . . .'; *Paradise Lost* IX, 21-4; and: 'He composed much of his poem in the night and morning, I suppose before his mind was disturbed with common business; and . . . he poured out with great fluency his *unpremeditated verse*.' Johnson's *Life of Milton*, para. 126. Johnson himself composed poetry in this way (see above, p. 208).

TRANSLATIONS OF THE MOTTOES AND QUOTATIONS IN THE *Rambler*

The *Rambler* was published bi-weekly from 20 March 1750 until 14 March 1752, in 208 twopenny numbers. Each number carried a motto, some of which had been used in preliminary newspaper advertisements indicating, in brief, what would be the tenor of the essays. It is possible that some of the mottoes were decided even before the essays were written, so that they may represent the germ from which the complete essay was to grow.

The mottoes and quotations were not at first translated. The original issues of the *Rambler* were reprinted and published in penny numbers in Edinburgh by James Elphinston, who provided translations of his own: these seem to have stimulated Johnson to supply translations when title leaves and tables of contents were issued for the original numbers in 1753, and they were also included in the second London edition of the *Rambler* in six volumes, which appeared in 1752.

The author most frequently quarried for mottoes is Horace (70), with Juvenal second (31); Martial and Ovid supplied 22 each, and Virgil 12. Johnson's translations are not as numerous as the passages quoted, for he made use of accessible translations. He was also assisted by the obscure Mr Francis Lewis (who 'lived in London, and hung loose upon society'). The translations provided by Johnson show a more even distribution: Ovid 10, Horace and Juvenal 8 each, Virgil 6, and 12 from Greek authors.

The 1752 edition of the *Rambler* is the authoritative text, but a few revisions and additions were introduced into the fourth edition in 1754. *Poems* 127-41; *Works* VI, 241-55.

The numbers before the notes refer to the numbers of the *Rambler*.

6 See Johnson's other translation from Boethius III, metre vi, 19-20 (p. 125).

7 *darkling* See note on *Vanity* 346 (p. 213, above).

45 see further translations from *Medea* (pp. 137-8).

65 *counsel* 1754] council 1750, 1752

67 The passage from Euripides replaces, in 1752, a quotation from the Greek Anthology in the original number. Compare also *Vanity* 9-10 (p. 83, above).

105 Compare with *Vanity* 345-6 (pp. 91-2, above), and motto of *Adventurer* 118 (p. 120, above).

130 Attributed by Johnson to 'Elphinston', but his version is so extensive a revision of Elphinston's translation as to amount to a new one. Elphinston rendered the passage thus:

> No mist so blights the vernal meads,
> When summer's sultry heat succeeds,
> As one fell moment blasts the blow
> That gave the tender cheek to glow.
> Some beauty's snatch'd each day, each hour;
> For beauty is a fleeting flow'r:
> Then who that's wise, will e'er confide
> In such a frail, so poor a pride?
> (*Poems* 382; *Works* VI, 360.)

153 Compare *Vanity* 79 (p. 84, above).

168 Taken from Rowe's translation, changing 'bark' into 'grove'.
183 Compare with motto for *Adventurer* 45 (p. 115, above).
199 Added in 1754 instead of a translation by F. Lewis.
208 Added in 1754 instead of a translation of Diogenes Laertius by F. Lewis.

THE ANT

First published in Anna Williams's *Miscellanies* (1766), but the now untraced manuscript is reported as bearing the date 14 April 1752. The poem is a paraphrase of the passage cited in the Book of Proverbs:

Go to the ant, thou sluggard; consider her ways, and be wise:
Which having no guide, overseer, or ruler,
Provideth her meat in the summer, and gathereth her food in the harvest.
How long wilt thou sleep, O sluggard? When wilt thou arise out of thy sleep?
Yet a little sleep, a little slumber, a little folding of the hands to sleep;
So shall thy poverty come as one that travelleth, and thy want as an armed man.

Johnson's *Works*, 1787 (*W*), followed 'the original in Dr Johnson's own handwriting' and differs in a few readings from the version in Anna Williams's *Miscellanies* (1766). As the only known manuscript was dated 1752 it presumably exhibited an early version which was revised for 1766. *Poems* 151–2; *Works* VI, 263–4.

Title] Paraphrase of Proverbs, Chap. VI. verses 6, 7, 8, 9, 10, 11.
    'Go to the Ant thou Sluggard' *W*
8 *gleans*] crops *W*
9 *useless* 'Answering no purpose; having no end'; *Dict*. One of Johnson's strongly condemnatory words. His own propensity to idleness made him the more vehement in his attacks on Sloth.
10 *Dissolve*] Unnerve *W*
11 *artful* produced by art or skill: a word of approval.
12 *soft* 'Effeminate; viciously nice'; *Dict*.

TRANSLATIONS OF THE MOTTOES AND QUOTATIONS IN THE *Adventurer*

Published with the tables of contents and the title leaves for the bound volumes of the collected bi-weekly numbers of the *Adventurer* (1752–4).
    The 140 numbers of the *Adventurer*, published between Tuesday 7 November 1752 and Saturday 9 March 1754, were edited by John

Hawkesworth. The periodical was modelled on the *Rambler*. Johnson contributed twenty-nine of the essays (see W. J. Bate, J. M. Bullitt and L. F. Powell (eds.), *The Idler and The Adventurer, Yale Edition of Johnson's Works*, vol. 2, 1963).

According to Thomas Percy, Johnson was largely responsible for the selection of the mottoes; the translations are less easily attributed to him, except on the analogy of the unsigned translations in the *Rambler*. (See a full discussion by A. Sherbo, 'Translation of the Mottos and Quotations in the *Adventurer*', in his *Samuel Johnson, Editor of Shakespeare*, 1956.) Despite the evidence that Joseph Warton (who contributed over the signature 'Z') disapproved of the translations, those which are to be found in Warton's papers have not here been attributed to Johnson. Warton was capable of making his own translations; Hawkesworth was not.

Of the 140 mottoes, 45 came from Horace, 30 from Virgil, 18 from Juvenal and 13 from Ovid; the rest are from a variety of sources, not all of which are in verse. Occasionally the same original was used in the *Rambler*.

Although the second edition of the *Adventurer* (1754) was revised, no changes were made in the mottoes and quotations. The text is therefore taken from the original numbers. *Works* VI, 371–86.

The numbers before the notes refer to the numbers of the *Adventurer*.

Title-page Johnson applied the closing phrase in Virgil to the Earl of Chesterfield (*Life* II, 329; 28 March 1775).

14 Compare with *Rambler* 81 (p. 98, above).

18 Used again as the motto for the collected edition of the *Idler* (1761).

19 Boswell alluded to this passage as being most characteristic of Johnson (*Life* III, 229; 31 March 1778).

33 Compare with no. 135 (p. 121).

34 Not rendered in *Vanity*, but compare lines 99–120 and 251–4 (pp. 85 and 89, above).

45 See *Rambler* 183 (p. 107, above).

50 *verum*] vera *in all editions, incorrectly*

54 *Sensim*] Rursus *in modern editions*

58 On his deathbed Johnson quoted the second line to his old friend Bennet Langton. Tibullus' mistress was Delia, not Cynthia, who was celebrated by Propertius; both poets (together with Catullus) were commonly collected together in a single volume. In the second piece, Ovid is himself quoting from Tibullus.

70 Boswell applied Horace's lines to the House of Lords (*Life* III, 204; 23 September 1777).

74 Used also as the motto for *Rambler* 95 (21 February 1751). When Langton doubted the propriety of the phrase 'sapientiæ consultus', Johnson pointed out that 'consultus' was, though an adjective, here used as a noun, 'So we have *Juris consultus*, a consult in law' (*Life* III, 280; 13 April 1778).

77 In 1754 the second line was corrected to read 'monet', but the translation was unchanged.

82 Johnson alluded to this line in the celebrated letter to Lord Chesterfield (7 February 1755), where he wrote, 'The Shepherd in Virgil grew at last acquainted with Love, and found him a Native of the Rocks'.

92 This, and the following eleven lines in Horace's *Epistle*, formed the motto on the title-page of Johnson's *Dictionary*.

104 Not rendered in *Vanity*.

118 Compare with *Rambler* 105 (p. 100, above), and *Vanity* 345-6 (pp. 91-2, above).

132 Compare with Milton: 'And through the palpable obscure find out / His uncouth way'; *Paradise Lost* II, 406.

135 See no. 33. At first both versions were identical, but in the second edition (1754), 'Within' was changed to 'Beneath'.

TRANSLATIONS FROM BOETHIUS:
DE CONSOLATIONE PHILOSOPHIÆ

The translations were undertaken 'about the year 1765' according to Mrs Thrale, who published them in her edition of Johnson's *Letters* in 1788. She and Johnson collaborated on the following portions and then dropped the venture. Mrs Thrale's lines are printed in italics.

Text from Mrs Thrale's original manuscripts, now in the John Rylands Library, Manchester; the manuscript of III 3 formerly belonged to Lord Harmsworth. The readings have been modified by versions published in Mrs Piozzi's edition of Johnson's *Letters* (1788). Roman numerals refer to numbers of books, arabic to numbers of metres. *Poems* 143-50; *Works* VI, 257-63.

II **2, 8** *hunger of the mind* a recurrent theme in Johnson's writings is the impulse of intellectual desire (see W. J. Bate, *The Achievement of Samuel Johnson*, 1955, ch. 2, and *Rasselas* xxxii).

III **6, 19-20** Compare with *Rambler* 6 (p. 93, above).

III **12** Mrs Thrale translated the whole of 12, and Johnson corrected her version, so preserving the earlier forms of his own lines.

5 *Moan* 'Lamentation; audible sorrow; grief expressed in words or cries'; *Dict.* It does not simply mean incoherent noises or groans, but may be used of a composition.

5ff] Tho' when Orpheus sweetly sighing
    Woods to evry Sigh replying,
    Hebrus heard her Poet groan,
    For his lovely Consort gone,
    Listning Forests learnt the Strain,
    Rivers rested as they ran,
    Tho' the

11 *danc'd*] crowd

36 *Hell's fierce Hawk* the vulture which perpetually feeds upon the entrails of Tityus, imprisoned in Tartarus.

   his] her *MS*

52 *losing*] loving *MS draft*

A REPLY TO IMPROMPTU VERSES BY BARETTI

The date of these verses is unknown. Johnson first met Baretti in 1751, but they are arbitrarily placed here in the later 1760s after Johnson had met the Thrales (1765) and whilst he and Baretti were members of the Streatham circle. In Baretti's Commonplace Book he had written down two extempore stanzas in Italian in praise of the Tuscan practice of impromptu verse composition; these lines are entitled *Rispossa del Johnson*.

    From the original Commonplace Book, recently identified by Professor Alan T. McKenzie, in the Furness Collection, University of Pennsylvania. *Poems* 142; *Works* VI, 256. See *Notes and Queries*, September 1971, pp. 336–7.

PROLOGUE TO GOLDSMITH'S *The Good Natur'd Man*

Goldsmith's play was first produced at Covent Garden on 29 January 1768, when Johnson's *Prologue* was spoken by Robert Bensly. Numerous versions were published in the newspapers, apparently from playhouse reports, but since they refer to Goldsmith as 'Our little Bard' (line 5) they cannot be close to what Johnson actually wrote, for Goldsmith was notoriously touchy about his shortness.

    The text published with the first edition of the play itself is presumed to be closest to Johnson's manuscript. The many newspaper versions differ in various readings. *Poems* 58–60; *Works* VI, 264–6.

4ʌ5] Amidst the toils of this returning year, / When senators and
    nobles learn to fear *Newspapers* – alluding to the General
    Election of March 1768.

5 *anxious*] little *Newspapers*

7 *Cæsar's pilot*   forced by the Emperor to sail into a storm.
15 *loud rabbles vent their*] caprice may vent its *Newspapers*
16 *mongrels bay*] children fret *Newspapers*
18 See note on line 97 of *Vanity* (p. 209, above).
19] The poet's foes their schemes of spite dismiss *Newspapers*
21-4 *Not in Newspapers*
30 *merit*] candour *Newspapers*

PARODIES OF BISHOP PERCY'S *Hermit of Warkworth*

The Hermit of Warkworth, Percy's imitation ballad, was published in March 1771. Johnson parodied it on various occasions: all three are here placed together. There are several versions of each, since they seem to have been much passed around at the time.

1 from Boswell's *Journal* (7 April 1773); 2 from *Thraliana*, modified by the version in Johnson's *Works* (1787); and 3 from the *St James's Chronicle*, 13 January 1785, where George Steevens noted that, like no. 1, it was improvised at Miss Reynolds's tea-table when Percy himself was present. *Poems* 157-9; *Works* VI, 268-70.

AN EPITAPH ON WILLIAM HOGARTH

Garrick submitted a draft of an epitaph to Johnson, who replied on 12 December 1771: 'Suppose you worked upon something like this . . .'

From the original letter to Garrick, now in the Berg Collection of the New York Public Library. The variant in l. 2 was deliberately left by Johnson so that Garrick could decide. The final version is inscribed on Hogarth's monument at Chiswick and only slightly follows Johnson:

'Farewel, great Painter of Mankind! / Who reach'd the noblest point of Art, / Whose *pictur'd Morals* charm the mind, / And through the Eye correct the Heart. / If *Genius* fire thee, Reader, stay: / If *Nature* touch thee, drop a Tear; / If neither move thee, turn away, / For HOGARTH's honour'd dust lies here.' Mrs Thrale recorded another version of Johnson's first stanza in her *Thraliana* (p. 41), which she perhaps received at his dictation:

'The hand of him here torpid lies / That drew th'essential Form of Grace; / Here clos'd in Death th'attentive Eyes / That saw the Manners in the Face.' *Poems* 153-5; *Works* VI, 267-8; *Letters* no. 269.

2 *wav'd*] *written above* trac'd *in MS*
essential Form of Grace Hogarth's famous 'Line of Beauty', a double curve which appeared on the title-page of his *Analysis of Beauty* (1753).
3 *curious* Lat. *cura*, care; hence careful, meticulously observant.

FRENCH DISTICHS

On 18 September 1775, Johnson's birthday, he and the Thrales crossed the Channel to Calais on their way to Paris. They reached St Omer on the 19th, Arras on the 20th, Amiens on the 21st, and Neufchatel (where they sampled the fare at the inn called Mouton d'Or) and Rouen on the 22nd. Mrs Thrale recorded these lines on the 22nd when they were at Rouen: 'Mr Johnson has made a little Distich at every place we have slept at.' (See M. Tyson and H. Guppy (eds.), *The French Journals of Mrs Thrale and Dr Johnson*, John Rylands Library, 1932.)

From Mrs Thrale's manuscript of her French Journal in the John Rylands Library, Manchester. *Poems* 172; *Works* VI, 285-6.

TRANSLATION FROM A PANTOMIME VERSION OF BENSERADE'S *Balet de Cassandre*

Probably made during the visit to Paris in September and October 1775. On 19 October Johnson noted in his diary: 'At night we went to a comedy.' Perhaps it was the occasion of these lines.

From *Thraliana*, where it is undated, though written in the volume for 1777-8; modified by the version in Mrs Piozzi's *Anecdotes* (1785). Mrs Thrale gives the original as: 'Je suis Cassandre descendu des Cieux / Pour vous faire entendre Mesdames et Messieurs, / Que je suis Cassandre descendu des Cieux', and notes that Johnson translated it impromptu. The original in Benserade's *Balet* is not so fatuous, but presumably the pantomime version strayed a good deal from it. *Poems* 173; *Works* VI, 295.

TRANSLATIONS FROM METASTASIO

The first volume of Mrs Thrale's Commonplace Book, *Thraliana*, covers the years 1776-7. In it she records several examples of Johnson's 'almost Tuscan' powers as an improviser of verses.

From *Thraliana*, modified by the version in Mrs Piozzi's *Anecdotes* (1786). Both translations were improvised. The first is from *La Clemenza di Tito* I, 2, and the second from *Adriano in Syria* II, 1. In 1767 Johnson had furnished the Dedication to the Duke of Northumberland for John Hoole's translation of *The Works of Metastasio*, but Hoole's versions of these passages have nothing in common with Johnson's. *Poems* 175-6; *Works* VI, 286-7.

TRANSLATION OF DU BELLAY'S *Epigram on a Dog*

From *Thraliana*. The original epigram is in *Menagiana* (1713, II, 162): 'Du Bellay a fait cette belle Epigramme sur un Chien qui etoit de bonne garde contre les voleurs, mais qui laissoit entrer les Amans sans abboyer: Latratu fures excepti; mutus, amantes: / Sic placui Domino; sic placui Dominæ.' *Poems* 173-4; *Works* VI, 287.

TRANSLATION OF THE BEGINNING OF *Rio Verde*

From *Thraliana*, modified by the version in Mrs Piozzi's *Anecdotes* (1786), where Johnson's impromptu composition is described: 'A famous ballad . . . beginning *Rio Verde, Rio Verde*, when I commended the translation of it, he said he could do better himself – as thus. . . . But Sir, said I, this is not ridiculous at all. "Why no (replied he), why should I always write ridiculously?"' For the whole ballad see Percy's *Reliques* (1765) I, 318. *Poems* 159; *Works* VI, 292.

TRANSLATION OF BENSERADE'S VERSES *à son Lit*

From *Thraliana*, modified by the version in Mrs Piozzi's *Anecdotes* (1786). Mrs Thrale supplies the original verses: 'Theatre des Ris et des Pleurs, / Lit ou je nais et ou je meurs; / Tu nous fais voir comment Voisins / Sont nos Plaisirs et nos Chagrins.' Johnson extemporized his translation. *Poems* 183-4; *Works* VI, 293.

TRANSLATION OF A DISTICH ON THE DUKE OF MODENA

From *Thraliana*, modified by the version in Mrs Piozzi's *Anecdotes* (1786). Mrs Thrale quotes the original Italian epigram as the work of an *improvisatore*, which Johnson immediately translated. In 1742, after the appearance of a Comet, presumed an evil omen, the Duke of Modena fled from his dominions before an attack by the Sardinians. *Poems* 176-7; *Works* VI, 295-6.

BURLESQUE TRANSLATION OF LINES FROM LOPE DE VEGA'S *Arcadia*

From *Thraliana*, also an improvised composition, for it is less a translation than an equivalent rendering of a play on words. *Poems* 182-3; *Works* VI, 296.

TRANSLATION OF LINES IN BARETTI'S *Easy Phraseology*

In 1775 Baretti published his *Easy Phraseology, for the Use of Young Ladies that wish to learn the Colloquial Part of the Italian Language*, ending it with a short Italian poem in praise of his *padrona*, Hester Maria Thrale.

Poems 174–5; *Works* VI, 291–2.

From *Easy Phraseology*, 1775, p. 424: 'Viva! viva la padrona! / Tutta bella, e tutta buona, / La padrona è un angiolella / Tutta buona e tutta bella; / Tutta bella e tutta buona; / Viva! viva la padrona!' A transcript of Johnson's version, by Baretti, is owned by the Marquess of Lansdowne; it varies in a few readings:

1 *my lovely*] our charming *throughout*
3,4 *transposed*
7] *an extra line added:* 'Huzza! Huzza! Huzza!'

LINES ON THOMAS WARTON'S POEMS

Warton's poems were published in January 1777. Johnson composed this commentary verse soon afterwards. The first stanza is recorded by Boswell on 18 September 1777 (Johnson's sixty-eighth birthday). The second was added on 9 May 1778, but Boswell failed to catch the whole of it and Johnson refused to repeat it for him. In spring 1779 Boswell found Johnson 'in better humour', and recorded the whole of the second stanza as it is printed here, except that Johnson at first described the sage as 'hoary', but changed it at Boswell's suggestion to 'smiling' (line 7).

The first piece is from *Thraliana*: 'When Tom Warton published his Poems in Jan:1777 – nobody read 'em – Warton's Poems are *come out* says Mr Johnson; yes replied I, & this cold Weather *has struck them in* again: I have written Verses to abuse them says he, but I can but repeat two or three of them, & those you must say nothing of, for I love Thomas look you – tho' I laugh at him' (p. 209).

The second is from Boswell's *Life of Johnson*. Boswell's account explains Johnson's attitude to Warton: 'He observed, that a gentleman of eminence in literature had got into a bad style of poetry of late. "He puts (said he) a very common thing into a strange dress till he does not know it himself, and thinks other people do not know it." *Boswell*. "That is owing to his being so much versant in old English poetry." *Johnson*. "What is that to the purpose, Sir? If I say a man is drunk, and you tell me it is owing to his taking much drink, the matter is not mended."' *Poems* 179–81; *Works* VI, 288, 294–5.

CHARADE ON DR THOMAS BARNARD

Written on a card left as a farewell note for Barnard who was about to return to Ireland, it is preceded by: 'Mr Johnson, not being to dine at the Club this day, as he intended, waits on the Dean of Derry to take leave, and wish him a prosperous voyage. Friday Jan: 17th (1777).'

From the original note in the possession of the Earl of Crawford and Balcarres. *Poems* 178-9; *Works* VI, 288-9; *Letters* II, 160.

TO MRS THRALE ON HER THIRTY-FIFTH BIRTHDAY

Mrs Thrale records the poem under 1777 in her *Thraliana*, but her thirty-fifth birthday was actually 24 January 1776. In her published *Anecdotes* (1786) she added that Johnson's comment was: 'And now ... you may see what it is to come for poetry to a Dictionary-maker; you may observe that the rhymes run in alphabetical order exactly.'

From a copy taken down by Mrs Thrale at Johnson's dictation, now in the John Rylands Library. Despite Johnson's remark, the alphabetical order is not exact, for 'drive' (7) precedes 'dive' (9). *Poems* 177-8; *Works* VI, 292-3.

1 Mrs Thrale had several dangerous pregnancies.
14 *declines* because it is exactly half of man's allotted span: three-score years and ten.

PROLOGUE TO HUGH KELLY'S *A Word to the Wise*

Written for the benefit performance for Kelly's widow and children on 29 May 1777, and published in the *Public Advertiser* and other newspapers on 31 May 1777.

From the *Public Advertiser*, 31 May 1777. Johnson was not fond of Kelly, whose vanity led him to display his spurs on the sideboard along with his other plate. When he was teased over his helping Kelly's widow and Dr Dodd, the clerical forger, his reply was: 'Why, Sir, when they come to me with a dead stay-maker [Kelly] and a dying parson [Dodd], what can a man do?' *Poems* 60-62; *Works* VI, 290-91.

2 Kelly's play, first produced in 1770, was 'damned' by the audience.
4 Compare with 'I war not with the dead.' Pope's Homer, *Iliad*, VII, 485.
9 *resentful petulance   Public Advertiser*] renew'd hostilities *all other versions*

The Reverend John Hussey recorded in his copy of Boswell's *Life of Johnson* (1791) that when he read the Prologue to Johnson the morning after it was spoken, 'The Doctor told me instead of *renew'd hostilities* he wrote *revengeful petulance*, and did not seem pleased with the alteration.' In a much earlier note in his '*Memorandums*', sent to Boswell in August 1787, he noted apropos this piece: 'for renew'd hostilities, read resentful petulance' (M. Waingrow (ed.), *The Correspondence &c of James Boswell relating to the making of the 'Life of Johnson'*, 1969, p. 235). 'Revengeful' is awkward and may represent a lapse of memory.

20   *best*] last *in some versions*

TRANSLATION OF ANACREON'S *Dove*

According to Mrs Thrale, who recorded the poem in her *Thraliana* on 15 January 1778, Johnson said 'they were the first Greek Verses that had struck him when a Boy; so says he they continue to please me as well as any Greek Verses now I am Three score'. Johnson's sixtieth birthday was 18 September 1769, but his comment seems not intended to be precise.

From *Thraliana*, modified by the version in Mrs Piozzi's *Anecdotes* (1786). *Poems* 184-6; *Works* VI, 296-8.

35   *luscious*   in his Dictionary, Johnson accepted the derivation from and equivalence with 'luxurious'.

44   *pye*   a magpie. 'From *pie*, *pica*, Latin, and *mag*. contracted from *Margaret*, as *phil* is used to a *sparrow*, and *poll* to a *parrot*. A bird sometimes taught to talk'; *Dict*.

A SONG COMPOSED FOR FANNY BURNEY

Recorded in Fanny Burney's diary under November 1778.

Published from the manuscript diary in the Berg Collection of the New York Public Library, by Professor J. Hemlow in her *History of Fanny Burney* (1958, p. 114). *Works* VI, 299-300.

AN EXTEMPORE ELEGY

According to Fanny Burney's account, the elegy was composed by 'Dr Johnson, Mrs Thrale and myself, spouting it out alternately'. Whether the alternate contributions were single lines, couplets or stanzas is uncertain, but Johnson's responsibility for the clumsy sixteenth line may be doubted. The piece is undated and is arbitrarily associated with the preceding verses.

Published from the manuscript of Fanny Burney's diary in the Berg Collection of the New York Public Library, by Professor J. Hemlow in her *History of Fanny Burney* (1958, pp. 114-15). *Works* VI, 300-301.

It has been suggested that stanzas three and four are in the wrong order (*Johnsonian Newsletter*, March 1966).

5 *once as cherry*] once a cherry *MS*

14 *Pug* 'A kind name for a monkey, or any thing tenderly loved'; *Dict.*

18 *Dram* 'Such a quantity of distilled spirits as is usually drank at once'; *Dict.*

EPILOGUE TO HORACE'S *Carmen Seculare*

First published in Baretti's *The Carmen Seculare of Horace* (1779). Set to music by Philidor, it was performed in February and March of that year.

From the original edition, pp. 18-19. Johnson wrote the Latin stanza also: 'Quæ fausta Romæ dixit Horatius, / Hæc fausta vobis dicimus, Angliæ / Opes, triumphos, et subacti / Imperium pelagi precantes.' The Bodleian copy bears manuscript revisions (*MS*) in an unidentified hand, which were followed in some later reprints. Their authority is not known. *Poems* 187-9; *Works* VI, 301-2.

2 *future greatness*] generous Ardour *MS*

3 *England*] Britain *MS*

5 *the varied*] th'alternate *MS*

8 *Masters*] Rulers *MS*

ON SEEING A PORTRAIT OF MRS MONTAGU

Johnson was given a portrait of Mrs Montagu in March 1779, and was on friendly terms with her until his *Life of Lyttelton*, published in May 1781, produced an estrangement. This estrangement is described by Boswell, 1781 (*Life* VI, 64); 'his (Johnson's) expressing with a dignified freedom what he really thought of George, Lord Lyttelton, gave offence to some of the friends of that nobleman, and particularly produced a declaration of war against him from Mrs Montagu, the ingenious Essayist on Shakespeare, between whom and his Lordship a commerce of reciprocal compliments had long been carried on.'

From Johnson's *Works* (1787), which refers to a 'Bust' rather than a 'Portrait', though the reference to a *frame* in line 1 still stands. The *Poems* point out that Mrs Montagu was the subject of one of James Tassie's cameos in 1775, which might explain the difficulty. *Poems* 189-90; *Works* VI, 302.

ON HEARING MISS THRALE DELIBERATE ABOUT HER HAT

Recorded by Mrs Thrale in *Thraliana* under 5 January 1780. 'Hester was deliberating whether She should put on her fine new dressed hat to dine at Mrs Montagus next Friday – *do* my Darling say Johnson. . . .'

From *Thraliana*, where the lines are recorded as composed extempore. *Poems* 194; *Works* VI, 306.

2   *your*] *emended to* thy *in Mrs Thrale's Anecdotes (1786).*

TRANSLATIONS FROM THE *Medea* OF EURIPIDES

The first version is a burlesque of the style (Johnson described it as 'verbiage') of Robert Potter's translation of Aeschylus, published in 1777.

The second was written seriously as a contribution to Charles Burney's *History of Music*, and was published in his second volume in 1782.

Both translate the same passage: *Medea* 193–203.

I. From *Thraliana*, modified by the version in Mrs Piozzi's *Anecdotes* (1786); II. from Burney's *History of Music*. Johnson also translated the same passage into Latin verse in an undated text, printed in his *Works* (1787). *Poems* 190–93; *Works* VI, 302–5. See also H. D. Weinbrot in *Notes and Queries* CCXII (November 1967) 410–11.

I 16   *blood-bolter'd* Compare 'The Blood-bolter'd Banquo smiles upon me' (*Macbeth* IV i 123).

17   *cates* 'Viands; food; dish of meat: generally employed to signify nice and luxurious food'; *Dict.*

A SHORT SONG OF CONGRATULATION

The manuscript was sent to Mrs Thrale with a covering letter on 8 August 1780. Sir John Lade came of age on 1 August.

From the manuscript, now in the Huntington Library. Johnson's letter says: 'You have heard in the papers how Sir John Lade is come to age. I have enclosed a short song of congratulation, which You must not shew to any body.' Lade was the son of Henry Thrale's sister: he fulfilled Johnson's predictions by marrying the notorious Laetitia Darby – formerly mistress of 'Sixteen-string Jack' Rann, the highwayman and of Frederick Augustus, Duke of York – and by squandering his fortune. He lived, however, until 1838. Housman's *A Shropshire Lad* is said to have been conceived with this poem in mind.

Other versions of the poem are found in *Thraliana* and in Mrs Piozzi's *British Synonymy* (1794, *MS* in Rylands Library). All are corruptions from Johnson's original. *Poems* 194-7; *Works* VI, 306-8.

VERSES MODELLED ON POPE

Printed in Johnson's *Life of Pope* (1781) without attribution. No source has been discovered, and it is presumed to be by Johnson himself.

From the *Prefaces to the Poets*, VII (Pope, 1781), where it is introduced: 'Motion, however, may be in some sort exemplified; and yet it may be suspected that even in such resemblances the mind often governs the ear, and the sounds are estimated by their meaning. One of the most successful attempts has been to describe the labour of Sisyphus: With many a weary step, and many a groan, / Up a high hill he heaves a huge round stone; / The huge round stone, resulting with a bound, / Thunders impetuous down, and smoaks along the ground [Pope's Homer: *Odyssey* XI, 735-8]. Who does not perceive the stone to move slowly upwards, and roll violently back? But set the same numbers to another sense . . .' The verses were first included in Johnson's Poems in *Works* VI, 309-10. Slight corruptions were introduced into later editions of the *Lives of the Poets*.

ON THE DEATH OF DR ROBERT LEVET

Levet was 'an obscure practiser in physick amongst the lower people' whom Johnson met about 1746 and whom he later sheltered in his house until his death on 17 January 1782. The poem was first published in the *GM* in August 1783. Levet, a native of Kirk Ella near Hull, was one of the indigent dependants who formed Johnson's extraordinary household which he described: 'Williams hates every body; Levet hates Desmoulins, and does not love Williams; Desmoulins hates them both; Poll loves none of them.'

The restrained sincerity of deep personal grief which informs the poem illustrates something of Johnson's theory of elegy which led him to denigrate *Lycidas* in his *Life of Milton*.

From *GM*, August 1783. There are many other versions of unequal authority, but none to displace the text of the Magazine. *Poems* 199-202; *Works* VI, 313-15.

1 Compare motto of *Rambler* 67 (p. 97 above). A common punish-

ment in ancient Rome was *damnare in metallum*, to condemn to the lead mines, and the phrase became current for unremitting drudgery.

7   *Officious*   'Kind; doing good offices'; *Dict.*
   innocent   'Pure from mischief. Unhurtful'; *Dict.*
   sincere   'Honest; undissembling; uncorrupt'; *Dict.*
10   *Obscurely*   'Out of sight; privately; without notice'; *Dict.*
11   *arrogance*] Ignorance *Hawkins's* Life of Johnson (1787)
20   Boswell records that Johnson repeated this line as: 'And Labour steals an hour to die', but then changed it to the present reading (*Life* IV, 138, 20 January 1782).
28   *The*] His *Boswell*
   single talent   See Matthew xxv 14–30 '. . . and unto one he gave five talents, to another two, and to another one; to every man according to his several ability.' Johnson was throughout his life profoundly disturbed by the parable of the talents, and by the severe punishment of the 'unprofitable servant' who failed to improve his single talent. See also the close of *Rambler* 77.
33   *throbbing fiery*] throb[s] of fiery / fiery throbbing *other versions*
36   *free'd*] forc'd *other versions*

TRANSLATIONS OF ROY'S VERSES ON SKATERS

In *Thraliana* under November 1782 Mrs Thrale recorded her acquisition of a French print of skaters, bearing Roy's verses underneath. The second translation was impromptu. *Poems* 202–3; *Works* VI, 311–12. Johnson's diary records on Monday 11 November 1782, 'did the French skating.'

From *Thraliana* modified by the version in Mrs Piozzi's *Anecdotes* (1786). Mrs Thrale gives Roy's original verses as: 'Sur un mince chrystal l'hyver conduit leurs pas, / Le précipice est sous la glace; / Telle est de nos plaisirs la légère surface; / Glissez, mortels, n'appuyez pas.' She encouraged members of her circle to supply translations, and Johnson gave her the first, but when he discovered that there had been a kind of competition he was 'most exceedingly enraged . . . and said, it was a piece of treachery, and done to make every body else look little when compared to my favourite friends the *Pepyses*.' After seeing William Pepys's version, Johnson composed the second translation impromptu.

2   *Skaiter*   this spelling is not given in *Dict.*, which has both 'Skate' and 'Scate'.

TRANSLATION OF HORACE: *Odes* IV vii (*Diffugere nives*)

Dated in the manuscript 'Nov. 1784'. On 27 September Johnson went to Lichfield for the last time, staying until 10 November, when he left for London and arrived home at Bolt Court on 16 November. The latter months of his life were filled with a sense of the transitoriness of human existence.

From the original dated manuscript now in the Hyde Collection. *Poems* 231-2; *Works* VI, 343-4. Some corrections in the manuscript and the general absence of punctuation suggest that it is close to the time of composition. It was first printed in his *Works* (1787 *W*).

2 *behold*] again *orig. MS*
10 *yields*] yield MS
   Summer's] Summer *MS*
18 *toss*] *misread as* rouse *in W*
24 *replace on*] restore to *W*
28 *his friend* Pirithous.

APPENDIX I

AURORA EST MUSIS AMICA

The manuscript derives from Charles Congreve, one of Johnson's Lichfield schoolfellows and later a contemporary at Oxford. It is undated, but was probably written at college in 1728.

From the manuscript owned by Major C. Congreve, deposited in the Bodleian Library. *Works* VI, 28. The manuscript is a working draft with some revisions.

Title Compare Milton's first *Prolusion*: 'exaudiatque Aurora Musis amica, exaudiat et Phoebus . . .' (May Aurora, the friend of the Muses, hearken, and may Phoebus give heed . . .). Johnson adopts the point made by Milton that the early morning is a time of poetic inspiration. The title is common among the 'themes' or undergraduate exercises preserved from the eighteenth century in Pembroke College library.

VERSES ON THE DEATH OF HIS MOTHER

Printed in the *Universal Chronicle* for 27 January 1759, with the original no. 42 of the *Idler* (renumbered 41 in collected editions). Sarah Johnson died in her ninetieth year on 20-21 January 1759.

The lines are not attributed to any author until Johnson's *Works* (1825), when they are given to Ovid; but they cannot be found in that author's works. The editors of *Works* VI, 387, suggest that they were composed by Johnson: it is certainly characteristic that he should have expressed his feelings on the death of his mother in Latin verse.

Γνωθι σεαυτον

(POST LEXICON ANGLICANUM AUCTUM ET EMENDATUM)

Johnson began the revision and correction of his great *Dictionary* in the summer of 1771. On 8 October 1772 he wrote to William Strahan, the printer; 'I am now within about two hours or less of my work. I purpose to go into the country for a month.' He spent somewhat longer than a month with his friend the Reverend John Taylor at Ashbourne in Derbyshire and with other friends in Lichfield, before returning to London where he arrived on Friday night, 11 December 1772. He dated this poem the following day and it seems that he had largely composed it in his mind beforehand, perhaps as he rode in the coach. The revised *Dictionary*, the fourth edition, was published in March 1773.

From the dated manuscript in Yale University Library. *Poems* 159–62; *Works* VI, 271–4. The manuscript contains revisions.

Title Compare *Rambler* 24, para. 1. The injunction, though of classical origin, was congenial to Protestant habits of self-scrutiny.

22 *discordia concors* See Horace, *Epistles* I xxi 19, 'Concordia discors' and Johnson's *Life of Cowley*, 'Wit, abstracted from its effects upon the hearer, may be ... considered as a kind of *discordia concors*; a combination of dissimilar images, or discovery of occult resemblances in things apparently unlike' (para. 56). See also *Rambler* 167, para. 9.

25 *Desidiae* See *Vanity*, note on l. 150 (p. 211, above).

41 *Res angusta domi* See Juvenal, *Satires*, III, 164–5, 'Haud facile emergunt quorum virtutibus opstat / Res angusta domi' *(It is not easy for them to make progress, whose narrow circumstances stand in the way of their merits)*, which Johnson rendered in *London* 177 as: 'Slow rises worth, by Poverty deprest.'

SKIA, AN ODE ON THE ISLE OF SKYE

Recorded by Boswell in his Journal under 5 September 1773, when the travellers spent Sunday at Armadale House with Sir Alexander Macdonald: 'I am inclined to think that it was on this day he composed the following Ode upon the *Isle of Skye*, which a few days afterwards he shewed me at Raasay.'

The original manuscript from which Boswell made his copy is now lost, but it was seen by Bennet Langton who published his transcript in

Johnson's *Works* (1787). The two versions differ slightly. *Poems* 165–6; *Works* VI, 278–9.

ODE, DE SKIA INSULA

On 6 September 1773 Johnson and Boswell rode northwards through Skye from Sleat to Broadford until they reached the farmhouse called Corriechatachan (The Corrie of the Cats), the home of Lachlan Mackinnon, where they spent the next two days. Boswell noted in his Journal: 'Dr Johnson, being fatigued with his journey, retired early to his chamber, where he composed the following Ode, addressed to Mrs Thrale.'

From the original manuscript in the Hyde Collection. The text in Johnson's *Works* (1787), edited by Langton, derives from a different source and seems to be more authoritative. *Poems* 167–8; *Works* VI, 280–81; *Life* V, 158.

INSULA SANCTI KENNETHI

On Sunday 17 October 1773 the travellers crossed to the island of Inchkenneth off the western coast of Mull, and stayed with Sir Allan Maclean. Boswell describes an evening service held in the house at which Miss Maclean, Sir Allan's daughter, read from the Prayer Book. 'Dr Johnson said that it was the most agreeable Sunday he had ever passed; and it made such an impression on his mind, that he afterwards wrote the following Latin verses upon Inchkenneth.'

A manuscript dated '2d Dec. 1773' was followed by Bennet Langton when he published the poem in Johnson's *Works* (1787), and the same manuscript was used by J. W. Croker in 1831 when he recorded further details of the variant readings in it. That manuscript has not been seen since 1896. A second, revised, version was sent to Boswell on 21 January 1775, and was published in the *Journal of a Tour to the Hebrides* (1785). That Boswell's text derives from the later revised version is implied by Croker's report that the earlier lost manuscript was slightly longer (26 lines). *Poems* 168–70; *Works* VI, 283–5; *Life* V, 325–6.

ON LOSING THE POWER OF SPEECH

Langton added the following explanation to these verses: 'The night above referred to by Dr Johnson was that in which a paralytick stroke had deprived him of his voice, and, in the anxiety he felt lest it should likewise have impaired his understanding, he composed the above Lines, and said concerning them, that he knew at the time that they were not good, but that he deemed his discerning this, to be sufficient for the quieting the anxiety before mentioned, as it shewed him that his power of judging was not diminished.' Johnson's own diary simply reports: 'I went to bed, and as I conceive, about 3 in the morning, I had a stroke of the palsy.'

First published by Langton in Johnson's *Works* (1787), apparently from a manuscript which bore alternative readings. *Poems* 204; *Works* VI, 313.

IN RIVUM A MOLA STOANA LICHFELDIAE DIFFLUENTEM

First published by Bennet Langton in Johnson's *Works* (1787), the verses were undated, but were probably written on Johnson's last visit to Lichfield in November 1784.

Stowe Mill stood near St Chad's Church, which is on a small islet between divisions of the stream; the confluence probably formed a natural bathing place.

From Langton's text in Johnson's *Works* (1787); *Poems* 227-8; *Works* VI, 342-3.

12 *Nisus* perhaps refers to Edmund Hector, who wrote to Boswell on 1 February 1785 in connection with Johnson's last visit to him in Birmingham in November 1784: 'He was very sollicitous with me to recollect some of our most early transactions and transmit them to him; for I perceived nothing gave him greater pleasure, than calling to mind, those days of our innocence.' Nisus and Euryalus were proverbial for their friendship (see Virgil, *Aeneid* IX, 176 ff). See also *Adventurer* 109.

PRAYER

Langton noted on the date: 'The day on which he received the sacrament for the last time; and eight days before his decease.' On this same day Johnson composed his last prayer in English: 'Almighty and most merciful Father, I am now, as to human eyes it seems, about to commemorate for the last time, the Death of thy son Jesus Christ, our Saviour and Redeemer. Grant, O Lord, that my whole hope and confidence may be in his merits and in thy mercy: forgive and accept my late conversion, enforce and accept my imperfect repentance; make this commemoration of him available to the confirmation of my Faith, that establishment of my hope, and the enlargement of my Charity, and make the Death of thy son Jesus effectual to my redemption. Have mercy upon me and pardon the multitude of my offences. Bless my Friends, have mercy upon all men. Support me by the Grace of thy

Holy Spirit in the days of weakness, and at the hour of death, and receive me at my death, to everlasting happiness, for the Sake of Jesus Christ. Amen.'

These verses are a paraphrase of the Collect in the Communion Service: 'Almighty God, unto whom all hearts be open, all desires known, and from whom no secrets are hid; Cleanse the thoughts of our hearts by the inspiration of thy Holy Spirit, that we may perfectly love thee, and worthily magnify thy Holy Name; through Jesus Christ our Lord. Amen.'

He died peacefully in the early evening of Monday 13 December 1784.

From Langton's text in Johnson's *Works* (1787). *Poems* 232; *Works* VI, 351-2.

APPENDIX 2

LINES IN HAWKESWORTH'S TRAGEDY

From a letter in the Hyde Collection from R. Ryland, Hawkesworth's nephew, to William Hayley, 7 April 1809: – 'the greatest Loss is the Tragedy, which I really think was a very fine One – that Johnson thought so and Mrs Thrale, I have Evidence in his own hand writing – it was a perfectly fair Copy . . . the Scene was laid in Spain and among Peruvian Connections. The Story is much in my memory but no lines of it wholly except 2 which Johnson substituted at the Close of one of the Acts for a Couplet which did not please his Ear, without altering the sentiment. . . .' Mrs Thrale noted that the tragedy was 'call'd the *Rival*' (*Thraliana*, i. 328).

The original letter is in the Hyde Collection. It refers to the bulk of Hawkesworth's literary papers, which had been sent to Johnson for his opinion on a possible edition of Hawkesworth's works. The edition never appeared and the papers remain undiscovered.

ANNA WILLIAMS: *On the Death of Stephen Grey*

Published in Anna Williams, *Miscellanies* (1766). Johnson told Boswell: 'She wrote it before she was acquainted with me; but she has not told you that I wrote it all over again, except two lines.' Anna Williams noted that she had been 'the first that observed and notified the emission of the electrical spark from a human body'. Grey or Gray was an early experimenter in static electricity, and died in 1736. Anna Williams's father was, like Grey, a pensioner at the Charterhouse, having come up to London with his daughter in 1730; later he was removed. Anna went blind in 1740 and was befriended by Johnson's wife, upon whose death in 1752 she became his housekeeper. Her father died in 1755, and she herself in 1783.

From Anna Williams's *Miscellanies* (1766). Johnson's part in compiling that collection seems to have been an important one, and few pieces in it can have escaped some revision by him. This and the passage from the *Excursion* are given as examples. *Poems* 378-80; *Works* VI, 354-5.

ANNA WILLIAMS: *The Excursion*

Published in Anna Williams, *Miscellanies* (1766). The whole poem of 176 lines, in praise of rural retirement, is alien to Johnson's thinking. His contribution, alleged by Boswell, was probably confined to a few stylistic points. I have admitted the exordium (lines 171-6) as possibly from his pen; most of the rest of the poem would have qualified for his own description: 'a despicable effusion of pastoral; a composition in which all is unnatural, and yet nothing is new.'

From Anna Williams's *Miscellanies* (1766). Malone also thought Johnson had had a hand in this piece. *Poems* 379; *Works* VI, 353.

OLIVER GOLDSMITH: *The Traveller*

Boswell's copy of the 'Fifth' edition of *The Traveller* (1770) is inscribed on the title-page: 'In Spring 1783 Dr Johnson at my desire marked with a pencil the lines in this admirable Poem which he furnished viz. l. 18 on p. 23 [=420] and from the 3 line on the last page to the end except the last couplet but one. "These (he said) are all of which I can be sure."'

Boswell's copy of the book bearing Johnson's marks is now in the Hyde Collection. *Poems* 380; *Works* VI, 355-6. The lines are characteristic of Johnson's view of political states: 'I would not give half a guinea to live under one form of government rather than another. It is of no moment to the happiness of an individual' (*Life* II 170).

420] And faintly fainter, fainter seems to go. *Goldsmith's original.*
435-6 The bracketed couplet is Goldsmith's.

OLIVER GOLDSMITH: *The Deserted Village*

Boswell's copy of this poem is bound together with his copy of *The Traveller* (see above). On the last page of *The Deserted Village* he noted: 'The last four lines were marked at my desire by Dr Johnson spring 1783 as all that he wrote of this admirable Poem.' *Poems* 381; *Works* VI, 356.

HANNAH MORE: *Sir Eldred of the Bower*

The second edition of *Sir Eldred* (1778) contains the following revisions from the first of 1776. Hannah More recorded in a letter that Johnson came to tea: 'Our tea was not over till nine, we then fell upon Sir Eldred: He read both poems through [*Sir Eldred* and *The Bleeding Rock*], suggested some little alterations in the first [*Sir Eldred*], and did me the honour to write one whole stanza; but in the Rock he has not altered a word' (see H. W. Liebert, 'We fell upon Sir Eldred', in *New Light on Johnson*, 1959). *Works* VI, 356–9.

Mr Liebert's study argues persuasively for Johnson's responsibility for all the changes. Hannah More's original versions were as follows:

Part I

2/2   *feed*] crown

6/2   *claim*] tax

8/2   ] He *doubly* served him *then*;

   4   ] He thought they still were *men*.

   11   ] Yet if distrust his thoughts engage, / Or jealousy inspires, / His bosom wild and boundless rage / Inflames with all its fires.

18/1   *vernal*] amorous

   2   *thick'ning*] vernal

   3   *And*] Their

33/1   *by*] with

37   ] While the sweet pink, and scented rose, / In precious odours last; / And when no more the colour glows, / The sweetness is not past

40/1   *cloudless*] liquid

   2   ] It pours its lambent light.

41/1   *So*] Such

45/1   *The virgin blush which spreads*] The mountain breeze which paints

   3   *beams*] fires

   4   *Like morning*] Illustrious

46/1   *raptur'd*] ravish'd

49   ] *Beauty* with coldness I've beheld, / And 'scaped the shaft divine; / But what my guardless heart can shield / From *Piety* like thine?

50   ] She cast her mild eyes on the ground, / And rais'd their beams as fast; / And close her father dear she found, / Who haply that way past.

Part II

3/2 *casque*] targe
66/2 *imbrued*] imbued. See *Translation of Addison's Battle of the Pygmies and Cranes*, note to line 47 (p. 188, above).

VERSES BY FRANCES REYNOLDS

The revisions are undated, but on 16 June 1780 Johnson wrote to Frances Reynolds: 'Do not, my Love, burn your papers. I have mended little but some bad rhymes. I thought them very pretty, and was moved in reading them.'

From Frances Reynolds's manuscripts in the Hyde Collection, first published by G. B. Hill in *Johnsonian Miscellanies* (1897). *Poems* 378; *Works* VI, 353. Johnson's revisions begin with line 5. The original readings were:

5   ] In prospect view the dismal scene to come
6   ] Of gloomy age should Fate my Days prolong,
7   ] ... linger on the doubtful steep
8   ] Where youth declining seems with age to meet
9   ] Nature to her own Laws appears averse
10] Still prompts resistance where there's no redress;
11] Chears every sense the common air I breathe
12] ... prompts to prayer and praise.

GEORGE CRABBE: *The Village*

By the agency of Sir Joshua Reynolds, Crabbe's manuscript of *The Village* was corrected by Johnson. Before Reynolds returned it to Crabbe in March 1783, Boswell borrowed it and copied out all Johnson's alterations.

The manuscript remains undiscovered. *Poems* 381-2; *Works* VI, 359-60; *Life* IV, 175, March 1783. Johnson preserved one line (19) of what Crabbe originally wrote: In fairer scenes where peaceful pleasures spring, / Tityrus, the pride of Mantuan swains, might sing: / But charmed by him, or smitten with his views, / Shall modern poets court the Mantuan muse? / From Truth and Nature shall we widely stray, / Where Fancy leads, or Virgil led the way?

APPENDIX 3

A TRANSCRIPT OF THE ORIGINAL MANUSCRIPT OF
The Vanity of Human Wishes

Boswell preserved the original manuscript of the *Vanity*, which is written in leaves from small blank-paper notebooks, ten leaves altogether. They are now in the Hyde Collection. A facsimile was privately printed by Mr and Mrs Hyde in September 1962, and the manuscript was used extensively by the editors of the Yale Edition of *The Works of Samuel Johnson: Poems* (1964), i.e. *Works* VI, 90–109. It is here printed from the facsimile, so that the curious reader may see for himself the progress of Johnson's mind and art.

The numbering of the lines is designed to help the reader to find the corresponding passage in the finished version, and does not represent a true count of the lines in the manuscript.

A Dictionary of Proper Names

Cross-references are indicated by ◊

Aeneas A Trojan, founder of Rome and hero of Virgil's *Aeneid*.
Aethra Sea nymph, daughter of Oceanus and mother of the Pleiades; she ruled the upper air.
Achilles Greek hero in the Trojan war; killed Hector.
Alecto One of the Furies.
Alexander Surnamed the Great, King of Macedonia, son of Philip, and conqueror of the ancient world.
Alfred King of Wessex, whose reign was characterized as a golden age.
Alphius A celebrated usurer, ridiculed in Horace, Epode 2.
Amerillis (*alias* Amaryllis) A countrywoman in Virgil's eclogues, hence a rustic sweetheart. See Milton: 'To sport with Amaryllis in the shade' (*Lycidas*, 68).
Anacreon An Ionic lyric poet much given to self-indulgence, who choked to death on a grape-stone.
Andromache Daughter of Eëtion and wife of Hector.
Anne, Queen (1665-1714) Reigned 1702-14.
Antilochus Son of Nestor, killed in the Trojan war.
Apollo Sun god, often called Phoebus; also god of music and poetry.
Apulia A region of Italy, now Puglia, famous for its wool.
Argive Name used by Homer for all the Greeks.
Argo The ship in which Jason sailed to Colchis in quest of the Golden Fleece.
Aristius Fuscus Satirist, friend of Horace, whose *Odes* I xxii and *Epistles* I x are addressed to him.
Aspasia (Greek, ἀσπάσιος, pleasing, welcome) The most famous of the name was the intelligent and beautiful mistress of Pericles.
Assyria The most ancient empire of the ancient world.
Astyanax Son of Hector, killed by Achilles.
Atlas A Titan, turned by Perseus by means of the Gorgon's Head into a high mountain which was supposed to bear the heavens on its top.
Atridae The patronymic given by Homer to Agamemnon and Menelaus as the sons of Atreus, an extravagantly wicked king of Argos.
Augustus Caesar and patron of the arts. He was celebrated by Horace, Ovid and Virgil.
Aurora Goddess of the dawn, mother of Memnon.
Auster A south wind.
Austria Maria Theresa. ◊
Bacchus The god of wine and drinkers.

Bacon, Francis (1561–1626) Lord Chancellor, philosopher and author much admired by Johnson, who often quotes him in the *Dictionary*.

Bacon, Roger (1214–94) Philosopher and scientist. His study beside Folly Bridge at Oxford was reputed to be liable to fall if one greater than Bacon himself passed by.

Balbo A stammerer.

Baretti, Joseph (1719–89) Critic, linguist and writer.

Barnard, Dr Thomas (1728–1806) Dean of Derry and Bishop of Killaloe in Limerick. A friend of Johnson and fellow member of The Club.

Bavaria's Lord ◊ Charles Albert

Bavarian, the bold ◊ Charles Albert

Behn, Mrs Aphra (1640–89) Dramatist and novelist.

Belinda Heroine of Pope's *Rape of the Lock* (who took the name from an epigram by Martial); a poetic name cognate with *bella*, a beautiful girl.

Benserade, Isaac de (1613–91) French poet.

Birtha Heroine of Hannah More's *Sir Eldred of the Bower*.

Bodley, Sir Thomas (1545–1613) Founder of the Bodleian Library at Oxford.

Boethius, Anicius Manlius Severinus (d. 525) Medieval philosopher and poet.

Boreas The north wind.

Boyle, Hon. Robert (1627–91) Scientist.

Briareus A giant with a hundred hands and fifty heads who joined in the war against the gods, and was supposed to have been thrown under Mount Etna.

Bryan, W., of Bury St Edmunds Eccentric and contributor of occasional verse to the *Gentleman's Magazine*.

Burney, Frances ('Fanny') (1752–1840) Novelist and memorialist.

Bury St Edmunds County town of Suffolk.

Cadmus Founder of Thebes, who in an infirm old age prayed for death.

Caesar's pilot Was forced by the Emperor to sail into a storm.

Cambria Wales, of which St David is patron saint.

Carpathian coast The Carpathian sea lay between Rhodes and Crete.

Carpenter, Hon. Alicia Maria (1729–94) Daughter of the second Lord Carpenter.

Carter, Elizabeth (1717–1806) Poetess and miscellaneous writer; early friend of Johnson.

Cassandra A prophetess doomed to be disregarded.

Cato, Marcus Uticensis Great grandson of the famous Censor, gave his wife to his friend to bear him children, and received her again after his friend's death.

Cäyster A river flowing into the Aegean; frequented by swans.

Cerberus The many-headed dog which guarded the entrance to Hades.

Ceres Goddess of corn and harvests.

Charles XII (1682–1718) King of Sweden; a brave, ambitious, reckless yet skilful general who was sympathetic to the Jacobite cause in Britain and therefore a hero to the Tories.

Charles Albert (1697–1745) Elector of Bavaria; later Emperor Charles VII. He was defeated by Maria Theresa in the War of the Austrian Succession. Johnson described the course of the war in his *Memoirs of Frederick the Great* (1756).

Chloe Sometimes a surname of Ceres; the name signifies young green corn, hence often an adolescent girl, the beloved of the pastoral poet.

Cibber, Colley (1671–1757) Poet laureate from 1730 to 1757; he produced an annual ode on the King's birthday.

Cleora Unidentified.

Clodio A lame or clumsy person.

Crispin The patron saint of shoemakers and hence of tradesmen and citizens in general.

Croesus King of Lydia, who was warned by Solon of the fate awaiting the very rich.

Cupid The youthful god of love.

Curio Someone who takes care; a cautious man.

Cynthia A surname of Diana, the huntress and goddess of the moon.

Daedalus An ingenious inventor who escaped from Minos, King of Crete, by means of artificial wings.

Danaus King of Egypt who, in consequence of a prophecy, caused his fifty daughters to murder their bridegrooms; inevitably one did not, and the survivor fulfilled the prophecy by killing Danaus.

Danube The Magyars of Hungary, through which the Danube flows, were a byword for lawless cruelty.

Daphne A nymph pursued by Apollo, whom the gods metamorphosed into a laurel. The laurel was thereafter sacred to Apollo and the arts.

Daphnis A Sicilian shepherd, supposedly the first pastoral poet.

Democritus Experimental philosopher who laughed at the follies of mankind.

de Vega, Lope (1562–1635) Spanish dramatist and poet.

Diana Goddess of the moon, of hunting and of chastity.

Du Bellay, Joachim (1522–60) French poet and critic.

Durfey, Thomas (1635–1723) Song-writer and dramatist; butt of both Dryden and Pope.

Edward III (1312–77) With his son the Black Prince, defeated the French at Crecy in 1346.

Eëtion King of Thebes, killed by Achilles.

Eliza Elizabeth I, Queen of England, 1533–1603; born at Greenwich.

Eliza Elizabeth Carter.◊

Elphinston, James (1721–1809) Scot, schoolmaster, spelling reformer and friend of Johnson.

Elysian plain The Elysian Fields were the home of the virtuous after death.

Erasmus, Desiderius (1466–1536) Renaissance scholar.

Euripides Greek tragic poet.

Eurus The east wind.

Eurydice Wife of the poet Orpheus who descended into Hades to recover her, but lost her at the last moment by looking back at her.

Fabius Named *Cunctator*, the delayer, renowned for his caution. He was one of the few Roman generals to be a match for Hannibal.

Fates Three goddesses, *alias* the Parcæ, who presided over the birth, life and death of man. Clotho was responsible for birth and held a distaff, Lachesis spun out the events of life, and Atropos cut the thread with her shears to signal death.

Firebrace, Bridget, Lady Second wife of Sir Cordell Firebrace of Ipswich; she died in 1782.

Flaminius A Roman consul, slain by Hannibal near Lake Thrasymene.

Fuscus, Aristius ◊ Aristius Fuscus

Galileo, Galilei (1564–1642) Was, by tradition, tormented by the Inquisition for his scientific and astronomical theories.

Gaul A Frenchman.

George, King George II (1683–1760) Was also Elector of Hanover and made frequent visits, apparently to see his mistresses; he appointed Colley Cibber to be Poet Laureate in 1730 and was a regular subject of Cibber's verses.

Giffard, Henry (1699–1772) Actor and manager of the theatre in Goodman's Fields until its closure by the Licensing Act of 1737. Garrick made his stage début with Giffard's touring company at Ipswich in 1741.

Goldsmith, Oliver (1730–74) Poet, dramatist and critic, friend of Johnson.

Greenwich Birthplace of Queen Elizabeth I.

Grey, Stephen (d. 1736) Early experimenter with static electricity; a Fellow of the Royal Society.

Gripus A stingy or grasping man.

Hanmer, Sir Thomas (1677–1746) Speaker of the House of Commons and editor in 1744 of the 'Oxford' Shakespeare.

Harley, Robert (1661–1724) First Earl of Oxford, Tory statesman, was disgraced for Jacobitism.

Hector Trojan hero, son of King Priam, slain by Achilles.

Hector, Edmund (1708–94) Schoolfellow and life-long friend of Johnson. He practised medicine in Birmingham and supplied Boswell with much information about Johnson.

Hecuba Mother of Hector.

Helicon A mountain of Boeotia, sacred to the Muses, from which flowed the fountain Hippocrene, source of inspiration.

Henry V (1387–1422) Defeated the French at Agincourt in 1415.

Heraclitus A pessimistic philosopher.

Hesperia A western country, home of Hesper or Vesper, the setting sun.

Hibernia Ireland.

Hickman, Dorothy (1714–44) Daughter of Gregory Hickman of Stourbridge and a distant cousin of Johnson.

Hippolytus Son of Theseus who, rejecting the advances of Phaedra his mother, was falsely accused of assaulting her and accidentally killed.

Hogarth, William (1697–1764) Painter and engraver of satirical caricatures. He and Johnson first met in the house of Samuel Richardson the novelist in 1753.

Homer Greatest of the epic poets.

Hunt, Edward (*fl.* 1747) A boxer who in June 1746 defeated an equally famous pugilist, Hawksley.

Hydaspes A river of Asia, probably the Indus, whose annual flooding brought fertility to the region.

Hyde, Edward (1609–74) First Earl of Clarendon, father-in-law of King James II, grandfather of Queens Mary and Anne, was legal adviser to both Charles I and Charles II. Exiled in 1667.

Hydra A many-headed monster, which grew two new ones each time a head was cut off. It was eventually killed by Hercules.

Hyperia A fountain in Thessaly.

Hypoplacus The region lying below the Trojan mountain, whose plains were densely wooded.

Icarus Son of Daedalus, who flew with his father from Crete, but flew too near the sun, which melted the wax holding his wings, and he was drowned.

Idomeneus King of Crete, who accompanied the Greeks in the war against Troy.

Ilion Troy.

Inachia A courtesan.

Irene (Greek, εἰρήνη, peace, *or* time of peace) In Knollys' *Generall Historie of the Turkes* (Johnson's source) Irene was a beautiful Greek captured by the Sultan Mahomet II at the sack of Constantinople in 1453. Despite her great beauty Mahomet slew her publicly to demonstrate his war like fortitude and his control over his passions.

Isther The Danube, which was, for the Romans, the boundary between the empire and the barbarians to the north.

Ixion Punished in Hades by being bound to a perpetually turning wheel.

Jove Chief of the gods, *alias* Jupiter or Zeus.

Juba King of Numidia, a country corresponding roughly to modern Algeria and Lybia.

Jude, St A carpenter, often identified as one of the brethren of Christ; he was traditionally martyred in Persia. ◊ Simon, St.

Kelly, Hugh (1739–77) Staymaker, author and playwright.

Kenneth, St (d. 599) Companion of St Columba, to whom the chapel on the island of Inchkenneth was dedicated.

Lade, Sir John (1759–1838) Second baronet, nephew of Henry Thrale. He squandered his fortune but lived to his eightieth year.

Lalage One of Horace's favourite mistresses.

Latian state (*alias* Latium) The region of Italy near the river Tiber, which rose to importance when the city of Rome was founded there, thus bringing about the pre-eminence of its inhabitants, the Latins.

Latona Mother of Apollo and Diana.

Laud, William (1572–1645) Archbishop of Canterbury, executed in 1645 not because of his learning but because his zealous rigour for Anglo-Catholicism brought him into conflict with the Protestantism of Parliament.

Leniades The Latin form of the name Maclean. Sir Allan Maclean (1710–83), sixth baronet of Duart in Mull, was Chief of the Clan Maclean.

Levet, Dr Robert (1705–82) A poor physician befriended by Johnson, who sheltered him in his house.

Lucilius An early Roman satiric poet.

Luna The moon.

Lybia In ancient times the name of all of north Africa.

Lyce An Amazon, but here an unattractive woman.

Lyciscus A beautiful youth.

Lydia's monarch Croesus, who ignored Solon's caution against great riches, was defeated by Cyrus, lost his empire, and was only spared from execution by the recital of Solon's warning *Respice finem* ('Look to the end').

Lydiat, Thomas (1572–1646) Mathematician and divine who, despite a great contemporary reputation, lived and died in poverty.

Maecenas Statesman and adviser to the Emperor Augustus, and patron of both Horace and Virgil. The type of enlightened patronage.

Maeon's lake Lake Thrasymene in Etruria, where Hannibal defeated the Romans in 217 BC.

Maeonian bard Homer, supposedly born in Mæonia.

Mahomet (*fl.* 1747) A rope dancer.

Mantua The birthplace of Virgil, who was therefore often known as 'the Mantuan'.

Mareotis fen A lake in Egypt.

Maria Theresa (1717–80) Empress of Austria.

Marlborough, John Churchill, first Duke (1650–1722) Accused of enriching himself by protracting the campaigns in the War of the Spanish Succession, 1702–11; he suffered two paralytic strokes in 1716 but lived for a further six years.

Maro Surname of Virgil: Publius Virgilius Maro.

Megaera One of the Furies, who punished with disease.

Melibaeus A shepherd.

Melissa (Greek, a bee) A sweet young girl.

Memnon Son of Aurora, killed by Achilles, commemorated by a statue which uttered melodious sounds at dawn and dirges at sunset.

Memphis A town of ancient Egypt where Apis the bull-god was worshipped. Appropriate flowers were perhaps ox-eyes and cowslips.

Metastasio, Pietro (1698–1782) Italian poet and dramatist.

Mincio A river of Venetia on whose banks Virgil was born.

Minerva Goddess of wisdom, war and the liberal arts.

Minos First King of Crete of that name was a wise legislator who became the supreme judge in Hades; he shakes the fatal urn containing men's destinies.

Minos Second King of Crete of that name, husband of Pasiphæ, keeper of the Minotaur, imprisoned Dædalus.

Modena, Francis III d'Este, Duke of (1698–1780) Italian general in the war against the Sardinians.

Montagu, Mrs Elizabeth (1720–1800) Authoress and 'blue-stocking', was known as the 'Queen of the Blues'.

Mopsus A shepherd.

Muses Nine daughters of Jupiter and Mnemosyne, who presided over poetry, music and the liberal arts. 'The Muse' means inspiration.

Myrtale A girl. ◇ Myrtle.

Myrtle The symbol of true love, sometimes unrequited. 'A fragrant tree, sacred to Venus'; *Dict.*

Mystes Son of Valgius Rufus, to whom Horace wrote his Ode II ix, to relieve his grief.

Nassau Count Maurice of Nassau (1604–79), who outgeneralled the French in the campaigns of 1672–4.

Nemesis Goddess of vengeance and inexorable fate.

Nero Tyrannical emperor of Rome, whose name became a byword for cruelty and extravagant self-indulgence.

Nestor The aged hero of the Greeks in the Trojan war, famous for his wisdom and virtue.

Newton, Sir Isaac (1642–1727) Natural philosopher, astronomer and mathematician.

Nilus The river Nile, which enters the Mediterranean through seven mouths or estuaries, which form the Delta.

Niphates A river flowing from Armenia into the Tigris.

Nisus Nisus and Euryalus were Trojans, famous for their friendship. When Euryalus was captured by the Rutulians, Nisus gave his life in the attempt to rescue his friend.

Numidia An inland country of north Africa.

Ogilby, John (1600–76) Dancing master, author and printer.

Orestes Son of Agamemnon and Clytemnestra, he was saved by his sister Electra from the wrath of his mother, whom he later killed to avenge his father.

Orgilio A vain, proud and pompous man.

Orpheus A musician whose playing stopped rivers, tamed wild beasts and moved mountains; he recovered his wife Eurydice from Hades, but lost her by looking too eagerly back.

Pactolus A Lydian river touched by Midas and thereafter remarkable for its golden sands.

Parcae The Fates. ◊

Peleus Father of Achilles, whose death grieved him severely.

Pelides Patronymic of Achilles.

Percy, Bishop Thomas (1729–1811) Editor of the *Reliques of Ancient English Poetry* (1765), and author of a ballad-imitation, *The Hermit of Warkworth* (1771).

Persia's tyrant Xerxes. ◊

Pettius Friend of Horace, to whom Epode 11 is addressed.

Phasis An eastern river visited by the Argonauts, and the resort of birds hence called 'pheasants'.

Phidias Celebrated Athenian sculptor of statues of Minerva and Zeus.

Phidyle Horace's servant girl, to whom he addressed Ode III xxiii.

Philander (Greek, literally, a lover of men) Since Ariosto's *Orlando Furioso*, a young lover.

Phillips, Claudy (d. 1732) An itinerant Welsh violinist.

Phoebus One of the names of Apollo, god of the sun.

Pirithous Son of Ixion, imprisoned in Hades, but rescued by Theseus.◊

Plato (c. 519–438 BC) Greatest of the ancient Greek philosophers.

Pluto God of death and ruler of the underworld.

Pompey Surnamed the Great; a successful but imprudent general, defeated at Pharsalia by Julius Caesar, and later assassinated.

Pope, Alexander (1688–1744) Poet and satirist.

Priam Last of the Kings of Troy, father of many children including Cassandra, Hector and Paris; despite his venerable age he was at last killed by Achilles.

Pultowa Scene of the defeat of Charles XII of Sweden by Peter the Great of Russia in 1709.

Renny Frances Reynolds. ◊

Reynolds, Frances (1729–1807) Sister of Sir Joshua Reynolds, minor artist and 'blue-stocking'.

Ross, James Boswell's servant and occasional amanuensis from about 1785 to 1791.

Roy, Pierre (1683–1764) French poet and dramatist.

Sabines Early inhabitants of Italy, celebrated for virtuous living.

Sage, the Nestor, father of Antilochus, who was killed at Troy.

Saturn Banished by his son Jupiter to Italy, which was therefore called Latium (Latin, *latere*, to hide). There he civilized the people and ruled wisely and with moderation in what became known as the 'Golden Age'.

Scaean Gate The gate into Troy through which the Wooden Horse was introduced.

Scaliger, Joseph Justus (1540–1609) Scholar and polymath.

Scamander A river of Troas which imparted beauty to all who bathed in it.

Scythia The lands to the north-east of the Black Sea, later called Tartary, and regarded by the Romans as the home of barbarians.

Sedley, Catherine (1657–1717) Mistress of the Duke of York, later James II. Of her Charles II said that his brother had her for a mistress 'by way of penance', such was her lack of beauty.

Settle, Elkanah (1648–1724) Minor poet satirized as Doeg by Dryden in his *Absalom and Achitophel*, II.

Simon, St Also called Zelotes; a fishmonger, supposed to be one of Christ's brethren: 'Is not this the carpenter's son? is not his mother called Mary? and his brethren, James, and Joses, and Simon, and Judas?' (Matthew xiii 55). Simon was said to have been martyred with a saw on a missionary journey to Britain.

Sirius The Dog-star which was in the ascendant from 3 July to 11 August; hence the 'Dog-days', when the weather was unhealthily close and hot.

Sisters, the sacred The Muses. ◊

Sisters, the inexorable The Fates or Parcae. ◊

Sol The sun.

Solon Greek philosopher and law-giver, who warned Croesus of the fate of the grossly rich.

Spenser, Edmund (1552–99) Elizabethan poet, author of *The Faerie Queene*.

Stella (Latin, a star) Unidentified girl to whom several of Johnson's juvenile pieces are addressed.

Stoics A philosophical sect who sought absolute command over the passions and were therefore best known as despising bodily comfort and pain.

Strymon A river dividing Thrace and Macedonia; the haunt of cranes.

Stygian ◊ Styx

Styx The cold and venomous river which encircled Hades nine times and had to be crossed at death.

Swedish Charles Charles XII of Sweden. ◊

Swift, Jonathan (1667–1745) Poet and satirist, was intermittently insane before his death and was said to have been exhibited in that condition by his servants for a fee.

Sybilla A prophetess.

Sylvia A rustic girl (Latin, *sylva*, a wood); perhaps the Hon. Alicia Maria Carpenter ◊ is meant.

Tantalus Punished in Hades by being confined to his neck in water which he could not drink, beneath a bough of fruit which he could not reach to eat.

Telamon Father of Ajax, one of the Greek heroes in the Trojan war.

Thales One of the seven wise men of ancient Greece; Johnson gives the name to the addressee of *London*, though Juvenal's Satire iii was addressed to Umbricius.

Theban brothers Eteocles and Polynices, sons of Oedipus and Jocasta, who quarrelled over the throne and died in mutual combat. Their ashes on their funeral pyre were said to have separated, so intense was the hatred between them.

Thebes A city of Bœotia, said to have built itself at the sound of Amphion's lyre. It was destroyed by Alexander the Great.

Theseus King of Athens, performed many heroic exploits, but was eventually imprisoned with his friend Pirithous in Hades. Hercules rescued Theseus and together they released Pirithous, who had been fastened to the wheel of Ixion his father.

Thrale, Mrs Hester Lynch (1741–1821) 'Blue-stocking' wife of Henry Thrale, a wealthy brewer in Southwark, who entertained and paid court to Johnson from 1765 until her second marriage in 1784 to Gabriel Piozzi.

Thrale, Hester Maria (1764–1857) 'Queeney', later Viscountess Keith, eldest daughter of Mrs Thrale.

Thralia Latinized form of Mrs Thrale.◊

Thyrsis A shepherd lover in pastoral poetry.

Tigris With the Euphrates, one of the major rivers of Persia.

Timotheus Court poet and musician to Alexander the Great.

Titan A name applied by Ovid and Virgil to the sun, and by Juvenal to Prometheus, who stole fire from heaven and gave it to mankind.

Tityrus A shepherd named in Virgil's pastorals.

Tityus A giant imprisoned in perpetual torment in Hades.

Torquatus Torquatus Manlius, renowned for his inflexible rectitude and severity; friend of Horace.

Turnus King of the Rutuli, of great physical strength, defeated in single combat by Aeneas (*Aeneid* VII).

Tydeus Father of Diomedes, a Greek hero in the Trojan war, who figures in the later stories of Troilus and Cressida.

Tyrian purple The Phœnecians of Tyre were credited with the invention of scarlet and purple dyes.

Urbanus A signature used by Johnson, apparently to indicate that the piece emanates from Urban's office. Sylvanus Urban was the pseudonym of Edward Cave (1691–1754), the founder and editor of the *Gentleman's Magazine* in 1731. The name implies both a countryman (Latin, *sylva*, a wood) and a townsman (Latin, *urbs*, a town), and so suggests that the magazine will cater for all tastes.

Valgius Rufus Fellow-poet and friend of Horace, who wrote Ode II ix to alleviate his grief for the death of his son Mystes.

Vane, Anne (1705–36) Maid of honour to Queen Caroline, and mistress of Frederick, Prince of Wales. She was described by Viscount Perceval as 'This fat, and ill-shaped dwarf' who 'has neither sense nor wit, and is besides (if report be true) the leavings of others'. Lord Hailes commented on 17 August 1773 on the inappropriateness of Johnson's allusions to Vane and Sedley (◊); see *Life* V, 49, 470–71, 17 August 1773.

Venus Goddess of love.

Villiers, George (1592–1628) First Duke of Buckingham, was murdered in 1628.

Villiers, George (1628–87) Second Duke of Buckingham, characterized by Dryden as Zimri (*Absalom and Achitophel* 500). 'Chymist, fidler, statesman and buffoon', was a spendthrift profligate who died, according to Pope, 'In the worst inn's worst room' (*Epistle to Bathurst: Of the Use of Riches*, 299–314).

Warton, Thomas (1728–90) Miscellaneous author and poet, critic and literary historian.

Wentworth, John (*c*. 1677–1741) Headmaster of Stourbridge school, 1704–32 (he was dismissed for absenteeism and 'giving too long a holiday during Whitsuntide'). He preserved twelve of Johnson's schoolboy exercises, which were lent to Boswell by his nephew, also John Wentworth.

Wentworth, Thomas (1593–1641) Earl of Strafford, statesman, served Charles I, who assented under pressure to his execution in 1641.

Wolsey, Thomas (1475–1530) Cardinal and statesman, confidant of Henry VIII, who eventually destroyed him. He is characterized in Shakespeare's *Henry VIII*.

Xerxes Son of Darius, King of Persia, whose invasion of Europe with a vast army was stopped by a handful of Spartans at Thermopylae. Thereafter his power declined, until he barely escaped with his life.

Zelinda A girl's name, implying jealousy (Greek, ζῆλος, jealous).

Index of Titles

Index of First Lines